mistreatment
ed CIA moles

Cy
ale who,
War, op-
n.

he agency for
954 until 1974,
Al-
ncy officials dis-
like Colby say the
gence excesses of
n period nearly para-
CIA's efforts to spy on
mlin. Angleton died in

that

were actually investigated and a
least 16 were treated as serious sus
pects, although former directors o
central intelligence, like William F
Colby, say that not a single Soviet
penetration was ever uncovered.

The mole hunt had cost Karlow
er and Kovich their reputa
betrayed their loyalty an
their careers. Kovich an
d lawyers who lobbie
compensation bil
into law in Octo
sident Jimm

sought an
981. Bu
cutiv
th

CIA/Cold War spawn

From page 1

Soviet spies for the CIA until his
career slid into limbo, also received
compensation. Three other unidentified CIA employes sought payments, but the agency rejected their
claims.

Mark Mansfield, a CIA spokes-
ment on Wise's book be-
said agency officials declined
had not yet seen it. But
"Several agency em-
ceive compensation
ften been referred
f Act,"
three former
from news
ks about
ing.

Anatoly M. Golitsin, a KGB office
who became one of the best-kno
Soviet defectors, turned up
snowy doorstep of the CI
tion chief in Helsinki, Fi
Golitsin touched
reaction at the CI
officials that he
tion at KGB
came from
CIA.

"several agency employes did receive compensation under what has often been referred to as the Mole Relief Act."
CIA spokesman

die
cy o
Colby
excesses
nearly para
to spy on th
To
tors
G

To Bill Balaz - a dear friend, a solid contributor, and someone you can always count on in a crisis - with best regards

[signature]
Newtown Square PA March 2002

TARGETED BY THE CIA

AN INTELLIGENCE PROFESSIONAL SPEAKS OUT ON THE SCANDAL THAT TURNED THE CIA UPSIDE DOWN

By S. Peter Karlow

TURNER PUBLISHING COMPANY
Paducah, Kentucky

Turner Publishing Company
412 Broadway • P.O. Box 3101
Paducah, Kentucky 42002-3101
(270) 443-0121

Turner Publishing Company Staff:
Bill Schiller, Editor
Dayna Spear Williams, Editor
Susan L. Harwood, Designer

S. Peter Karlow, Author

Publishing Rights:
Turner Publishing Company

ISBN: 1-56311-653-7
Library of Congress Control #: 2001087254

For Lib – the rest of the story.

The information in this book is from my recollections and records, from Freedom of Information documents finally received under threat of legal action, and from data and records provided by friends and former colleagues and associates. Any opinions expressed, or conclusions reached, are mine. Some persons, places, or operations have had names altered for security reasons. The manuscript was submitted to the CIA Records Board for review. The CIA neither endorses nor opposes any part of this manuscript.

S.P.K.
Newtown Square, PA
July 2001

So we die before our own eyes; so some chapters of our lives come to their natural end.
-Sarah Orne Jewet

Prologue...

The two FBI men were in a hurry.

They led me briskly down the marble corridor of the old post office building, that out-of place red brick structure set back from Pennsylvania Avenue at 12th Street in mid-town Washington. The Federal Bureau of Investigation uses this old turreted building as its operations center for the National Capital area, as it is located catty-corner across Pennsylvania Avenue from FBI headquarters in what has become known as the J. Edgar Hoover Building.

I kept up with them as they turned left and approached what was obviously a special security area. Double doors, mounted with electronic security locks, yawned open at us like huge jaws. In front of them was a gray steel desk manned by a burly security guard looking doubly forbidding in a dark blue uniform complete with black Sam Brown belt. There was a large walkie-talkie on his shoulder strap and what looked like a pristine new .45 in its holster on his belt. A large electric sign on the wall behind him kept blinking the word "OPEN." The standard three-month government-issue calendar showed January, February, and March 1963. Each date in January and half in February were meticulously crossed out with a red "x."

The guard waved us through. We soon came to a black steel sliding door that was opening slowly, pulled by an unseen electric motor. On an impulse, I deliberately walked a few steps further down the hall and turned into a usual style wooden office door that was part open. I knew it was the wrong door for me at the moment. I was sure it led to the concealed observation room that is part of any polygraphing complex. It was, and I waved pleasantly at the four men in the room whose expressions of pained surprise reflected their shock at seeing me in person. I was not surprised at the near-frantic reactions of my FBI escorts to catch me and pull me back before I could go any further through the door.

The metal sliding door opened into the main polygraph room, the notorious "lie detector center." It was a large, brightly lit inside room with one wall dominated by an imposing framed glass window area that glistened like an oversized modernistic work of art. This window with its one-way mirror glass concealed the observation room. It was a cubicle where others, without being seen, could watch at close range the facial expressions and emotional reactions of the person being questioned.

The polygraph equipment was on one side of the main room. The polygraph machine, like a large, old model electrocardiograph, stood on an office table arranged at an angle behind the chair used by the person being interrogated. In this way the person faced the observation window and could hear but not see the machine. When in use, the machine would give out whining and scratching sounds which inevitably served to increase the anxiety of the person being interrogated as to whether the machine was "detecting" any "lies."

Three sets of black wires on the floor reached out like tentacles towards the chair. They would be attached to the three elements of the polygraph. The heavier wire went to the Baumanometer blood pressure cuff, which would be wrapped around the upper arm of the person being interrogated. The smaller wire, actually a twisted pair cable, went to the flexible belt that would be strapped around the person's chest to measure frequency and depth of breathing. The thin black wire went to the waxed pad that would be placed in the palm of the person's hand to register nervous perspiration.

On the other side of the room stood a wooden Government Issue conference table that could seat ten. Four men were already there. I knew only Aubrey and Maurice—the unlikely pair of first names that I read from the identification cards of the two FBI men with whom I had spent most of this past week. They were special agents Aubrey "Pete" Brent and Maurice "Gook" Taylor. They perfunctorily introduced the two others there as fellow FBI special agents, an older man apparently in charge, and a young man, like a trainee. They all took seats and the older man motioned me to the head of the table.

There was no small talk. The older man, introduced as Alex Neale, began a dry, canned explanation of how the polygraph worked. This irritated me. The first time he stopped for breath, I cut in quietly but firmly to say that after my twenty years in intelligence, fifteen of which in the CIA, I was no stranger to the polygraph. I added that I knew the rule that I must be told in advance what questions I was to be asked if (and I stressed the "if") I agreed to be polygraphed at all. This was greeted by silence and I realized that I must not let this silence game rattle me. It was a classic interrogation act, to let things drag along to see how the subject reacts to uncertainty.

After a while I spoke up again, as calmly as I could, to ask them not to play games with me. Now was the time, I continued, for them to tell me why I was there. It had all seemed like a blind fishing expedition, going over details of my personal history from A to Z, including that of my parents and grandparents, all kinds of people I had ever known or worked with, their sexual preferences and whatnot…without any apparent focus or purpose. In the absence of any reasonable explanation, I stated flatly, I'd stop right here, and exercise my rights to have a lawyer present.

The FBI agents exchanged glances, and looked over at Neale who nodded his head as if in agreement. He straightened up, put both palms of his hands flat on the table, and looked over at me, his face flushed with emotion.

"All right, I'll tell you." He took a deep breath. "We have been investigating a major security penetration in the top ranks of the CIA. You are the principal suspect of being a Soviet spy...a mole in the CIA."

I remember the moment clearly. All eyes were fixed on me.

I began to laugh.

I couldn't help it.

I felt suddenly relaxed, as if a weight had been lifted off my shoulders.

The circle of faces around the table did not relax one bit. I could not resist a comment, which I meant to be lightly sarcastic, "I thought this was going to be about something serious."

"Why are you laughing?" Neale asked. "I don't think this is very funny."

But this was ridiculous. So ridiculous that there ought to be a ready way of disposing of this wild allegation and letting me get on with my life.

"Are you really being serious?" I asked.

From the looks on their faces it was obvious that they were serious.

Neale spoke up. "What did you expect this to be about?"

"Oh, I thought I was being checked out for a new job, or perhaps something happened in the State Department that might have somehow involved me."

Stony silence. They were obviously still watching my every reaction. The seriousness of all this dawned on me.

"Wait a minute," I picked up the dialog. "Let me get this straight. You are telling me that I am accused of being a Soviet spy?"

"Not accused...suspected."

"All right, suspect. Well, what am I supposed...I mean, what am I charged with?"

"No charges, this is just an investigation."

"Can't you tell me what I'm accused of doing...or having done, where, when...and with whom?"

"Well," he retorted, "that is the purpose of this investigation...and the next step is polygraphing."

"Polygraphing?" I asked incredulously, "What in Hell good would that do for a sweeping and wild accusation like this?"

Not accusation. Suspicion; the purpose of the investigation. Neale explained the polygraph was the essential tool in a serious case like this.

I urged them to be realistic. Before we talked polygraph or anything else, could there be some mistake in identification? Just what had implicated or identified me as the traitor they were looking for? My walk? I do have a slight limp. My accent? I have a slight accent in English, because I learned to speak German and French about the same time I learned English. What about German, I speak it with little or no regional accent. Pretty much the same in French, no regional accent.

There was no reaction.

I assured them that then I would cooperate in any way that I could.

"Good," they said. Then the next step was the polygraph.

But no line of questions has been defined for anyone to cover on the polygraph. Or, I said sarcastically, would you ask me whether I am a spy and watch needles wiggle on the machine like an ouija board?

The polygraph, they explained carefully, can be validated by science. "Are you by any chance concerned about taking a polygraph test?" Neale asked.

"Look," I said trying again, "I'm glad we are finally getting at what has been overhanging me. It has been obvious to me that something was wrong over the past three months or more. Still, how can I answer the suspicions I'm under if I have no idea of how I became involved in all this?"

They said the polygraph would cover this. What bunk!

I thought briefly of the psychologists I had been working with some years back in the CIA, and their strong scientific reservations about the effectiveness of the polygraph. There was for several years an ad hoc CIA taskforce on the polygraph back in the late 1950s, and I was one of several non-technical members. I smiled to myself that here would be a chance to take a full-dress FBI polygraph test on a subject that was obviously fail-safe. This was something the task force members had been unable to arrange because of the open hostility by the FBI to any study or second thoughts about the so-called lie detector.

Just speaking professionally, I asked them, how could anyone think I would ever go over to the Russians, or defect? Purely personally, or psychologically, why would I do something like that? I have had a good life, at least to this point. I was happily married with an ideal family. I had adequate means, no debts, no vices like drink or drugs, or gambling. No homosexuality, or womanizing for that matter.

Again there was silence.

In other words, I asked again, what did they think could in any way induce me to defect, to become a traitor to my country, and work for the USSR?

Neale looked over at me.

"You tell us," he said.

"Tell you *what*?" I asked.

"How you could become a Soviet spy."

"Bullshit."

It was the only word that came to my mind at the time.

Even after four days of intense interrogation, I couldn't begin to fathom what had led to this inquisition. They were calling me a traitor! What was the motivation behind this personal and professional defilement? Had I done something wrong? What was the evidence being used against me? Whatever, I reasoned, it couldn't possibly amount to much, yet it somehow seemed to be enough to have an official FBI group call me a spy and a traitor. These words would become increasingly familiar as I was sucked ever deeper into this whirlpool.

Whatever, I began to review to myself what I had done in twenty years of professional intelligence work, and forty-one years of lifetime, and what could have gone wrong. This wrong.

CHAPTER 1

STARTING OUT...

There is a certain fascination with intelligence work...a certain air of mystery, excitement and power. It invokes images of one who is on the inside, behind the scenes and somehow in the know. Of travel, new places, new faces; of intrigue and, idealistically, of being on the side of right, of virtue, of the way things should be, and with special powers to help get things done.

Intelligence work in my mind is not a career. It is a calling, a tradecraft, and a way of looking at a problem, making judgments on the best sources for the most needed information and how to make the best use out of it.

Romantic? Idealistic? Perhaps, but I was bitten by the intelligence bug early in life. My interest was fed by mystery stories, movies, and actual events after the first World War. In looking back I see that my high school yearbook write-up from 1937 says something about a probable career in the FBI. In 1940, a year before graduating from college, I did go to the FBI office in Philadelphia to see about job opportunities after graduation or over the summer. My knowledge of French and German did not produce much of a reaction, as there was more interest in whether I intended to get a law degree. Just from reading the headlines I realized that there would be opportunities in the intelligence field somewhere, although I had little idea of how it all worked or how to get at it.

One thing I concluded, and this was almost prophetic: Intelligence work would give a great deal of responsibility early and often in a career.

Something I did not realize, and could not possibly have known, was how unorganized the U.S. intelligence effort was at the time.

Both these conclusions were brought home to me shortly after I got into what became the core of U.S. intelligence.

•••

My first intelligence mission started in New York City on the morning of March 5, 1942 . It was my twenty-first birthday.

I took a cab to Grand Central Terminal in Manhattan, boarded the New York Central's daytime express, the Great Lakes Limited, and set out for Schenectady. My assignment was to collect some information that might be necessary for the war effort without specifically giving away what I was after, concerning what country or area, or why my employer, the cryptically named Office of the Coordinator of Information, wanted it. If pressed, I was authorized to say that my employer was an office of the United States Government. I didn't expect to be pressed, but it was less than three months after the Japanese attack on Pearl Harbor, and Americans were shifting to a war footing and becoming vaguely aware of the nature and importance of secrecy in national defense. As the latest Government security poster warned, "Button your lip; save a ship!"

Even if pressed, I would have had difficulty in describing the Office of the Coordinator of Information. It was very new, established only in July 1941 by President Franklin D. Roosevelt in a broadly worded, one-page Executive Order. His action created a new agency, the Office of the Coordinator of Information, to be known as the COI. Colonel William Joseph Donovan, "Wild Bill" Donovan, was designated its director. I "entered on duty"-governmentese for "came to work" -on September 15, 1941.

The COI headquarters in Washington grew quickly as Donovan went about recruiting top-level businessmen, bankers, engineers, lawyers, writers, from all branches of private life, and researchers and faculty members from universities and colleges around the country. The Oral Intelligence unit in New York, to which I was recruited, was organized within a month's time, in August 1941. When I took off for Schenectady, I had been working there about five months. To be honest, I really was not yet aware of the background or the complexity of inter-agency turf warfare in Washington, or what we were doing in New York that other agencies were not already doing. I had no idea what administrative bloodshed was involved in building an intelligence organization whose mandate would cut across all sorts of established jurisdictional lines. More directly, it was hard for me to realize that there was not much organized intelligence on foreign countries available in the U.S. government. Or was it that I had not yet had access to it?

The Oral Intelligence unit was off by itself in a modest office suite at the corner of 41st Street and Madison Avenue on the fourth floor. The unit was headed by G. Edward Buxton, a Rhode Island businessman. He, like Donovan, had been a colonel with a distinguished record in World War I. He had assembled a staff of six professionals including an assistant district attorney, a labor union official, a psychologist, an advertising man, and a historian on Central Europe. As his deputy he recruited William H. Vanderbilt, the former Governor of Rhode Island. Our job was to find new sources for information on conditions and developments in countries already affected by the war. At first we spent most of our time finding informed people among the stream of refugees arriving from Europe by ship in the port of New York. Since many did not speak English, I worked as an interpreter for others on the staff, using my fluent German and French acquired in childhood.

Very shortly after joining Oral Intelligence, I was assigned my own interrogation targets. As junior man in the office I was to specialize on interviewing people coming from Africa. My interview reports began to go to the Africa branch of the COI's new Research and Analysis (R&A) organization in Washington. This R&A Division grew into a collection of the ablest, most prominent scholars in the country in all major fields like history, sociology, economics, political science, geography, agriculture and natural resources, as well as having scholars in cartography and the latest techniques for presentation of information. The Africa branch was headed by an associate professor of history from Yale, Sherman Kent. Kent was a native Californian whose deliberately shaggy, casual style did nothing to hide his quick mind and warm sense of humor. The top of his desk, like a snow scene in the Arctic, was perpetually covered with documents, papers, books, and newspapers in many languages, which he somehow navigated and kept in order in his mind.

What had all this to do with Schenectady, a manufacturing town on Lake Erie? On one of my first trips to Washington, Kent showed me a photo from a French Moroccan newspaper. The accompanying article told how a rockslide high up in the Atlas Mountains had threatened a passenger train, but that "the American made locomotive remained on the track although several coaches behind were derailed." Kent asked if I could find out who had made that locomotive, and did any other American company make anything for the North African railroads? Further, what else could I discover about the Moroccan railroad system and its present condition?

Back in New York, I put the problem to Buxton's deputy director, Governor Vanderbilt. He was one of those well-connected people that Donovan knew and was able to gather about him in the COI. Vanderbilt suggested that I start with a call on the American Locomotive Company in Schenectady, New York, whose chief executive officer, George McWhorter, he knew. A discreet letter and phone call from Vanderbilt gained me a cordial invitation to visit the company at the Schenectady headquarters. The letter did not indicate the nature of my mission or what country and what details I was interested in. Two days later, I was aboard the Great Lakes Limited.

Yes, Schenectady seemed like an unlikely place to research Morocco. While it was seasonally overcast and cool in New York City, here in Schenectady the March weather was still slush on the ground and it was raining, a wet sleet-like drizzle, and windy, a steady biting moisture-filled blast. The taxi driver who took me from the railroad station to the downtown YMCA building proudly pointed out some street lights which had what he called horizontal icicles which literally grew out sideways, driven by the wind and the cold.

The "Y" was a brown, impersonal building and centrally located downtown. The price of a room was right: $7 for members, which I had been since attending a YMCA-sponsored high school in New York. I was scrimping on expenses as this was my first experience traveling on a government expense account and I was not yet familiar with per diem allowances or travel cost claims.

As I entered the "Y," I imagined to myself what it would be like if I were indeed an agent on a secret mission, a spy under cover. Would I be able to carry it off nonchalantly as in spy stories I had read, from "The Count of Monte Cristo" to the movie "Mata Hari?" Would my newness, my naiveté, give me away?

I pushed open the heavy door into the cavernous lobby, chilly and empty except for an elderly man behind the counter of the registration desk. He was slightly stooped, with thinning gray hair and wearing both a heavy turtleneck sweater and a tweed jacket with leather patched elbows. I went over to him. Without looking up from his sports magazine, he slid a clipboard towards me with registration forms to fill out. I entered my name, *S. Peter Karlow*, on the top registration sheet, and under "Company or Business," wrote a deliberately scribbled *Coord. of Information*—no reference to U.S. Government. With hardly an upward glance, he peeled the top sheet off the clipboard, stuck it into a bulky electric date/time stamper that marked it with a resounding snap that startled me. He then slid the sheet into a creased manila file folder on his desk. He handed me the room key, mumbled the room number, and pointed towards the single elevator. I went up, put my overnight bag up in the closet of the sparsely furnished but comfortable room. Well, so far so good.

I did not realize how cold it was in Schenectady until I looked out the window. There was a big illuminated car ad on the billboard across the street. The sign featured a frost-streaked brown 1942 four-door Chevrolet sedan driving up a highway on the face of a huge thermometer, whose big black pointer was swung way over to the left and pointed to 4 degrees—below zero. The night would be even colder.

Down the street, a red glow came from a large neon sign on the roof of a diner a block away. The sign read: "ALL YOU CAN EAT FOR 65 CENTS." The diner proved to be of the classic late art deco style, as if it had been a converted railroad car, on a concrete platform. It had a long brown and chrome counter down the middle and some small tables at the end, as well as an ornate Wurlitzer juke box on continuous play, putting out Glenn Miller and Artie Shaw numbers that were the classics of the time.

The only other customers, two men sitting at a table to the side, finished their meals in silence. They never looked up or across at me. If I were a secret agent, should I be more alert in case I was being followed or watched? I hung my coat and scarf up on the nearest coat rack, took a seat at the counter, and ordered the standard menu: thin-sliced meat, mashed potatoes splashed with brown gravy, canned-tasting green beans, a slice of white bread, a pat of butter, then two scoops of rich, creamy ice cream, and a cup of bitter coffee that tasted as if it had been warming all day.

Back in my room at the "Y," I had time to review my notes for the next day's meeting. I had pretty well memorized the general map of Morocco, and such features as the Meknès repair yard, the high pass at Taza, the port facilities at Casablanca. To think that I had almost gone there, to Morocco, at age twelve when my mother sent me to spend the summer in France with a family friend; but that's another story.

Promptly at nine the next morning, a slush-spattered gray Hudson Commodore pulled up before the "Y." The driver, a heavy-set man with graying hair, called my name through the open car window, opened the door and invited me in.

George McWhorter, who had been with ALCO for nineteen years, eyed me with some misgivings. "Frankly, I was expecting an older person," he said. It was said kindly, but it was not the last time I would have that comment made to me. Then he gave me another quizzical look. "What do you guys want to do, blow up locomotives?" Before I could think of an answer, he sighed and added, "Yes, I know. I shouldn't ask what you're after, so go ahead, you shoot the questions."

I saw the oval "ALCO" logo come into view, and he turned into the parking lot. He parked and led me into the building. The doorman greeted him with a warm "'Morning, George." I was interested in the informality and obvious camaraderie. Yet it still seemed strange to me to see this open access to the building, with no badges, no security sign-in.

Up in McWhorter's comfortable office, he motioned me to a chair next to his desk, but I was too absorbed in the magnificent hand-made locomotive models displayed on two layers of bookshelves around the walls of the office. Delighted by my show of interest, McWhorter told me about the various models and how most of the locomotives they depicted were still in operation in the U.S., in Central America, and in Canada, Alaska, and some of the European colonies in Africa. One in particular was striking, a big black and red job that looked as if it ran backwards, with the operator's cab out front and then what looked like twin steam engines attached tail-to-nose.

"Union Pacific," McWhorter said proudly. "Our biggest, the 'Big Boy,' see, like two locomotives together, and articulated so she can get around the curves. Boy, this baby can haul anything and everything across the Rockies without back up, you know, without the need to couple on extra locomotives. I worked on her, down in the wheel shop. Every day I'd be amazed at the size of those wheels. Would you like to see her?"

"Sure, is it here?"

"Yeah, only finished a few years ago and back for some check-ups. Let's go down and look her over; take your coat, we go outside to get there." McWhorter obviously wanted an excuse to go see "her" again.

The shop building had a large central space the length of the building, like an aircraft hangar, with workshops on the sides on two levels, and connecting conveyor belts. It was nearly as cold in the hangar as outdoors. Everything was scaled huge, even a screwdriver that was four feet long. And, of course, "Big Boy" was overwhelming in its scale. I also noted some electric and diesel locomotives in various states of assembly.

"I guess that's the future," McWhorter said somewhat sadly, as we returned to his office. "The diesel-electric has some things in its favor when it comes to operating time alone. The steamers need to be watered and cleaned out regularly while the diesels can just keep running, as long as you slosh in the fuel oil. That's what's tying up 'Big Boy,' it needs more water than we provided for."

Back in his office I went over to an engine model whose tender was marked "C.F.M.," which I assumed stood for *Chemins de Fer Maroccains*, and asked whether this was the model sold to the French for North Africa. It was a good guess, and I sensed that McWhorter was still not clear on what I knew or wanted to find out. I decided to push my luck further.

"Why did you pick this 4-4-0 model for the job?" The numbers stood for the wheel configuration, four weight-bearing wheels forward, four driving wheels, no trailing wheels. My years of fascination with toy trains paid off.

McWhorter sat back in his chair and put his hands behind his head.

"Funny you should ask. I worked on that Morocco job, pulling together the formal specifications. It's always a compromise," he explained. "Since you seem to know something about these things, you can realize it depends on the loads, the frequency of use, the location of watering points, the sharpest curves, the steepest grades, the narrowest tunnels, and, of course, cost. So, first of all, we need to know everything about the rail system, and I mean everything. You know, they have some good-size mountains over there, whatever they're called..."

"The Atlas Mountains," I volunteered.

"Yeah. Say, if you're interested in Morocco, you'll want to see what we collected by way of briefing data. I have it in our map room. Come with me." He rose from the chair, and led me to the next room.

"Did you send someone over to look at the situation first-hand?" I asked.

"Oh yes, but that was some years ago, back in the mid-twenties. As I remember, it was old Chuck Murray. He's retired now. He lives near-by though and I guess you could find him if you want to."

Yes, I wanted to. I made a mental note to get his address before I left.

"I remember he came back with one important detail," McWhorter continued. "He noted high calcium in the water, so we right off-the-bat designed in some linings in the water tanks. The French were impressed with this. They had always had to flush out the water pipes of their equipment in the area with acid every few months, which meant down-time."

In the files room he found the proper map drawer and spread out a finely detailed set of maps of Morocco: topographic, climate, bridges, tunnels, freight yards, round houses, signals, safety equipment, side-tracks and grade crossings. With his finger and, when that was not adequate, with a steel pointer, he pointed out some of the trouble spots that the ALCO team had identified. I was taking notes as fast as I could.

We broke for lunch at a nearby steak house.

"I'd have taken you to the company's officers' dining room," McWhorter explained, "but I figured there would be too many people there who would want to know what you're doing." I appreciated that. Over coffee and ice cream, McWhorter offered to let me take along anything and everything out of his files. Yes, he'd like to have them returned some day, and no, we should not, in principle, show them to Baldwin, Electro-Motive, or any other competitor.

We went back to his office to pore some more over other material he produced. McWhorter added some details as we went along, like on grade crossings, bridges, and repair facilities. I noticed that the most recent information was from 1926, 15 years earlier, but said I wanted all of it. He provided me with an artist's folio carrier, a cloth flat zipper case big enough to hold a bulletin board, to carry the material. Then I asked him to give me Chuck Murray's address and phone number. I was sure someone, probably I myself, would be back to look him up and write down what he knew about the Moroccan rail system when he was there back in the twenties.

As McWhorter drove me to the railroad station, I mentioned as casually as I could that our interests were not just in Morocco but in all of Europe and that others would probably call him for information on other countries. We were in ample time for me to catch the 4:14 back to Grand Central.

The next day at my Mother's apartment in New York I opened the material. I had the weekend to go through the various papers, charts, blueprints, and maps—numerous and detailed. I was particularly interested in those items I had not had a chance to see. They included specific details, like freight yard capacity, repair equipment, grade crossing warnings, water points, and turnouts. Some packets of photographs were interesting and gave life to the statistical material.

Although impressed by all the detail I had acquired, I could not understand that the U.S. Government did not already have heaps of this information solidly in hand for all over the world. After all, even an amateur would know that railroads are the lifelines of a country's economy and, yes, of its military potential, too. Something to consider now that we were at war.

Saturday morning I phoned Sherman Kent at the office in Washington, figuring correctly that he would be there, and ticked off to him some of the items I had. He was quiet for a moment, then came out with one of his pet four-letter expletives and commented that this could just be "hot as a pregnant pig." Kent enjoyed his interpretation of Western cowboy mannerisms. "How early Monday morning are you going to be here in the office?" I agreed to come down Sunday evening and be in Monday morning. It gave me time to finish typing what had become an eight page, single-spaced report on my notes.

Kent and his deputy, Rudy Winnacker, were already there when I reached the office before eight Monday morning. Kent with his off-center grin and Winnacker with his open, mid-western smile greeted me effusively. Winnacker was tall, solidly built, a blond, blue-eyed Scandinavian/German type. He was a full professor of history at the University of Wisconsin. He hurried to clear off the top of a table in Kent's office, stacking up the files and loose papers, along with the books and atlases, on the floor. Avidly, they tore into the contents of the folio I brought in.

"Boris," Kent boomed, somehow "Boris" had become his nickname for me, "Jesus Christ, this is a gold mine! This is just what we need for that Strategic Survey of North Africa that we proposed, and, hell if we haven't just been assigned to prepare it for the Army Engineers."

"Not only that," Winnacker added, his broad German accent particularly noticeable when he was excited. "It looks like we damn near have half the strategic data on the North African rail system right here in our hot hands. Look at these

photos of the repair shops, and here, the freight yards at Fez, and—would you believe, that goddam bridge at Guerçif..."

At nine o'clock the weekly staff meeting of the R&A Africa Division was
almost entirely about the material I had collected. Kent thoughtfully made it a point
to be sure I knew all of the dozen or so staffers he had there. He told them that he had
asked me to get this material more or less as a favor, since I was in the New York
"Buxton Office" as it was known.

"Look, this one trip just shows us the great resources for raw intelligence around
the country just waiting to be collected," Kent was saying. "If this is a sample of what
is available from open sources such as from information in the files of businesses..."

"And banks, and research centers," Winnacker chimed in.

"It's nothing that we all wouldn't be trying to do for ourselves while working
on our study papers or theses back on campus. Now it's wartime, now we're Government, and now we have 'Boris' here. If he can get gut stuff like this out of
people, why, with that innocent look on his face," Kent went on, "I tell you he can
charm the birds down out of the trees and bring us back their tail feathers."

"You know," Winnacker added, holding up a sheaf of yellowed printed
data, "He even got us an inventory of the rolling stock by code and model
number. If this is what I think it is, it'll apply to France too and we'll have all
we need to know about the freight and passenger car resources of the French
State railroad, exactly what we've been trying to decipher by trial and error
from these coded inventories."

He passed it over to researcher Henry Roberts, a smooth, serious, good-hu-
mored Yalie whom Kent had brought in with him. "Here, look at this." Roberts
whistled appreciatively and said, "You're right. I'll bet these same freight car designations will also apply to the whole French rail system. Now the inventories we
have will make sense."

Waldo Campbell, another researcher, tall, with the manner of a large sheep
dog, reacted particularly to my mention of the railroad man who had been to North
Africa. He took the card I had with the Chuck Morris's number, excused himself
and left the room.

"Boris," Kent took over. "Tell us how you came to get this stuff. Was there any
problem getting at it? How long were you working on this? Did they ask what you
were doing or what you wanted this all for? Were they suspicious about Morocco or
curious about what you were after? Did they in any way hesitate to lend it to you?"

I explained how I had made the date at ALCO and how, in the course of a morning
and part of an afternoon, they had let me take away what they had provided.

In the course of this discussion, Campbell came back into the room.

"Say, Shermo." He boomed in his deep voice. "This railroad guy, I reached
him on the phone. He'll be down next week, bringing us all sorts of newer pictures.
Apparently he went over to Morocco on what seems like a vacation, or maybe the
company sent him, in 1932 or 33, which isn't all that long ago. I offered to pay his
rail fare here to Washington and back, if that's OK."

"Hell, yes," Kent replied over his shoulder. Then he turned back to me, held
my arm up like a winner in a boxing match, and in a loud voice addressed the others
in the room.

"Look. This much is clear to me," he announced. "I want 'Boris' here to work
with us as closely as he can. I propose to make him our beagle to snoop out this
kind of stuff, to learn from us what we need and where he might get it, and then
turn him loose..."

I realized I was getting a new job description. And, indeed, by summer a new job was defined for me. When in June 1942 the COI was reorganized and most of it became the Office of Strategic Services, I was designated as "field investigator, OSS/R&A New York." I was in effect on my own in New York and reporting directly to Washington.

More than that, I had a private office and private secretary. The office was easy to get used to, but the secretary - she was Lillian Landsman, a young slim brown-haired woman about my age, and I remember the first memo I ever dictated. So as not to look new or naïve, I wrote it out in longhand and then read it to her.

Chapter 2

Background…

A recollection of one's life – it's strange where you sometimes start. My thoughts began with an incident involving my sister. She had rather plaintively and persistently been asking our mother to provide some details about our family ancestry. Sonja was thirteen and I was eight years old at the time.

It was one of those moments where Mother…it could happen to any mother…was busy or distracted with things around the apartment. It was a rainy autumn weekend in New York and she was in the midst of rearranging the linen storage in the dining room, napkins, doilies, tablecloths, several sets of each, several in heavy white damask.

"What in the world brings that up?"

"It's the school. I have an assignment, to do the story of my life, what they call my family tree, and my ancestors, who was famous, who did what. Who were my ancestors? What can I…"

"Oh, come. Not now. I must get this place straightened up or we will never be ready for guests Friday," my mother replied as she set about looking for a rose bordered set, but my sister was emphatic.

"Give me the name of one ancestor and what he did," Sonja persisted.

"As far as I'm concerned, none of your ancestors amounted to a row of pins," my mother chided.

And some months later, we saw the end product, a two page hand-written report on lined paper in the meticulous left-leaning print script that girls were taught in those days at private schools. Sonja's report started with a candid sentence: "My ancestors do not seem to have amounted to very much." From there, the report went on to delve into our personal family history.

My father, Sergei Klibansky, had worked in Berlin as head of the Berlin Music Conservatory and, in his early 30s, was the youngest person ever to have held the position. He was a gifted musician, had perfect pitch, and had developed a technique for teaching the importance of deep and measured breathing to opera singers.

As a young man, he apparently had failed a physical examination, perhaps for military service, on the grounds that he had a low-level tuberculosis that had affected his lungs. Undaunted, Sergei became a health enthusiast and could often be seen performing exercises and visiting health centers such as the baths of Reichenhall on Lake Constanz in southern Germany. At Reichenhall, vast amounts of salt-heavy brine water cascaded down wooden trellises where the patient walked. Deep breathing, especially salt water, was said to have been excellent for any lung problems. It was in this setting that Sergei soon developed a deep breathing technique he considered critical to the foundation for those learning to sing opera. It was a style of breathing which when learned...would provide the singer with such magnificent audibility, the voice would crescendo off the walls of even the most expansive of opera houses. And, at a time prior to the introduction of microphones and amplifier systems, the technique developed and promoted through my father would understandably go on to cause quite a buzz among those people and patrons of the arts most esteemed within the society of opera.

My mother Ferida was the older daughter of Alfred and Frederika Weinert, a pretty 19-year old, with long brown hair braided and worn fetchingly in circular twists in back of the head or over the ears. She was fascinated by languages and etymology, and passed language teachers' exams in French, English, and Italian. Her parents were owners of a small textile factory that made linens and printed cloth largely for export to the German colonies overseas. Their domestic arrangements seemed very much like "Life with Father," with Alfred the absolute, unquestioned authority in the home.

My mother used to tell the story of how my father came to call on her family in Silesia, in southeastern Germany. His visit was originally planned to arrange a marriage between her and his younger brother, Leon, who was an up-and-coming banker. Leon had newly moved to Paris and wanted a German wife. How the contact was made, I never knew. I would guess a marriage broker was involved, but Sergei made a formal call of this visit. At some point, he quit acting on his brother's behalf and decided he wanted her hand for himself instead. My mother and father apparently went out to a dinner and dance that evening. They had a great time, got in at 2:30 in the morning, and next morning there was a large bouquet of a dozen red roses delivered to the house for her, with the card that said, "To My Beloved Fiancée".

There was a preliminary step; however, as Sergei would have to confer at some length with Alfred before any vows could be exchanged. The two discussed the marriage while all the women folk held their collective breath in the next room. At long last, the living room door opened and there stood Sergei and Alfred arm-in-arm, a sign that paternal consent had been given. Sergei and Ferida were married in 1910 and came to the United States practically immediately after their honeymoon.

Father had accepted a position at a school of music in New York City to give master classes based on his technique. They sailed on the *Nieuw Amsterdam* in August 1910, spent the first night in New York at the Algonquin Hotel, at that time the artists' and musicians' favorite spa. Those were the golden days of the opera and classical music, and the young couple was quickly taken up by wealthy patrons of the arts.

My father became known as the "German Baritone." However, World War I loomed on the horizon. As cultural attitudes began to sway against those of German descent and war with Germany became imminent, there were many who persuaded my father to disassociate from his title as "the German Baritone." They argued it would be more politically correct to refer to him as the "Russian Baritone" and father did not hesitate to facilitate the change.

My parents took a house on 1190 Madison Avenue, at 87th Street, in the German-populated Yorkville section of Manhattan. I was actually born in that house. My mother was a faddist, ready to try new methods if they appealed to her sense of "fitting"...that which she personally deemed as appropriate and progressive. She elected to give birth to me at home, attended by a nurse, following some new approach that promised painless natural childbirth and that was prominent at the time. This involved her administering her own anesthetic. She was in labor with me for 21 hours. I was her last child and I doubt that my birth did much to gain more following for that painless childbirth theory.

My sister was bitterly disappointed that the little sister she had hoped for turned out to be a boy. She came into the room with a bouquet, and with tears in her eyes, and sobbingly asked whether we could return something we hadn't ordered. It was one of Mother's favorite stories, also that my father came in, beaming, to report that his friends didn't say that oh, it was a baby, but they said "Ah! It's a boy!"

My father became well known in musical circles, and taught at home as well as at the school. We moved into a large apartment opposite Carnegie Hall, with four bedrooms and maid's quarters. The studio was the front living room of the apartment. My young life echoed with the reverberations of scales and chords, sung and re-sung, in strenuous private coaching.

There were some prominent pupils; names like Metropolitan stars Lauritz Melchior and Geraldine Farrar—a charming lady, a personal friend as well as pupil—and Zazu Pitts, a well known character actress in the movies who wished to work on developing her singing voice.

One incident was outright humorous. A lady named Florence Foster Jenkins was a fabulously wealthy patron of the arts in New York City, and by all descriptions a person of charm and taste who was very popular in musical circles of the day. One weakness: She wanted to be a coloratura soprano. Every year or so she hired the Grand Ballroom of the Plaza Hotel and had 200 specially invited guests in for a white tie reception, dinner, and recital. She studied for a while with my father. He could not turn her down; she was too nice a person and it just wasn't prudent to turn down that kind of money. He scheduled her at 8:00 in the morning so that she wouldn't overlap with any other pupil. Then came the next Concert, again a gala affair. She would dress in appropriate costume for each aria that she sang. The trouble was, she had a way of frequently missing that high note in the coloratura repertoire. It became famous; all in the audience would steel themselves for that high note. There it came and it was about 4 cycles off.

She was such a lovely person that nobody really minded, but at the end of her last program she called my father to the stage and said, with a flourish, "And now I want you to meet the person to whom I owe it all, my teacher Serge Klibansky." My father had a great sense of humor and an infectious laugh, and tears were flowing down his cheeks he was laughing so hard. The audience laughed with him. There is a 78 or 33 rpm Red Seal record outstanding, a collector's item, where some RCA engineers transcribed a concert but they only made it available after her death and then only to be privately circulated.

Sonja's report went on to account for our travels abroad. Every year or two, my parents returned to Europe, meaning Germany or France, to determine whether personally or professionally if they wanted to be back in Europe. As a result my schooling also started in Germany, in Berlin in the public school near where we lived in Charlottenburg, not far from the Kurfuerstendamm, the "Broadway" of Berlin. I remember that my parents engaged one of my schoolteachers, with the epitypical name of Herr Schultze, for late-afternoon visits to give me tutoring in German some days of the week. Herr Schultze was out of a book. High shoes, a shock of brown hair, mustache, in his early 50's, dark mohair coat. He enjoyed a sandwich with the tea that my mother served him. I recall he took out a pocketknife to help cut the sandwich into small pieces. Then I noted his teeth, a full set but the first time I had ever seen dentures, particularly ones that had a spring action all of their own. Herr Schultze insisted I write a "7" the German way, with a crossed line like a "t." He taught me Gothic script, that angular up-and-down stylized writing that remained preeminent until finally abolished under Hitler. In the nearly two years in Berlin, I practically forgot my English.

Would my parents stay back in Germany? Time and distance had taken their toll. After nearly two years in Berlin, they decided to return to the U.S. for good. I was sent to a Quaker school in downtown Manhattan, and I remember that I literally had to learn English all over again. The American "r" was particularly hard for me, like in the word "gridiron," and I didn't understand American football anyway, even though my throat had become adapted to Germanic gutturals and French vowels. I think I have more accent in my spoken English to this day than I have in my German or for that matter in my French.

My sister had a more difficult transition to school in Germany. As often happens to children who are taken overseas, she had become a super U.S. nationalist. Whenever the teacher said, "We Germans think..." Sonja raised her hand vigorously and announced that she was not German, and did not think that way at all. German teachers could not be expected to have the sense of humor that Americans have. She was regularly grounded or faced-to-the-wall, or sent home in Berlin.

Looking back on it, I realize that my parents were not an ideally matched couple. My Father was the extrovert, the dramatic artist, the pioneer and experimenter with not too much attention to prosaic details such as those related to business. Despite my Mother's repeated urging he could not get himself to sit down and write out how his technique worked and why it was so successful. He was verbal person, he could make it work and, in his "master classes," he could instruct others in some of the basic techniques. He was substantively very strong, and shrewdly never gave away too much. It was a different story in practical matters of business. He trusted people and respected advice, good or not; most often, not.

My mother was shy by comparison, made more so by extreme near-sightedness, a matter in which she deferred to Sergei who did not like her to wear glasses with company. She was cautious, skeptical of strangers. She had her small circle of warm friends but did not enjoy the swirl of what she regarded as superficial New York social life. She was a cautious bookkeeper openly critical of some of my father's financial advisors. The term "margin" as in "buy on margin" was anathema to her. Then there came the crash of 1929, deteriorating further the next two years.

I noticed increasing arguments between my parents, often loud enough to overhear even some rooms away. It seemed my mother wanted us to move out to a small house in the Long Island suburbs and in effect have my father start a new career all over again.

The memories came back in fleeting snatches as I was interrogated. I contemplated my sister's report, her statement that our ancestors never "amounted to much" and how different things may have been were it not for 1929, the year of the stock market crash and great depression which followed. Indeed, my father, with all his prominence, seemed poised for greatness. None of us could foresee what would happen next...or how those events would play a role in my future life as an agent in the world's most powerful intelligence force.

•••

It would have been reasonable to assume that I was destined for a career in the arts...certainly if environment had played a factor. My father and mother had always been on hand for openings at Carnegie Hall. He associated with some of the best and brightest performers of the time and I suspect, like any father, he would have hoped his son would somehow follow in his footsteps. I'll never know.

The great depression, set off by the 1929 stock market crash, severely cut back support to the artistic world, and ended the glamorous days of Carnegie Hall and the Metropolitan Opera. And also ended my father's income and life style. Oh, yes, the advice from his trusted good friends played a part, encouraging him to keep his money invested in the booming stock market of the 20s. In those days, on 10% margin, you could build up a broad portfolio that looked good on paper but was on borrowed money. And it was good, until 1931, when the paper portfolio vanished overnight in a flurry of margin calls. For my father it meant starting over again, all over, and starting small. We were left with nothing, except for a $20,000 life insurance policy that my father had the foresight to take out.

One afternoon in October, when he was through giving lessons, he came into my bedroom in the apartment and saw me playing with some toys on the floor. I was a little shy with my father; with his work and travel schedule I saw much less of him than I did of my mother. He did take me out every now and then on weekends to museums or to the movies, just he and I. There were only silent pictures. I recall several installments of "The Perils of Pauline" which typically left her stranded on a narrow railroad bridge with the train thundering at her...and then I recall we saw one of the earliest sound pictures, which seemed so strange! He often took me on the subway to Coney Island or Brooklyn Beach where he loved the boardwalks with the gadget shops. He once bought an apple peeler, a little hand-held gadget that he couldn't possibly make work, and this tickled his funny bone and aroused his soft but infectious laugh. He was entirely unmechanical, tried three times to pass the driver's test but saw no reason for the gear shift lever to be where it was or do what it did, and laughed at himself and his ineptitude.

On this afternoon he sat down on the armchair and held his arms out and asked me to give him a hug and a kiss. I climbed on his lap and put my arms around his neck. He asked me to say, "Daddy, I love you," which I did. Then he told me he was going away on a long trip. He always brought me souvenirs or little toys on his trips, and I asked whether he was going to remember to bring me something. Well, it was going to be a very long trip and he just might not be back. Oh, no, I said, bring me something. Somehow I sensed something was not right. He gave me another hug and let me down. He left and I resumed my puttering around on the floor.

I remember tiptoeing into my parents' bedroom early the next morning for a quick morning hug from my mother. My father wasn't there; he frequently slept in the front guest bedroom because he had become a restless sleeper. That particular morning the maid knocked frantically at the bedroom door and burst into the room, a terrified look on her face. She babbled almost incoherently and held her hands up next to her cheek as a sign of sleep. She had come into the kitchen only to find my father slumped down with his head in the open gas oven. With a cry, my mother told me to go back into my bedroom and stay there until called, and ran off to the kitchen. It was October 17, 1931.

My father's death changed our lives dramatically. We could not afford, nor did we need, the large apartment. My mother, Sonja and I moved to a small residential hotel only a few blocks away, on a side street in back of Carnegie Hall. Mother sold off several rooms full of excess furniture and many of our nice things. I remember an Eleventh Edition leather bound Encyclopedia Britannica set being carried out, even my beloved shoe-box size heavy steel "Buddy-L" truck, modeled after the blunt-nosed Mack trucks with solid hard tires so common on the streets at the time.

There was the life insurance from my father, and for income my mother took on translating jobs and did some language coaching for opera singers.

One time-consuming job she had was to translate from German into English a book recently published in Germany called "The Riddle: Man" by Dr. Paul Alsberg, a German gynecologist and anthropologist. He was reasonably well known in the field at the time, and moved to England with the advent of Hitler in Germany. Dr. Alsberg's scholarly treatise analyzed fossil findings in East Africa as the most comprehensive to date, and postulated that further research and excavation in the Kenya area would produce evidences of a species of man-ape that would prove to be the missing link between apes and humanoids. While the English version of the book when completed never received much notice, in retrospect it did anticipate by forty years the work of the Leakey family in the African Rift valley.

We could also no longer afford the tuition at Friends Seminary, the private Quaker grammar school that Sonja and I had been attending. Sonja shifted to a professional children's school, near Columbus Circle on the West Side, which had flexible hours that fitted in with her ballet work. I applied for and won a partial scholarship at the McBurney School, a YMCA-sponsored progressive education venture located in the big "Y" building on 63rd Street just off Central Park West.

The next summer, 1932, the first summer after my father's death seemed long and very hot in the small apartment. My sister kept up her ballet lessons and had her first professional jobs with a well-known corps de ballet in the New York area. My mother took me with her to Connecticut for a few weeks to stay with Isabel Ely Lord, a close friend and a genius on indexes for books, or indices as she called them. Isabel was an imposing woman with rebellious graying hair. Her casual approach to clothes belied her deserved reputation as the publishing industry's top index maker. She had inherited two adjoining summer cabins at the end of an isolated dirt road on a scenic bend of the Connecticut River near Hadlyme. Neither cabin had electricity or indoor plumbing. The main cabin had a screened porch the full length of the second floor with a magnificent view up and across the river. Here she compiled her "indices" working on a roomy improvised desk made from an eight-foot long door panel mounted on solid wooden legs. Underneath were file cabinets for three-by-five index cards; the desk top was largely covered with additional file cards in boxes, a mountain of pencils for writing, an array of reference works and dictionaries, and two large ashtrays to keep up with her chain smoking. There were also several comfortable canvas deck chairs and directors' chairs for guests. Just then she was working for Harcourt Brace on an index for the three-volume Lincoln series by Carl Sandburg who I recall as a tall, somewhat frail and shaggily dressed figure who visited for a few days during our stay there.

Another visitor was Edgar Hamilton, a cousin of some friends from Connecticut that my parents had first met on their first ocean voyage to America. Hamilton was a charming and eccentric leftover misfit from World War I days. Before the U.S. entered the war, he interrupted his college work at Carnegie Tech, took pilot training, and enrolled in the Lafayette Escadrille, the squadron of American pilots who volunteered to fight for France as a unit of the French army. After the war he tried to resettle in Connecticut but somehow drifted back to France and took a commission in the French Foreign Legion. He had since seen service in Southeast Asia and several parts of French North Africa. A tall man of athletic build, Hamilton was recovering from wounds received in the Berber Campaign in Morocco where he was serving as artillery officer and forward spotter plane pilot. In 1931 an open revolt by the Berbers, an independent minded nomadic people in the Atlas Mountains, broke out in Morocco and Algeria. In an ambush a bullet grazed his cheek, a remarkably close call, leaving the left side of his face slightly paralyzed; he was on recuperation leave in the U.S. for the summer.

In talking with my mother and me, Hamilton suggested that I visit him in France next summer. It should not be expensive. The idea was that he would arrange invitations for me to visit for two weeks at a time in different parts of France with French families whom he knew and who had children my age. He could arrange all this because he knew he would be stationed in Paris that summer, studying part of the time at the Artillery School in Metz but available to take me and call for me at intervals as scheduled. If time permitted, he would plan as climax a brief trip with him to Morocco. It sounded like a great opportunity to learn French and visit France.

CHAPTER 3

EDUCATION AND TRAINING...

I liked McBurney School. It was small and well equipped, with access to all the YMCA facilities including two swimming pools, five gyms, and vocational workshops on radios and auto motors. I was eleven, and entered the "sub-freshman" or eighth grade. Early that year an essay contest was announced to select the next editor of the school paper. Apparently the competition for the position between three members of the Junior Class was too close to call, so the faculty decided on holding a school-wide contest to resolve the succession. The contest, open to all students, involved submitting a three to five page interview with a real or imagined person. I heard about it and decided to enter just for the heck of it, even though I was not even on the paper's staff.

Influenced by my mother's translating job, I made up an interview with a "Professor Quintus Thimbletop," an imaginary fuddy-duddy archaeologist. I laced it with scholarly jargon I had overheard from my mother's translation work, about how "primitive man" adopted "tools" to be "extensions of his hand," and how he began to walk upright not just from tree to tree in the jungle but out in open non-forested terrain. I described how "Thimbletop" used the lower jawbone of an anthropoid ape as a paperweight on his cluttered desk.

My hand-written three-page entry won the contest. No, I wasn't made editor; but with some embarrassment the faculty advisor to the newspaper congratulated me and invited me to join the paper as a cub reporter. The headmaster, a wise man named Thomas Hemenway who had a strong impact on my life, had a better idea. He told me he was recommending me for a four-year McBurney High School full scholarship, which made it possible for me to matriculate there.

Came summer 1933 and after final arrangements with Hamilton, I duly sailed by myself on the SS *Samaria*, a veteran Cunard liner of 20,000 tons on which I had an indoor third-class cabin. The ship was not full and I had students' rate. As happens with children traveling alone, the staff and crew of the ship made a mascot of me. The captain showed me the bridge; the chief engineer took me through the engine room, and the chief steward gave me a tour of the kitchen and food facilities.

Most impressive, and frightening, was the time when the quartermaster navigator took me up the inside of the forward mast to see the lookout's perch, the so-called Crow's Nest. We reached this by climbing up iron rungs inside the hollow steel shaft of the mast. I had a wild case of acrophobia, not helped at all by the lateral movement of the mast as the ship rolled gently back and forth with the ocean swell, a motion sweepingly exaggerated in its effect on the Crow's Nest itself. I still have no memory of how I managed to climb back down the inside of the mast, except that I was terrified until I got to the bottom rung, out the hatch and back on deck.

The *Samaria* reached Havre, but there was no Hamilton on the dock to greet me, just a telegram delivered to me as I debarked, instructing me to take the boat train, the special rail connection for boat passengers to Paris. The train reached the terminal in Paris, the Gâre du Nord, and again no Hamilton on the platform. As the crowd thinned, I noticed a French family, a couple with a boy my age and an older sister, looking over at me uncertainly. Seeing me as the only unaccompanied twelve-year-old, the father came over to me and asked hesitantly, *"Peet-air?"* I realized he was trying to say my name, and it turned out to be the only word of English he knew without resorting to his shiny new French-English dictionary. The mother gave me a hug that required no translation and introduced herself as Madame Marina Lenoir, her husband Charles, her son Lucien, and her daughter Marguerite, called Margo. Lucien handed me a note from Hamilton in that exact tight handwriting I had come to recognize, commending me to the Lenoirs and asking me to go with them. He wrote that he would join me "tomorrow as I am detained at the Artillery School." He added, "I have been promoted to Captain, a real honor for me." I opened my English-French dictionary to "ready" and was surprised to see the word "prêt." Rather than mispronounce it, I showed it to Lucien. He laughed, pronounced the word, then said "allons, vee go" in minimal English.

It was total immersion in French for me; Hamilton had planned itineraries for every day of the week we were to be in Paris. I moved into his comfortable room in a small but very conveniently located hotel near the Etoile where the concierge and the chambermaid made special efforts to see that I was comfortable. For two days I spent every day with Lucien, who had no school at this time. We "did" the Eiffel Tower, rode up the Seine on a river barge, and took on a bus tour through Montmartre. That second evening Hamilton arrived in a black Ford Model A sedan that he said he rented from a friend. He had time off and took over showing me around.

In the succeeding days we went to Versailles, through the principal sightseeing sights such as the Louvre and the Invalides military museum, and to some most interesting museums including one on arts and measures where he bought me a bar compass that came in a bamboo case. It seemed to fascinate me to see the compass needle repeatedly point northward. We also visited a museum featuring medieval artifacts including copper chastity belts with locks that the knights who went off on the Crusades had made for their wives to wear, to keep them virtuous in their absence. Apparently, stories have been written about the sudden demand for skilled locksmiths to cope with this. I had no idea anything like this had existed or had a place in life.

Next, Uncle Edgar, as he asked me to call him, drove me to Normandie to stay with the Charles Walhain family; the father was the engraver who had designed the 1,000 Franc note among other things. Michel, his son, was slightly older than I, but good company, and I spent two most pleasant weeks at Trouville, a beach resort where the Walhains had a beachfront home. Then Hamilton reappeared in that same black Ford. We drove to the Dijon area, to a farm town called Poncey-les-Athées near the Saône River. I stayed with a charming family named Garnier; the father had served with Edgar in the Lafayette Escadrille. They had no children my age but treated me like their son. As a city boy, I was fascinated with life on a working farm. I remember bicycling all over the area and the delicious aromas of fresh baked bread and local wine used in the Sunday Catholic service to which the Garniers took me.

When Hamilton and the Model A reappeared, we drove southward to the area of Carcassone, a beautiful walled city in Provence where the des Vallières family had a magnificent country estate. They had a daughter my age with whom I felt I had little in common; they regretted their son had not returned from a camping trip, but they made me feel most welcome. I recall the huge fig tree in the front courtyard, with the ladder perched against its trunk for use in climbing up to pick the figs. The figs were the size of pears, purple-black on the outside and fiery red inside, and the well alongside to provide clear, cool water as a chaser — which led to my spending at least two days with a wild case of the runs, never out of sight of the bathroom.

Hamilton called for me and we drove back to Paris. We talked about Morocco and about seeing Tangier and perhaps Fez, the capital, a scenic city in the Atlas Mountains, or Arzew, the headquarters of the Foreign Legion regiment with which he served. But time had run out. We had three days left in Paris before my scheduled sailing date, and on one of them he had to be back at the school in Metz.

That day was a wildly rainy day, and I went over to visit Lucien at his parents' apartment in southern Paris. The Lenoirs had a four-bedroom flat on the second floor of an apartment complex near the Denfert-Rochereau cemetery not far from the Boulevard Raspail. I took the subway over, being by this time expert in Paris public transport. The parents were both away at work: Charles worked in a construction company, and Marina was a practical nurse and, I though she said, a midwife.

Lucien's sister Margo was there, and her friend Mireille, grouped around a bridge table in the living room trying out a game that looked like a French version of Parcheesi. It was basically throwing the dice to move pieces around a patterned board. Mireille and Margo were both 14. Margo was very slim like Lucien, also shared his straight, dark brown hair, hers cut in a bob at the neck, and had slightly freckled skin. Mireille was youthfully chubby but not fat. Her light brown slightly curly hair fell below her shoulders and was caught up in a ponytail, and her v-necked sweater more than hinted at early and full adolescence.

They were giggling when I came in, trying to see how they could teach me the game despite the language barrier. My French was by then quite fluent; I noted wryly that Lucien hadn't learned much English from teaching me French. Still, there had been heavy use of Lucien's French-English dictionary which, like its partner which I carried, was well dog-eared by this time. We played a card game for a while; it was not a particularly exciting game. We spoke of schools in America and everyday life for kids. What kind of games did we play back home? Somehow we drifted into Margo's small bedroom that was decorated with movie posters and a double bed covered with various colored pillows and stuffed animals that she moved to one side. Mireille had Lucien's pants open and was feeling him with her fingers. Margo was soon opening my trousers, which embarrassed me because I realized I was having an erection that she ultimately found with her mouth. My utter amazement was drowned in a cascade of newfound sensations. I was somewhat distracted for the rest of the afternoon.

Lucien and I took off to have lunch at the nearby "Coachmens' and Chauffeurs' Restaurant." Obviously the games with the girls had little effect on him, while I was still breathless. The restaurant served an excellent Petite Marmite, a casserole with veal, sausages, potatoes and cabbage, and then to see a movie. The near-by movie house was showing "Fra Diavolo," a Laurel and Hardy picture dubbed in French. The dubbing seemed strange; I had not seen a dubbed movie before. I remember very little about it except it was a riotous slapstick comedy set in Mexico. One scene had Hardy trying to reach a balcony from the street by building a ladder of restaurant tables and chairs which, when he tried to climb up on them, began to sway and finally collapse.

Hamilton returned to Paris early that evening. We had a light dinner in a small Russian style restaurant across from the hotel on the rue Jean Giraudoux. He was telling me some light anecdotes about his stay at the artillery school and how much difference it makes for him now to be a captain and not just a lieutenant. He then suddenly became serious and asked me whether we could have a serious talk. Did I have any questions that he could answer for me about sex, about girls, or about growing up physically? I blushed deeply with thoughts of the afternoon; did he, could he know about that? Apparently not, as he asked did I know what a girl looked like? Yes, I said, what with my sister in her ballet exercises sometimes prancing around in the altogether, this was no novelty to me. He went on to say that he appreciated that without my father I might not have a grown man to talk frankly with, and my mother had mentioned to him that we might find time for a father-son talk. No, I said, I really hadn't thought about it. We returned to the hotel.

The subject came up again that evening at bedtime. Hamilton wanted to go on with the conversation. I remember I was tired and yawned most inopportunely. I kissed him goodnight on the cheek and he held me and gently reached his fingers through the fly of my pajama pants. "Does this shock you?" he asked. I felt his fingers and pulled back and out of his grasp. "No," I said, "it's not shock; it's that I'm sleepy." And I got into my bed; yes, I was shocked but I did not know from what. Too much had happened today.

The next evening, my last evening in Paris, Hamilton again brought up the subject. He asked what I had thought of when I had expressed surprise at the chastity belts in the museum. Then he launched into an interesting enough exposition on the sex act and the feelings it unleashes, and how touching and petting are important in sex. I told him that I had not really thought much about this yet. He did not seem to notice my blush, as a vivid memory of yesterday crossed my mind. He mentioned wet dreams and suggested I would have them soon and to keep a small towel with me in bed just in case. This registered with me as it had happened and surprised me. He asked me to write him any time I felt I wanted some confidential talk with him. And then, the conversation having run its course, I turned over and went to sleep.

My last day we visited a museum with Impressionists' works, which made no particular impression on me. We packed my things in the afternoon, followed by another evening at the theater, Molière's "Le Bourgeois Gentilhomme," a comedy and, I realized, I understood most of the conversation on stage. Next morning Lucien and his mother came by the hotel to say good-bye and leave me a small Eiffel Tower with thermometer as a souvenir of my visit. I read nothing in Lucien's expression about that afternoon, so simply thanked them for their great hospitality. Then I was off to the boat train at the Gâre du Nord. I said good-bye to Hamilton on the platform, and was again on my own, back to Le Havre and the *Samaria*, and home. My mother met me in New York at the dock.

●●●

My sister started her career as a ballet dancer and appeared with the corps de ballet in several New York vaudeville theaters and on a coast-to-coast road touring company doing live stage shows in some of the larger theaters. She used the professional name "Karlow" as it was easier to spell and would not appear to capitalize on the family name, still fairly well known in musical circles. She was generous in sending home some of her salary to help on everyday expenses. After several years her interests changed to merchandising and fashions, and she went into the retail business. She won admittance to the famous R.H. Macy executive training program, very much sought after by business school students. With her keen mind for business and her deep sense of style she was off on a career as buyer in the leading stores around the country.

More and more my mother and I were also called Karlow by my sister's friends and contacts, and then by our own as well. We decided to make a formal change of name when I finished high school in 1937. Until then I used both names hyphenated, or either name as the occasion warranted.

Came time for college, early for me because I was barely 16. Headmaster Hemenway suggested I apply to some of the smaller colleges, most of which I had never heard of—Swarthmore, Haverford, Middlebury, Hamilton, Hobart, etc. Having gone to a Quaker elementary school, I applied for Swarthmore, a Quaker school near Philadelphia. It was suburban, a contrast to my city life, and it was co-ed, in contrast to McBurney. I went down for scholarship interviews one Spring weekend and fell in love with the place.

I had one anxious moment that week-end: All the other applicants were dressed in blue suits with white shirts and dark ties; I was wearing a light brown sports jacket with dark shirt and light tie, and had on the brown and white saddle shoes popular at the time. In the formal interview, crusty old Nicholas Pittenger, the comptroller of the College, commented to me that I looked as if I already attended Swarthmore! It broke the ice or, as the Quakers say, let the light shine on me and I won one of the full four-year scholarships.

I treasure the memories of my college years from September 1937 to June 1941. Swarthmore College had six hundred students then, evenly divided between men and women. At age sixteen and the second youngest in the class, I felt socially immature. I had had precious little chance to learn about dating and etiquette. Perhaps because of this, I found co-ed life great after my all-male high school days. Although I felt shy at first, the informal and congenial life style on the campus quickly made up for this. Freshman Week, a time when the freshmen had the campus to themselves, was a good social icebreaker for me. It was the custom for students to say "hello" when meeting on campus walks and, with less than 175 classmates, I came to know them and most of my fellow-students in the adjoining classes as well.

Swarthmore's campus had a life of its own. Even when classwork picked up and its demands on students' time grew to staggering proportions; there was an active core of extracurricular social and intellectual activity that centered on the campus.

The town of Swarthmore was small indeed; basically a suburban bedroom community with a drug store and services like laundry and hardware; no liquor. The sidewalks did seem to roll up early after dark. The students joked that the town fathers had only recently allowed the sale of something as heady as soda water. The fact that Philadelphia was near, less than an hour's time by train or bus, made up for any feeling of remoteness. I could get home to New York City in some three hours by Pennsylvania Railroad; four hours by Greyhound Bus.

Above all, my political senses were increased and reinforced at Swarthmore. There were lectures, discussion groups, debates, and general awareness of national events even if from the somewhat removed ivory tower perspective of a cloistered campus. I say national events because most of the political discussion among students and faculty was about whether Franklin D. Roosevelt was going to save the country from the Depression or would his socialistic policies ruin the country in as little as the next six months?

Meanwhile my attention was on international matters. I read with growing alarm how Nazi Germany expanded in Europe to reoccupy the Saar and the Rhineland without British or French protests or opposition. Newsreels were beginning to show the growing body of Nazi uniformed troopers marching and demonstrating. Open civil war broke out in Spain in 1936 as its army mutinied and moved to take over the country with thinly disguised German and Italian support. Reports from the Far East told of open warfare between Japan and China and of Japanese expansion. Hitler had renounced the Versailles Treaty that limited German rearmament, and Germany was overnight a military power again.

It took me a while to realize how absorbed the campus and, for that matter, American popular opinion was with domestic issues. It seemed that the relatively small amount of discussion in America of events abroad became polarized between the extremes of isolationism and its leader, the America First movement, on the one hand, and the conspiratorial communist-leaning groups on the other. Ironically, the measures advocated by the two extremes frequently overlapped, and at times supported each other.

Around Christmas time 1937, a program on Spain was held in the Quaker meeting house on campus. It featured some members of the Abraham Lincoln Brigade, a group of Americans who volunteered to go to Spain and fight on the government side. The meeting was sponsored by the American Student Union (ASU), a nation-wide college students' political action group which had a militantly active chapter at Swarthmore. The Spanish civil war, now with open German and Italian military participation, was going badly for the government there.

The program on the Spanish Civil War featured speakers who talked about the horrors of the warfare and showed slides of civilian casualties, broken bodies and scattered human limbs, and gloating fascist soldiers. They deplored the threat to Spanish democracy, whose only support was from the Soviet Union. They attacked Britain and France for appeasing the fascist aggressors, and for maintaining their misguided Chamberlain-Daladier non-intervention policies. The speakers described graphically how nothing was safe, not schools, not hospitals or homes. They said that fascists shot at any glimpse of light reflected from chromium parts of ambulances, even if they were plainly marked with red crosses. Then, on behalf of the ASU, they started a fund-raising drive for a new ambulance for the Spanish loyalists.

The drive continued into 1938 and finally materialized some months later in the form of a brand-new General Motors GMC suburban station wagon. This was a large four-door wagon, tan with huge chrome bumpers and hubcaps, white-wall tires, and wide chrome seatback rails. On its doors it had in bold gold letters "Gift of the students and friends of Swarthmore College." I found this offensive. It was inappropriate since the American Student Union chapter raised money for it and so, in my mind, had no right to use the name of the College as a whole. Even more than that: What about all that chrome trim? Was this vehicle appropriate or even useable under the circumstances? I joined some other students in protesting this, but the whole thing blew over. The vehicle was reportedly sent, with some fanfare, in the spring of 1938 on the *Mar Cantabria,* the last ship to leave New York for the loyalist cause. The *Mar Cantabria* was intercepted by the fascists off Gibraltar in the last days of the war. I'm sure the GMC wagon made a great staff car for a fascist general.

This wasted, over-sold, and aborted political cause made a great impression on me as an object lesson in what not to do in attacking the problems of the world. It was my first exposure to the bluster of a communist-front organization.

•••

In 1938, Hitler was openly expanding in Europe, repeatedly calling the bluff of the British-French appeasement advocates. Austria was annexed in the spring; the Munich Conference in the fall gave Hitler most of Czechoslovakia. It seemed obvious to me that Hitler had to be stopped, and the sooner the better.

In March 1939, I experienced my single most impressive classroom lecture. Two days after Hitler moved German troops into Prague and what was left of Czecho-Slovakia, Professor Richard Salomon announced the Modern European History class had a change in its schedule. He had prepared a special session just on Prague, Central Europe and the position in history of the three key provinces, Bohemia, Moravia, and Slovakia. Salomon was new at Swarthmore, a refugee from Prague who had come out only recently via England as anti-Jewish pressure mounted in Germany. He was middle aged, dark haired, slightly stooped and spoke excellent but careful English with a resonant German accent. This day he was very serious, waited for the class to settle down; it took a little longer as we felt something unusual was about to happen.

He began with a history of the earliest days in Europe, the Romans and the tribal invasions, the Holy Roman Empire, the invading hordes from the East, the pivotal position of the provinces between the Russian, Austrian, and later the Germanic empires. He pointed out that the splintering of the Austro-Hungarian Empire in World War I left a political vacuum in the area that competing forces sought to fill. After the recent attempt to appease Hitler in Munich, it was not a surprise to see the newspapers showing pictures of the weeping faces of the people of Prague as German troops marched into their city.

The bell rang, marking the end of the hour but no one stirred.

Salomon went right on talking. He dreaded the coming of another general war but felt it inevitable before peace could be restored in Europe and in the entire world. Yet another world war would not suffice. Even after such a war, he foresaw that confrontation and political imbalance would continue until the three provinces, Bohemia, Moravia, and Slovakia, were again able to live their own lives as the pivotal points of Europe.

He sat down, emotionally drained. For measurable moments no one moved. Finally there was the soft slap of notebooks closing and the rumble of chairs being pushed back as we rose. We all stopped by Salomon's desk in a slow line and without a word spoken we each shook hands with him on our way out.

I have thought back to this lecture many times. Salomon actually anticipated not just World War II but also the Cold War that followed it.

•••

Open war in Europe broke out on September 1 as Polish horse cavalry from World War I days tried to oppose Nazi mechanized divisions in Blitzkrieg mode. The strong and strident America First movement spoke out, with isolationists determined to keep "us" out of Europe's constant problems. To me, the problems of Europe and America were just too entwined for the United States to keep out of the war. The spreading Nazi Empire was too horrendous a prospect of spreading tyranny, particularly with a Hitler-type demagogue whipping up populations with waves of hatred.

The local chapter of the ASU was the only organized political group on campus. At that point, it supported the isolationist America First position on the grounds that the war in Europe was an imperialist colonialist war. It also opposed military draft, the selective service legislation then being debated.

I volunteered to attend a national student rally on the draft, held at Columbia University. I was one of three delegates from Swarthmore. After formal speeches, the floor was opened for comments. Mine was the last of two pro-draft comments from the floor—I said the draft was sensible for us, to get ready for what seemed a very real possibility, namely war. Every subsequent comment was opposed to the draft. Suddenly a ready-made resolution opposing the draft was read, starting with the words—"We, the students of America..." I told my two Swarthmore colleagues that I would not associate our college with this, and walked out. One of our delegation remained at the meeting, skeptical but saying "they may have a point..." It was my first experience with communist steamroller tactics to manipulate and take over an open meeting.

•••

In March of 1940 I won the college public speaking contest for the second year in a row. The prize was $35, just enough for the new electric shaver I coveted. My winning speech before the whole student body was on politics, and I called it "What this campus needs." I spoke about how the ASU chapter had repeatedly asserted it was speaking in the name of Swarthmore on issues like the draft, on which that group patently did not reflect the views on campus, and that we needed a new group to give voice to majority opinion. I was pleased that I won, because I really wanted that electric shaver.

The next day I was jolted when I received a personal letter from the College President, Dr. Frank Aydelotte, complimenting me on my speech and asking me to come see him and tell him what I planned to do and how he could help me. I hastily cobbled together an idea about recruiting a nucleus of twelve student leaders, half of us to join the ASU chapter and work to wean it out of the national organization, the other half to form a new middle-of-the-road organization that would work along "Town Meeting" lines. Aydelotte welcomed me in his office, listened attentively to my proposal, told me how important he thought my initiative was, and wished me well. At the next weekly all-students meeting, or "collection," as these sessions were called, I mentally cringed when he started his talk with — "I was excited when last week Peter Karlow called for a new student organization..."

Actually the Town Meeting did quite well for a short while. The best attendance was at a meeting we held featuring a Nazi spokesman, sent by the German Library of Information in New York, debating a faculty member, the chairman of our philosophy department, on the true nature of Hitlerism. It was a tense but exciting discussion. I remember the German spokesman as an oily young man who asked me to smooth the way for him by giving him a somewhat humorous introduction as "one of those nasty Nazis." I do not remember what he said; it was lost in the withering blast our philosophy professor gave him, an unreserved acid sharpness I never expected a faculty member to display inside or outside a classroom.

The Town Meeting held several more meetings on topics like why the League of Nations failed and definitions of neutrality in the face of open war. Its meetings died out with the end of the school year. Meanwhile the other members of our Town Meeting group who had joined the ASU managed to take over the chapter, which voted itself out of the national organization. It did, however, continue on campus under another name and under a far more subdued program.

In May 1940 the German attack broke out, overrunning the Low Countries and most of France. The air battle for Britain was on and the attitude of the American public towards the war became clearer, basically sympathetic towards the British but still not wanting to get directly involved, at least not too soon. On campus the atmosphere became more tense as we sensed we all most probably would be in what we could only think of as a repeat of 1914-18.

1941 — War in Europe was going badly, and die-hard America First isolationism was noisier than ever. President Roosevelt was trying out destroyer for bases deals to begin open military support to Britain.

In June we had ten days of final exams. Under the seminar or "Honors" system introduced by Aydelotte, this meant ending the senior year with eight final exams, one on each of the subjects covered in Junior and Senior years. It was a hell week exercise, followed by eight individual oral exams. The exams were prepared and given by outside professors briefed only on the particular course's suggested reading list.

Despite this difficult finale, I found the seminar system ideal. The student-run discussions at these seminars, usually held in the professor's homes, were instructive for the subject matter and for the ability to discuss ideas and alternatives.

With the war boiling in Europe, I shared a certain slap-happiness that inevitably pervaded our spirits at the time. The first war casualty among our classmates was Bert Marclay, a tall, handsome, popular scholar/athlete who had volunteered for the Army Air Force after the first semester of Senior year. Marclay was commissioned and assigned to basic pilot recruit training. He was killed when a student pilot he was instructing froze at the controls during a steep dive. A harbinger of more to come, we all realized. It seemed that our career planning depended on the draft, no longer a subject of discussion but a reality, or on being declared "4-F" as medically not qualified.

Hitler suddenly invaded Russia; it was final exam time and I met one of our former ASU leaders in front of the Library one day. He was elated and said that now it was indeed a holy war for national liberation, because we were now hand-in-hand with the Soviet Union, the "workers' paradise," fighting fascism. I was astounded that one of my fellow-students, one of my peers, a classmate, could be so completely manipulated by an outside influence.

CHAPTER 4

JOB HUNTING...

After graduation I returned to New York City and started job hunting. I applied to General Electric's executive training program and went to Bridgeport, Connecticut for an interview and a plant tour. Even thinking about being involved in something as prosaic as the manufacture of window and room fans when the war in Europe was breaking its bounds was, well, it was not for me.

I applied to National Broadcasting Company, in answer to an ad for their international newsroom, but they wanted someone with knowledge of six languages for their $35 a week job. But the NBC Guest Relations staff took me on, the blue uniformed guides to radio studios and tours, at the salary of $15 a week. I started as one of the ushers steering the nightly studio audiences. I learned a lot about studio layout and sound effects, then was promoted to an office boy job in the press room, running scripts to the news announcers for the twice-nightly news programs. My hours were from four p.m. to midnight, not a bad schedule for the summer, and it gave me time to look around for other jobs.

Guest Relations work for the press room usually meant that once every evening I was locked into the studio if a feature show was scheduled immediately after the news program. For example, for each day of several weeks I watched the seven p.m. Fred Waring show, the "It's Chesterfield Time" musical, pleasant but five times a week was sweet torture. For every day one week, Fred Waring introduced his featured singer, a slim brunette with bare-midriff dress. Then he would ask the studio audience if they liked her dress. After the applause subsided, he would look at the dress and say, "I made it!" After the laughter subsided, he would peek wolfishly at the bare midriff and bring down the house with the climax line, "I'll finish it."

During what I thought of as my intermission, a one-hour period I had in lieu of lunch hour, I sometimes took the subway for a brief date with my college flame, a delightful, bright and vivacious, longhaired blonde who lived in Brooklyn. I'd phone first; by agreement I would let the phone ring three times then hang up and call again. Since she was living with her parents, she explained, everyone would know that the call was for her and she would answer it with a warm "Hello, Peter." One day I apparently let the phone ring four times before hanging up and calling again, and she answered with a warm "Hello, George." I had a lot to learn.

One Sunday I saw a want ad looking for field people for market research. Applicants were to apply to "Roper" in Radio City. It turned out to be Elmo Roper, the prominent public opinion pioneer. He interviewed me, but not to be one of the field people counting cars in gas stations or whatever. He had a better idea. He was interested in me as his personal aide, a person who could save him time on details. At Roper's request, most of his staff interviewed me. They all turned me down flat, appalled at the idea of some young squirt fresh out of college starting to go to work in the boss' office, and possibly forming a barrier between the boss and his staff. Roper called me in a week later to tell me this would not work out after all. I brazenly asked what else could he suggest? He thought a moment, then said what about Colonel Donovan's, that's "Wild Bill" Donovan's, new assignment to build an intelligence organization? Some years later I saw the letter of recommendation Roper wrote to Donovan about me. He wrote "this young man's eyes fairly sparkled when I told him about your organization." Since Roper was one of the people Donovan relied on to recruit early candidates for the new COI which needed an interpreter of German and French, I was promptly interviewed, given personal history forms to fill out, and hired as soon as my security clearance came through. The process lasted less than a month.

On Monday, September 15, 1941, I arrived for work at the office on the fourth floor of a building at 41st Street and Madison Avenue. Emerging from the elevator, I saw that the glass pane had not yet been installed into the front door of the office suite. Seeing no reason to open the metal doorframe, I simply climbed in. Mary Florence Veronica Smith, a slim, middle-aged professional secretary with her red-blonde hair cut short in a becoming bob, greeted me with a smile. She had worked for years in Rhode Island for the boss, Col. G. Edward Buxton, "Something tells me," she said, "that you'll do well here with us." Florence became a real mentor for me, and a life-long personal friend.

I could not believe my luck. I seemed to have landed on the ground floor of what was to become a new U.S. national intelligence service. I began to realize how much this new service was the work of one inspired man. It was an achievement for one person to pull together a proposal for a national intelligence organization. It was an additional achievement to outflank its many detractors and obtain presidential approval to move ahead. Donovan was able to do this and more. He found key people who helped him build the organization, initiating the first independent intelligence activities.

On July 11, 1941, President Roosevelt issued a one-page order that read:

> *"1. ...established the position of Coordinator of Information, with authority to collect and analyze all information and data, which may bear upon national security; to correlate such information and data, and to make such information and data available to the President and to such other departments and officials of the Government as the President may determine; and to carry out, when requested by the President, such supplementary activities as may facilitate the securing of information important for national security not now available to the Government...*

> *6. William J. Donovan is hereby designated as Coordinator of Information."*

Donovan was born in Buffalo, New York. He worked his way through Columbia University and Law School. When war broke out in Europe in 1914, he took a reserve commission with the Sixty-ninth Regiment of the New York National Guard, a unit that was called up early and that saw heavy combat. He emerged from World War I as a colonel and a hero. He was one of the most decorated officers in the U.S. Army, receiving the Congressional Medal of Honor among other awards. His wartime exploits led to his becoming popularly known as "Wild Bill" Donovan. His popularity was so great that he was asked to lead the New York City victory parade down Fifth Avenue.

He gained a reputation as a lawyer of the highest integrity, specializing in business and banking problems. He was also, on several occasions, a state and national public servant. Undoubtedly, Donovan's foreign missions for his clients and for the federal government gave him a world-view of political, business, and banking activities that few other Americans in the 1920s and 1930s possessed.

In 1939, as the threat of another world war grew, Donovan undertook several missions in Europe for President Roosevelt. As he toured the Balkans and spent time in England, Donovan became more and more convinced of the need for a comprehensive national intelligence effort, and he reported this to Roosevelt. After war broke out, Donovan spent time in England and it was during this period that the British briefed him thoroughly on the workings of the British intelligence organizations. Donovan was convinced the U.S. needed an intelligence service like that of the British to be ready for whatever threat of war might arise.

How to staff this new organization? Donovan knew and kept in touch with a wide range of top-level people in business, banking, science and academia. He called upon them to volunteer their services. They responded positively and, in turn, recruited others.

How to start the wheels turning? Donovan called on "Ned" Buxton, his close friend whom he had just recruited to organize and head what became the Oral Intelligence unit in New York.

G. Edward Buxton's association with Donovan began when they were fellow-officers in World War I. Buxton was the Major who talked the conscientious objector Sgt. York out of his reluctance to kill. York subsequently single handedly rescued his pinned down platoon and wiped out a German machine gun company, for which he received the Congressional Medal. A movie, "Sergeant York," had just been released based on this story, starring Gary Cooper. Buxton told me it was not a bad representation of him and of the actual story, except that he was unhappy about his being depicted as having his officer's tunic open at the collar when he had his talk with York.

The Oral Intelligence unit was the first COI venture to collect original (or new) information. The basic idea was to bring together a nucleus of people with widely varied backgrounds who would be able to open contact with new or old professional, charitable, political and social groups with international ties that could be useful in providing information related to the war effort.

New York City, with its international focus, was an ideal location for such an office. New York was a magnet for groups and associations with agendas related to every phase of world cultural and political activity.

The most immediate opportunity to obtain information was in the stream of refugees arriving in New York from Europe and North Africa. All kinds of organizations stepped in to help or host as many refugees as possible. In the labor field, the Ladies Garment Workers Union became active. In the religious field, a number of Jewish organizations joined together to form HIAS, the Hebrew Immigrant Aid Service, that quickly had its hands full with the wave of Jewish refugees arriving. Catholics and Protestants also had centers for refugees. The émigré political and national groups pulled together forming political parties in the U.S. that matched those that were formerly influential in European countries.

It became obvious that more language skills, specifically knowledge of German and French, would be needed. It was just at this juncture that my application to the COI arrived and I was hired as a translator and interpreter. After just a short time on the job, I was turned loose to do my own interviews where the subjects spoke no English.

• • •

Many refugees came on "neutral country" ships like the Portuguese-flag *Serpa Pinto* that shuttled between New York and Lisbon. The Port Authority in New York had no ready way to handle these newcomers, to give them any more than the most cursory health check and interview. Any further information of interest that they might have would have to be elicited in German or French. The established agencies—State Department, Immigration, FBI, Navy Intelligence, Internal Revenue, and Coast Guard—were little better prepared. Buxton's Oral Intelligence unit stepped into the breach.

Buxton made arrangements with the Port Authority for his group to screen the new arrivals. It was Oral Intelligence's first commitment. These arrangements pointed the way to a growing circle of contacts that produced intelligence. They also opened the way for the operations group in Washington to gain access to several valuable recruits who subsequently were trained, then returned to their native countries as agents.

Collecting information was new to all of us. No one really knew what sort of questions to ask, what or whom to look for, and what to do with the information and data that was collected. When I went to Oral Intelligence, the office had been open for only four weeks. Our questionnaires, made by us, were mainly on everyday morale and living conditions in the places where the new arrivals had come from. The questionnaires also asked about military sites and production.

After a while, I gave this an added twist, thinking that if spies were to be sent into Europe at some time, they would need stage props. American toothpaste and clothes would be out. I noted that some refugees had wristwatches or wallets or books from their home areas. I offered to buy them American replacements if they would sell me theirs. Some wondered what kind of game this was and offered to give me their things; others smiled wisely and realized their belonging might be used for people being sent back to their countries. I found Europeans much more spy tolerant than we Americans were. I gathered quite a collection of materiel that included suits, toilet gear, wallets, shoes, and coats and, in some cases, just the store labels out of the clothes. One day Buxton, with some amusement, saw my growing collection and after reviewing it thought it was a good idea. He sent several parcels of materiel to some office at the Washington headquarters.

There were few rules or procedures in the Oral Intelligence Office. However, those that existed included: not losing documents; tearing up all carbon paper; keeping all papers in safes or safe repositories; keeping minimal subject files and relying as much as possible on central chronological files. Unwritten ground rules had to be compiled. The key one was that no word of the office or its activities or contacts must be allowed to reach anyone or anything related to the America First Committee. We assumed that the eyes, ears, and fingers of the anti-FDR people, or the anti-interventionists, or the plain outright isolationists, were everywhere. I had no idea about leaks or how they worked until articles about Donovan and the COI began to appear in the press. There were articles by anti-administration feature writers like the moderate, yet anti-FDR, Arthur Krock of the New York Times as well as embittered isolationist Walter Trohan of the Chicago Tribune.

Pearl Harbor ended isolationism. On Sunday, December 7, 1941, the nation was shocked and galvanized into action. I was home. I was living with my mother in a small, sixth floor three-bedroom apartment near Carnegie Hall. It was not fancy because the money reserves had nearly run out and my government salary checks, although very good by the standards of the time, $50 a week as GS-7 Assistant Field Investigator, had only recently begun.

The radio was on. At around two PM, as I recall, the announcer broke into the program with the stark words that the Japanese navy was attacking Pearl Harbor. I felt a tingle of excitement, and relief. The charade of isolationism had been put down in one sweep. But at what cost!

Monday at the office, we listened to each other's views about war and our future positions. Would we become a military unit? Or would the work be taken over by the military? Now we could be more open about our activities.

The week before Pearl Harbor, I had made a discreet call on the German Library of Information; the propaganda and news office of the German Consulate located on Sixth Avenue in the upper forties. It was an unproductive visit. This was the same office I had contacted while at Swarthmore to obtain a speaker for the Town Meeting organization I had helped found back there. The Tuesday after Pearl Harbor, I was asked by Washington's R&A office to assist Dr. Walter Dorn, the COI's leading political researcher on Germany in Washington, to close down the German Library.

I accompanied him and Bill Moran, special agent with the U.S. Treasury Department, through the Library's offices in search for material that might be intelligence or of research interest. We arrived at nine in the morning, were greeted politely by a lady receptionist, an American, and by the German-American office manager. We looked around and found some statistical data and a good deal of descriptive material on current German physical and economic features and infrastructure. These were duly shipped to R&A in Washington. Much of the material was pure Nazi propaganda, glowingly illustrated books and posters on public demonstrations cheering the new Nazi paramilitary, statistics on German economic revival, and happy German families cheering Hitler.

There was a thin veneer of cultural material, classic German art and literature. I spotted an exact reproduction of famous German children's book, *Sloppy Peter,* which dated from the 1840s and to which I had been exposed in my childhood in Berlin. I still know most of the rhymes by heart. With Dorn's and Moran's approval, I absconded with the little volume and have had many occasions to show my friends how German children were influenced in their childhood by simple parables based on sheer terror. For example, there was the story of the boy who sucked his thumbs until one day the Terrible Tailor came along in his black suit with his huge black shears and cut off both his thumbs. The refrain, roughly translated, was:

"There he stands without a thumb;
Wasn't he a little dumb?"

•••

I worked with a number of other senior researchers who came up from Washington at different times to collect material from companies, libraries, and informed people in the New York area. At one point, Sherman Kent called me to tell me that the man he called "Bill Langer's favorite spook" was coming to do work on British African countries. (I did not at first catch the word "spook" as meaning Negro.) A tall, charming man with swarthy complexion arrived. I had a number of things lined up for him and, at day's end; we were still not finished. I told my immediate boss at Oral Intelligence, former New York State assistant district attorney Malcolm A. Crusius, that we would be back after dinner. Crusius caught my arm and took me aside. He asked me in a low voice where I was going to take our guest. Though a born New Yorker, I only then put together the facts that our visitor was black and that some restaurants still did not welcome black patronage. Our visitor was Ralph Bunche, later Secretary General of the United Nations.

There were other personalities. Karl Adler was a German refugee businessman who found to his surprise— and regret— that he had a Jewish grandmother. I say regret as he would have been an avid Nazi given the chance. Now in the West, he was avidly anti-Nazi. In Germany, he had been arrested and he and his family deported to North Africa. He was one among many Jewish refugees who had been transported to Algeria and made to work in the Atlas Mountains on the "Trans-Sahara Railroad." This railroad was eventually supposed to connect Algeria with the Senegalese railroad across the Sahara and so provide a rail link to Dakar from the Mediterranean.

One of the new questions on our interview list concerned such a Trans-Sahara Railroad. Adler located and obtained statements from others that had worked on the railroad project, which quickly showed up the nature of this venture as pure propaganda. Instead of being Trans-Sahara, the railroad was to go only to the phosphate mines at Colomb-Béchar, just south of the Atlas Mountains at the northern edge of the Sahara. Other refugees reported that the railroad company was installing standard-gauge track where they were working. We knew from research sources that standard gauge would not be compatible with the narrow-gauge track on the Senegalese railroad. The whole Trans-Sahara thing seemed silly to me, at least as not being a military threat to the U.S., but I learned through this that my opinion was not the point. My job was to be sure to have the most complete and latest information possible, then, to evaluate the reporting for reliability of the sources and the timeliness of the information. I must leave behind any opinions I might have and present the intelligence in usable form to the customer to let him draw the final conclusions and determine what should be done or if more information was needed.

A number of missionaries came back from West Africa. I became familiar with active and interesting groups like the Phelps-Stokes Foundation and the Christian and Missionary Alliance, and with their various esoteric doctrinal differences. One returned missionary, the Rev. Francis Thornberry, reported a sighting of a German submarine off the Ghana coast just a few months before we talked with him. He brought two letters from others who had seen the sub as well. While their information was usually general, I did not realize until afterward that the reports of my interviews with them caught the eye of the operational people in Washington. Several missionaries were recruited to go back as agents. I had not thought of missionaries as open game for recruitment.

•••

There were lighter moments, too. One day a new staff member joined us. He was Tom Krock, the son of journalist Arthur Krock whose criticism of the Roosevelt administration was daily fodder in the press. Roosevelt had told Donovan to find a job for him hoping this might diffuse some of Arthur Krock's criticism. Donovan turned to Buxton, and Tom Krock appeared. We did not know where to use him, as his German was limited. We each were asked to work with him and to recommend where he could be best utilized.

Krock was easy to talk to, had stories to tell about a variety of interesting places in the Middle East, Romania, and Germany. He was in his mid-forties, with a small mustache and always well dressed in expensive looking suits. He often wore small ribbon rosettes in the lapel of his suits, the colors usually matching his ties. A colorful ribbon he wore one day represented, he said, a high decoration from Romania where he had done some consulting in the oil fields. A black and white ribbon was, he said, for the German Iron Cross that he received when he attended the German General Staff School in the mid-thirties. I pricked up my ears at this because of his limited German.

When I reported this to my office mates, we agreed to ask him to write up these experiences, especially the German General Staff School. He worked on a report; he talked to others and me about details of the report on several occasions, although no drafts were ever in evidence. At this stage we had an office caucus about Tom, and, late one afternoon, after he had left, we searched his desk. He was indeed working on a paper on the German General Staff school, but he had two volumes on the subject from the Public Library and we could see several paragraphs of his handwritten text directly cribbed from one or the other of the library volumes. Buxton called him in and fired him.

Later I saw a letter to Donovan from Arthur Krock, apologizing for Tom, expressing appreciation for his having been hired, and noting wistfully that he had hoped that Tom would have overcome his flights of fancy for which he had been under treatment. I wondered if this experience, of Roosevelt's having done him a favor, would in any way change the critical tone in Arthur Krock's articles. If it did, I could not detect it.

CHAPTER 5

IN THE NAVY...

In March 1942, I went on my own to local Navy headquarters in New York at 90 Church Street and applied for a Navy commission. There were rumors in the office that we might receive direct military commissions, but they sounded pretty vague. The Navy announced a V-7 program for college graduates, to involve three or possibly six months of training at a college campus followed by commissioning. This interested me. Strange, and possibly a throwback to my European background, the Navy seemed like the "elite" service to me. To be an officer in the Navy would mean something special. I filled out a detailed personal history questionnaire; very similar to the one I had filled out for the COI job. I don't recall whether I was completely consistent in my answers on the two questionnaires, nor whether it made any difference.

By early summer it was obvious that we in the Oral Intelligence unit were going our different ways. Malcolm Crusius, my mentor, was in the first group to be drafted. He had a warm sense of humor, was tall, slightly stooped, and constantly complaining about his bad feet. He was surprised to find himself in the induction line with his foot doctor. He was even more surprised when the foot doctor was exempted as 4-F while Crusius was inducted. Crusius, as much worried about his feet as about going into the Army, found that his new GI boots, even without arch supports, were, he said, the most comfortable shoes he had ever worn. He was inducted, then commissioned and assigned to the Judge Advocate Corps. Most of his service was in the U.S. and in England.

Jack O'Keefe was a journalist and labor lawyer. He went with the Labor Desk, the outfit that had the OSS' greatest success in penetrating Germany with well-placed agents. Emmy Rado, a psychologist, and Frances Kalnay, a professor of language and history, helped develop new organizations designed to deal specifically with foreign nationality groups and specialists. Les Fossel actively helped develop support for the Norwegian resistance, which turned in an impressive record of anti-Nazi activity and sabotage.

In early June 1943, I received a certified letter from the Navy, addressed "Ensign Serge P. Karlow," that asked me to report downtown for a physical exam at Church Street.

By mid-June the COI was closed down. Its "overt" information functions like the Voice of America were placed under a newly created Office of War Information. This met the objections of many prominent news and media people like producer

Robert Sherwood ("There Shall Be No Night") to separate the open statements by the U.S. from secret operations. The remaining functions were covered by a Military Order and assigned to the newly created Office of Strategic Services under the Joint Chiefs of Staff.

There was turmoil in our office, and also relief. That OSS was placed under the Joint Chiefs should make a broad range of operations possible and help define relations with other agencies like the military intelligence services, State Department and the FBI.

This was that very week that I received a letter stating that my commission as an officer in the Navy was ready and that I must come down to be sworn in. I was half elated and half-concerned. What do I tell the office? Just then Buxton was in England. His secretary, Florence Smith, told me that he and Donovan were in London to negotiate a vital intelligence working agreement with the British Services, Secret Intelligence Service (SIS or MI-5) and Special Operations Executive (SOE). Nonetheless, she cabled Buxton to ask him about my accepting the commission. In two days, Buxton's reply was in, in effect telling me to take the commission, that "we" had "him" on "our list" for an Army commission, but to go ahead and "we would get him back" from the Navy after commissioning.

Without knowing what that meant, I went down to Church Street again, had another physical, then attended a briefing on the V-7 program. We were lined up, perhaps 20 of us, all recent college graduates, and sworn in. After this, a Lt. Commander with a broad New York accent dismissed those for whom there were no orders. They were to await orders by mail or phone. There were orders for the two other men and me. The others went to MIT in Boston for technical training as engineering officers. Then the Lt. Commander looked at me with a quizzical expression, and said words I will never forget. "Kralow," he started, stumbling over my name. "Kralow, I got your orders here. But what the hell is the O-S-S, the office of sas-tregic sterbo-scopes?"

I went to Saks Fifth Avenue to buy a summer weight blue uniform; this was the object of numerous envious glances later. It was not of "regulation" material but oh, so comfortable in the early and late warm summer weather when heavy, winter blues were already the mandatory uniforms. I received from the Navy a fat packet of papers, a correspondence course in Navy rules and practices that I was to mail in, lesson by lesson, since my assignment to OSS precluded my attending the V-7 program. I also received a copy of the Blue Jacket's Manual, the basic sailor's bible on details, such as, drill, insignia, flags and pennants, knot tying, and what-not, on which I had more tests to mail in.

"Well, I'm in the Navy now," I said wonderingly to myself, "And an officer at that." The whole process of my militarization seemed unreal.

•••

As of Monday morning, June 15, 1942, it was OSS, the Office of Strategic Services. The change from Coordinator of Information gave a big boost to general morale and sense of purpose in our office. I called the R&A offices in Washington to get reactions from there. I heard only relief that the situation of the function had now been clarified and established. The controversial overt functions, the open news and propaganda activities of COI, like Voice of America, were off on their own in the new Office of War Information.

The intelligence functions were now together in OSS, including collection and analysis of intelligence from all possible sources, the mounting of psychological and paramilitary warfare operations, and the necessary auxiliary functions to support them. These activities were all developing into operations centers whose exact missions were not yet clear. The OSS was growing, but on an uncharted course. We were all new at it, but it was the challenge of developing these new operations and the romantic appeal of behind-the-scene operations that attracted all of us in varying degrees.

To avoid any gap in authority and funds, President Roosevelt issued a military order placing OSS under the Joint Chiefs of Staff. I saw the order at the time, and realize now that I did not appreciate its classic simplicity and to-the-point language:

> *"Pending the issuance of specific instructions as to its functions, the Joint Chiefs of Staff desire that the Office of Strategic Services continue the duties and activities of such Branches and Divisions of the former Office of the Coordinator of Information as have not been transferred to the Office of War Information."*

> *"This order is designed solely to clarify the relations of the Office of Strategic Services to other government agencies, to facilitate the transaction of current operations, and to make possible the continuance of existing contracts and services."*

This order did not reflect any of the intense inter-service rivalry that was rampant in Washington. Now that there was a state of war, the military wanted to keep control of the intelligence function, particularly the clandestine functions, and not trust these functions to civilians. I had felt some of this resentment by military personnel with whom I had dealt, even at my entry-level position in New York. It seemed to disappear overnight when I started to work in uniform.

"Joint Chiefs of Staff" sounded supremely impressive. I found out at the time that all service men in uniform had franking privilege, meaning they could mail letters without postage stamps as long as they put their name, rank, serial, and affiliation on the envelope. I couldn't resist sending Phil Wood, a college classmate, a letter on which I put this as the frank:

Ens. S. P. Karlow USNR 174975
Joint Chiefs of Staff
Office of Strategic Services
Washington, D.C.

I used Washington in the address as the home base of the OSS even though I could have used New York; with "Joint Chiefs of Staff" showing, nothing else mattered. The letter went through, and elicited a breezy answer from my classmate. He was impressed because it sounded like I was running the entire war effort. He hoped I would keep General George C. Marshall on as Chief of Staff to help me!

In September, Donovan came to the New York office to give a general briefing to the staff. The meeting was held in Allen Dulles' meeting room in the Radio City office building, which then housed the bulk of the New York office. There were offices on the 35th and 36th floors. I recall how impressed I was with the decision to build an inside stairway between the floors. Dulles was a perfectionist. I wondered how much this inside stairway must have cost. It did, however, improve the security of the office not to have to go between offices in the open corridors and elevators.

This meeting in September was the second time I had occasion to meet or at least to shake hands with Donovan. The first time had been on a visit he had made to the Oral Intelligence office early in January after Pearl Harbor. This time I noticed his controlled manner, clear blue eyes, and quiet smile. He spoke to everyone around the table, using his famous ability to remember the names of each person whom he had met before. To my surprise, when Donovan came to me, he remembered meeting me in Col. Buxton's office and made a comment about Oral Intelligence. I made a remark about hoping to get closer to the scene of action. He replied that he knew I was working with Sherman Kent and that he wanted to "get the professors to the front" to improve the caliber of intelligence processing and analysis. This was one of Donovan's pet goals.

During my assignment in New York, I became well acquainted with one of Donovan's personal aides, Wayne Nelson, a slender, high-strung former court reporter and amateur Thespian. His chain smoking and somewhat dissolute air hid an alert mind, a photographic memory, and keen powers of observation. Nelson once held a New York State record for high-speed court stenography, and was known for his ability to learn lines for a play in just a single rehearsal or two. Wayne was self-conscious about his "4-F" draft classification because of his poor eyesight and bad back. His photographic memory was fantastic, covering a variety of subjects, like knowing every line of Shakespeare, and most baseball statistics and modern history dates. We hit it off well, and met for lunch on his frequent trips to New York.

Nelson told me some stories about working for Donovan. Donovan slept only a few hours a night. He read a copy of every cable that went out from or came in to Washington headquarters. Donovan also read an array of newspapers and magazines and a book a day, scribbling comments to the author or letters to the editor right across the pages, and expecting Nelson, or someone, to catch the comments, transcribe them, and send them along.

One evening Nelson stayed on for dinner and a nightcap at my apartment. At around nine p.m., the telephone rang. It was Donovan from Washington to speak to Nelson. Donovan asked Nelson for a briefing on a particular problem discussed with a committee of the Joint Chiefs of Staff. "But Sir," Nelson said. "Those files are in Washington and I'm still in New York." "Take your time," Donovan said, "but have breakfast with me tomorrow morning." Nelson took a deep breath, then headed off to Pennsylvania Station to get the night train to Washington, which would give him a few pre-dawn hours to get the files together in the office.

In October 1942 Sherman Kent called me to come to Washington. He was still openly impressed with my work getting information from companies, associations, and research centers. He pointed out that he was in the midst of an overwhelming volume of work related to planning for the invasion of North Africa and needed all the help he could get. He asked me to spend considerable time in Washington so that we could work out the best and most effective way for me to become part of his unit, now called the R&A Africa Division. He wanted to replace me in my open sources collection work with his former colleague William B. Kipp, and use me to take advantage of my French.

The landings in North Africa were hardly a secret in the Africa Division, and Kent was thinking in terms of getting a team together that, after the landings, would be a portable R&A resource office and library and would operate overseas in the Theater of Operations. He told us that a sizeable group of R&A people in London would be working with American and British staffs on strategic planning that would be centered there. Kent assumed, correctly as it worked out, that the team in North

Africa would be giving closer tactical support to the operations that would be mounted from there. Since I was already commissioned, I could be sent abroad on short notice and be mobile in a changing military situation when conditions in North Africa were ready.

I was delighted at the prospect. Kent had a rigorous and intensive training program for me: move to Washington and be thoroughly drilled in research techniques, analysis, reporting, and in delivering information in its most useable forms.

I appeared in Washington the next Monday in Navy uniform and marched with exaggerated stride right into Kent's office, brass buttons flashing (I thought). I walked up to his desk, gave him a sweeping *"H.M.S. Pinafore"* salute, and said: "Ensign Karlow reporting, sir!"

Kent howled with laughter. "No good!" he barked out between guffaws. "You shouldn't look so goddam new." He turned around, reached for his huge ashtray with both hands and blew the ashes at me as hard as he could before saying, "Welcome, Ensign!" By that time most of the R&A people heard the commotion and came in to share the doughnuts and coffee that appeared. They had been lying in wait for me, not just to congratulate me but to ask me how I got the commission. They could not believe that I had just gone out and applied for it on my own.

The training was intensive, and concentrated. I was to do a Strategic Survey—a format that had been devised to present information on a geographic area in the most effective form to top military and strategic planners. I was given three days to work up a report on the Greek Island of Scarpanto. Where should I start? With the Encyclopedia Brittanica? As good as any place. And I should follow up every reference in the bibliography, and every reference in every reference, using the Library of Congress, the New York Public Library and any other library as needed. I should use the British-prepared *Nautical Almanac*, a detailed book containing coastal shore and offshore descriptions. Then I should visit the Greek Embassy and Information Center, the National Geographic, and an exiled Greek political leader. I should interview two professors who had recently left Greece, go through the files of Esso/Standard Oil and so on...

My first draft was rejected out of hand because of inadequate footnoting and referencing, and for editorializing on points that I could not specifically document.

My second draft was rejected. Why didn't I know that there was a more recent edition of the *Nautical Almanac* than the one I cited? Why did I overlook a U.S. Navy projection paper on the Aegean Sea, and another report of possible locations of submarine pens the Germans might use? Where was the triangulation into the continental map grid? What about health considerations, specifically water and insect-borne or endemic diseases; local customs to observe if a member of an occupation force. Did I date and evaluate the reliability of every source? My third draft was accepted.

The caliber of professors who agreed to force-feed me was something I appreciated only afterwards: Professor Richard Hartshorn of Wisconsin on geography, Professors Ed Mason and Emile Despres on economic projections and sociologic factors, Walter Langsam on political observation.

As it happened, Langsam had been my outside examiner on European Political Institutions in my final exams at Swarthmore. He did not remember me. I told him that I certainly remembered him. As I had come in for the oral examination, Langsam had harrumphed and said that I didn't seem to have covered much of value in my written exam, and that maybe he could find out something with a few questions. It was a shattering way to start an oral exam. When I recalled the scene to him, he said, with a shrug, "Oh, did I pull that old line on you, too?"

●●●

The North African landings took place November 8. The forces made rapid progress in taking over Morocco and Algeria. There was bitter fighting with the rear elements of the German Afrika Corps the whole length of Tunisia.

Pre-landings activities by COI and OSS in North Africa were new and obviously effective additions to the intelligence tools of the day. When the German armies overran France, the French surrender left certain territory, mostly southern France and North Africa, under the French "State" (État) but just called Vichy France, the collaborationist government in Vichy, headed by Marshal Pétain and his deputy, Admiral Darlan. An agreement was reached with Vichy France and, by extension, with the Germans, that North Africa should not be a war zone but be left disarmed, and that the U.S. had the right officially to monitor this agreement.

A number of American vice-consuls were stationed in key cities such as Tangiers, Casablanca, Oran, Algiers, and Tunis, overtly to serve as monitors. As it worked out, Donovan sponsored their designation, nominated some of the vice-consuls, and provided support and basic communications and operating equipment to them. The agent operations spawned by these vice-consuls were the COI's and, of course, also the OSS' first independent secret agent networks in the field.

U.S. military authorities recognized the value of the OSS reports and actions in planning and carrying out the North African landings. For example, top U.S. and British commanders had landed by submarine off Oran for a senior meeting directly with top French officers to try and head off resistance and large casualties during the coming Allied troop invasion. While they were meeting, two French officers, Lts. Georges LeNen and Charles Michel, immobilized the vehicles of the nearby Vichy-oriented police stations by removing distributor rotors or spark plugs from police cars and motorcycles. LeNen and Michel were arrested for this by the French military police. After the Allied landings, they were formally drummed out of the French Army, their rank and regiment insignia stripped off in front of their units. When this was reported to Donovan, he ordered that they be taken into the OSS and restored to their French Army rank. I learned later that Bill Kipp, who replaced me as Kent's man in New York, became involved. Kipp made a deal with Abercrombie & Fitch, the fancy sports supply store on Madison Avenue, to have new uniforms made for them. He used uniforms borrowed from a cooperative French military attaché in Washington as a model and had the copies shipped to North Africa in sizes to fit LeNen and Michel.

After the landings, a deal was made with Admiral Darlan for a joint administration of North Africa. The landings had left Admiral Darlan trapped in Algeria. The OSS national contacts from pre-landings days were appalled at this dealing with a person whom they termed a French traitor. The assassination of Admiral Darlan in December 1942 cleared the air. Most OSS intelligence sources were bitterly anti-Vichy and pro-DeGaulle. OSS reports highlighted the planned surprise attack being planned by DeGaulle on the city of Algiers. French colonial troopers from West Africa under Gen. de Lattre de Tassigny had trekked across the Sahara and were showing up clandestinely in Algiers ready to back the local Gaullists. This led to a confrontation between OSS in Algiers and the State department, which constantly seemed to downplay the popularity of DeGaulle. Our deputy chief was ordered back to Washington. Still, the OSS reports were accurate and shortly U.S. negotiations began with DeGaulle for his greater recognition.

•••

One of the R&A Africa Division's many assignments that caused some reper-cussions later was the preparation of "Soldiers' Guides" to the various areas U.S. soldiers would be sent. The one for North Africa, "Guide to North Africa," natu-rally became a task for the Africa Division. It was assigned to highly professional Arabists, Hibbard Cline and others steeped in North African Muslim cultures. Based on their own experience, they wrote out their advice for the GIs about Moslem social do's and don'ts. These included the famous strictures about never shake hands with your left hand, respect women's veils, take off your shoes at the door of a private home, and slurp your tea to show appreciation. The contrast between these strictures and the realities of getting around in modern Europeanized cities like Casablanca, Oran, and Algiers that the troops encountered, led to highly hilari-ous comments. In fact, the summer after the landings, Kent himself wrote a parody of these Soldiers' Guides, "A Soldier's Guide to Washington, D.C." The parody remained in longhand but circulated in the office and, I am told, on several college campuses after the war.

With North Africa secured, Sicily, Italy, France, and the Balkans beyond be-came the priority targets. Kent became head of a newly formed Europe-Africa Di-vision; now plans for an R&A intelligence library in North Africa could move ahead. OSS Headquarters was set up in Algiers, which was also headquarters for the Mediterranean Theater of Operations.

Administratively, the functions of the Africa Division broadened overnight thanks to its effective work. The R&A mission was to help others do their jobs better, right across the field of intelligence agencies. The key R&A people, profes-sors and experts, applied the highest standards of the academic world to the task, which was now the task of strategic planning, moving steadily towards tactical operational planning. In short order, R&A people and their contributions were readily accepted by military services as a valuable complement and not as competition. This was not the case, however, with secret intelligence penetrations, psychologi-cal or morale operations, or with para-military activities, all of which had to claw their way to acceptance often through bitter turf wars, particularly at senior policy and command levels.

Rudy Winnacker left Washington for Algiers in March, and was immediately swept up with preparations for the Sicily landings. We sent him materials that might help him contribute to last minute detail planning, but shipping by sea was uncer-tain and we were unsure about the materials arriving intact or in time. Winnacker urged by cable that I come to Algeria and bring him a number of items he felt were essential, and that four additional R&A people who were already designated to go abroad also come. The time was right to start the R&A center at the OSS Algiers headquarters.

•••

Travel arrangements for me were something else. Kent's invaluable secretary, Charlotte Bowman, opened negotiations with the newly established OSS Travel Office who mandated that I had to have military travel orders. She requested them from OSS Navy liaison channels. They were promptly cut and delivered to us. We gasped when we saw how broad the orders were:

> *"1. When directed by the Director of Strategic Services you will proceed to the port in which the Commander, North West Africa Sea Frontier may be, via such transportation as the Bureau of Naval Personnel may furnish, including via air..."*
> *2. You are hereby authorized to perform such travel as may be considered necessary in the proper performance of this duty, including via air. (Dated March 13, 1943)"*

Kent's only comment was that he had never seen such a clear "license to steal".

Next Charlotte reported the horrible possibility that I and four others of the team who were scheduled to go to North Africa might not obtain transportation for a month or six weeks since Army facilities were to be used for OSS travel. We had to take our place in line. I remember Charlotte telling me at lunch one day, with a laugh that wrinkled her snub nose, that the OSS travel office told her flatly to tell me that I may think I'm in the Navy, but I am to travel with Army orders, like everyone else in OSS! She challenged me to see if I could do better. Kent went further than this by reminding me that the landings on Sicily were imminent—they began on July 10—and that he wanted me and the rest of the R&A team out there. What was holding things up? I at once took my "license to steal" orders and contacted the downtown Potomac River Naval Command. It was Tuesday. Oh, they asked. Did I want to leave Friday or Monday?

I signed up for Monday July 12. Kent was delighted, and had the most needed materials assembled into two canvas duffel bags sealed officially for me to take along like diplomatic pouches. And, he said, "How about taking the weekend in New York as pre-trip vacation?"

I did. I had hardly made myself popular with the OSS transportation people by procuring my own transportation so readily. I showed them up and I didn't care. I was too new in government work to realize how important "channels" were to those who defined them, maintained them, and lived by them. I went back for final check-in with the Navy authorities in the Potomac River Naval Command to make sure everything was on track. While I was there, I asked innocently under what circumstances did Army channels apply to me? The Navy lieutenant on duty, an older man, just said, "Mister (term then used for all Navy officers below Commander), you're Navy, you have Navy orders and we're the part of the Navy here to see that you get there to carry them out. And, be sure to get your issue items."

Issue items? This was like hitting a jackpot on a quiz show. The supply officer, noting my destination and the areas to which I might be ordered, duly issued the best and the most that the Navy had to offer. I was given two beautiful white blankets marked "U S NAVY" (I still have them on the bed in my guest room); white puttees; two dark blue flannel long-sleeved so-called CPO (Chief Petty Officer) shirts made in the Brooklyn Navy Yard and, I noted, each with two right cuffs. They also provided a .45 caliber automatic in a leather case, still in pristine coat of cosmoline preservative; two clips for bullets with bullets; ear muffs, dark blue of course; and, to top it all, a white pith helmet on which I was to attach my Navy Officer's cap emblem. On the down side, I was sent to a dispensary and got all my shots, tetanus, cholera and whatnot. Despite sore arms, and laden with the goodies, I staggered back to the office, picked up the two duffel bags of documents, waved hasty good-byes to the group, got some last minute briefing and requests to look out for this and that. I made hasty notes. I was off to New York Friday at 4:30 p.m. on the Pennsylvania Congressional Limited, arriving in New York and at my mother's apartment after 9 p.m., exhausted.

We spent Saturday and the weekend packing it all together. My mother was a packing perfectionist; she could get more into a suitcase complete with tissue paper interlinings. It reach the point where my father used to joke about her packing for him and his having to buy a second suitcase for his return trip because he couldn't repack everything back in that small space. Well, I faced the same experience, but somehow in a duffel bag there always is some extra space.

Monday morning, July 12, was already warm and humid, promising a stiflingly hot day. I was glad for the lightweight khaki uniform. I carried my raincoat and hovered over the covey of bulky duffel bags. My mother was too tired or distracted to realize fully that her son was off to the War. A hurried good-bye and I was off by taxi to the Brooklyn Navy Yard dispatch point, then bus transport out Long Island to the seaport, Floyd Bennett field, usually used by Pan American Clipper seaplanes. There it was, not a Pan Am Clipper, but a large boxy-looking four-engine seaplane transport known as the Coronado, a PB2-Y3 made by the Martin Aircraft company. Drab gray outside with "U.S. Navy" lettering on body and wings. The inside was stark and stripped, hot as a furnace, with a half dozen passenger seats scattered around among the cargo wherever a set of floor cleats could be found to attach them to the cargo deck.

Pan Am ground crews handled the loading and the box lunches; I ended with my feet on a pile of Firestone tires, more comfortable than the footrest on the decrepit so-called passenger seat. Were there any seat belts? Seems to me there were, hooked into side rails or floor cleats. What kept the cabin tolerable? An air conditioner hose from a howling cooler compressor on the dock, foo-ing air forward and not quite able to keep control over the checkered contrasts between the hot and cold blasts of wind whistling around. I noticed an installed fan-like machine, a space heater unit in the rear, which I assumed was to keep things warm once air-borne. There were four other passengers, two other Navy officers, an Army captain on military courier duty, and a civilian engineer on a base construction contract. The plane was otherwise loaded with useful-looking cargo like auto tires, typewriters, and telephone sets.

We cast off. The engines on each side were roaring. We moved away from the dock. The air-cooling ceased. Suddenly it dawned on me that I had never flown on a passenger plane before. Before this thought was carried much further, one engine began to sputter and refused to settle down. Then it shut down. The pilot turned the plane around, taxied back the few yards to the dock and tied up. He said there would be no flight today and we should come back tomorrow. I "secured" my duffel bags with the Shore Patrol Security Officer, and was back in the bus headed home. Time for another cool bath at home that night and another good-bye the next morning. I was feeling a little blasé. I had now been a passenger on a plane.

It never occurred to me that that engine could also fail while in flight, which, as it turned out, actually happened. Or that the trip would be an adventure tour gone wild.

• • •

We took off successfully from Long Island the next morning, Tuesday, July 13, 1943, landing early afternoon in Bermuda. We were put up at a posh hotel overlooking the water. In its near-empty luxury dining room, a live band was playing languorous jazz music on the terrace. What a waste without a date, I thought. After a delicious breakfast the next morning, we took off for San Juan, Puerto Rico, arriving at the naval base in time for lunch, actually a box lunch on the pier, but it gave us a chance to stretch our legs.

Off to Trinidad, a six-hour flight with landing just at dusk. It was hot and humid. The Pan Am hostesses at the dock served us drinks of what I thought was grapefruit juice. I downed three since I was wildly thirsty. Things fairly quickly became hazy to me and I found myself sitting in the driver's seat of a 1941 Ford station wagon, the model with wooden sides. Soon we were moving smartly down a road but on the wrong side of the street. I had no steering wheel in front of me and sort of ducked down under the dashboard when a car came at us also driving on the wrong side. The next morning I knew I had never been that drunk in my life. The grapefruit juice of the evening before was a Jamaican rum drink, and three in a row on an empty stomach had taken their toll.

Fairly early next morning we were roused to a paper plate breakfast of scrambled powdered eggs, the first of many I was to eat—bread, coffee and orange juice which I avoided in case it had been near a rum bottle. The flight out from Trinidad was rough. We finally had to put down in a broad bay at Paramaribo, Dutch Guiana at a seaplane base taken over by the U.S. Navy. Another box lunch, this time at the pleasantly warm and breeze swept officers' club. After the plane was refueled, we flew along the north coast of South America, overflying Devil's Island off French Guiana, a frighteningly isolated set of islands.

From my porthole the coastline, flying at the relatively low altitude the PB2-Y3 maintained, was muddy brown with little or no way to tell where land ended and the ocean began. I was fascinated to see the mouths of the Amazon and the immense carpet of soil being washed out to sea along hundreds of miles of coastline. The plane headed inland across solid green jungle cut suddenly here and there by a straight ribbon of road or railroad, apparently starting nowhere and going nowhere. We picked up one of the branches of the Amazon and at a few thousand feet altitude browsed our way upstream, finally landing on the river. It was wretchedly hot and humid and the flying boat pitched interminably as it taxied upstream for the better part of an hour. I finally moved to the tail gunner's turret in a not too successful effort to avoid seasickness, to which I am not usually prone. At last the PB2-Y3 reached Belem and tied up, and we debarked, woozy and soaked with perspiration. A Brazilian officer greeted us. His jacket had epaulets bearing three stars and four stripes, and he carried a huge-looking .45 in a large black holster. Impressed, I saluted. Turned out he was only a first lieutenant, too. My rank seemed overly understated by one stripe and a half stripe, and the Navy star.

We were put up in a requisitioned hotel that had showers, however simple and rusty. We changed into dry clothes. Dinner in the hotel dining room consisted of tough beef, wildly strong coffee, and other food not memorable enough to recall. After dinner we went sightseeing for a few blocks downtown. It was quite a sight. There were small trolley cars with two trailers and with passengers swarming all over. A busy conductor collected fares from one and all as the contraptions collectively rattled down the tree-lined street on what seemed like hexagonal wheels. The streets were teeming after dark, especially because evening relieved the heat, if not the humidity.

The star-studded Brazilian lieutenant, now in a white uniform that made the shoulder boards appear even more prestigious, led us to the local casino. It was a little place with several roulette and blackjack tables. I have no idea if I won or lost at roulette as the paper currency was of all different sizes and was as covered with zeros as the lieutenant's shoulder boards were with insignia and stripes.

That night I shared a room with the Army captain, the courier who had the briefcase handcuffed to his wrist. He was a high school teacher from upstate New York, newly commissioned and on his first trip as a courier. He was most serious about his responsibility. When he was ready to take his shower, he asked me to hold the precious courier pouch that he detached from his wrist, but to remain where he could see. When he was through, he warned me not to disturb him while he slept because he might wake up shooting. I looked at his .45 in its brand new leather holster and was sure I could see the cosmoline oil still on it.

The next day, after taxiing interminably down the Amazon, we finally took off to Natal on the easternmost tip of Brazil. What a jangly frontier town, replete with people selling anything and anyone! Hawkers had watches strapped all the way up their arms under their jackets, and when they opened their jackets there were countless watches displayed in the countless pockets and straps all over the lining. I finally found one watch that intrigued me marked "Roamer," a make not unknown to me, but it lit up to show the time. I haggled, not knowing the value of the currency, and finally bought it for what I estimated was seven U.S. dollars. It ran for twenty-four hours.

We were billeted in Natal on the second floor of a barracks. The windows overlooked a narrow street filled with hooting; middle-aged women waving in a sinuous way that I suppose they thought was inviting. It was my first view of a working brothel, not a tempting one.

We stayed an extra day in Natal, waiting for a favorable tail wind without which we might not make it across the Atlantic. We were rounded up right after lunch, only to wait around the hot and breezeless landing area for several hours. It was dusk before the plane took off for the nearly one thousand mile run to Liberia. The night was a miserable one for me, wrapped around those Firestone tires.

The morning was something else. We landed at Robertsport in western Liberia in bright morning sunshine, touching down in a large bay surrounded by jungle. It was to be just a refueling and lunch stop. We went ashore anxious to stretch our legs.

I took up conversation with an American Army first lieutenant there. He was in command of a company of engineer troops, all but he were black. Their job was to maintain the seaport and complete a landing strip nearby. He offered to show me the countryside. We got into his jeep and drove into the thick jungle that surrounded the area. It was, to me, out of a stage set—the jungle, the dirt road, the cheerful natives waving as we passed, and the small teardrop shaped mud huts with locally made baskets and gold work displayed around them. My lieutenant friend was sure there was a gold mine or a vein of gold somewhere nearby, but he had not yet found any. While driving through the villages, he tossed out small packs of chewing gum like a medieval potentate tossing coins to the people. It was my first jungle experience.

After a lunch appetizingly served, with fruit I had not seen or tasted before, we headed north up the coast to Bathhurst, the capital of Gambia, known to me as a small British outpost from my high school stamp collecting days. For the first time I realized that the size of the country seems to be in inverse proportion to the size, number, and gaudiness of its postage stamps. At Bathhurst, we were put up at the British Royal Air Force base in Quonset huts. We gladly accepted an invitation to swim at the beautiful looking beaches we had seen on the flight in. The beaches were magnificent but the water was a warm, sticky, salty surfless swirl. Entirely unrefreshing.

Back at the Quonset huts, I saw two large lizards, perhaps three feet long each, resting motionless near the entrance. They had alternately light blue and tan four-inch stripes. I approached one of them slowly, managing to get within four feet of it when it whisked itself away about ten feet and resumed its motionless rest.

Without warning the skies darkened and a violent rainstorm hit. We dashed inside the Quonset huts. For about twenty minutes, the rain, pounding on the metal roofs, sounded like a solid wall of water descending, heralding the end of the world. As suddenly as it began, it stopped, as if someone had turned off the faucet. The rain did not relieve the humidity, although the ground dried quickly. The two lizards were still where they had been, unchanged and unfazed. This is an image that sustains from my first tropical monsoon.

The next stop was to be the Canary Islands, but we never made it. The pilot swung out wide to sea to avoid possible pockets of uncertain affiliation along French colonial coastlines. Waking suddenly from a nap, I saw that the plane was heading southward along the coast with one engine out. The pilot told us we were going to land at Dakar, the capital of French West Africa. In the distance we could see and hear some flashes and black explosions; it was anti-aircraft fire. The pilot swayed the plane back and forth and wagged the wings, signaling "friendly." We landed in the bay without further incident. Some shore gunners had not seen a Coronado before and decided it was easier to open fire than ask questions.

The engine of the Coronado was not readily repairable so we offloaded our baggage and headed for buses that would take us to the allied base in nearby Saint Louis. On the way, we were stopped at a grade crossing, and I realized I was having the good fortune to see the Peanut Line, the "Chemin de Fer des Arachides," the narrow-gauge Senegalese railroad, in action, with its toy-train-sized rolling stock. Thinking back to Oral Intelligence days, this was supposed to be the rail line that would link the Mediterranean with Dakar. I wondered how anyone could imagine feeling "Trans-Sahara" to North Africa, or anywhere far away, on this? Or was there really no information on this at home?

At the base adjutant's office we found a ride to Algiers. An Army DC-3 would be available in two days doing a milk and mail run to Atar and Marrakech, Morocco. The most exciting activity during our wait was drinking peanut beer. When the plane was ready, off we went, into the Sahara Desert. My first desert, and what a surprise! It was not flat but studded with thousand-foot high bluffs that, with oncoming evening, were stratified into multicolored layers of gold, orange and copper. A group of huts and an airstrip came into view as I looked down into a deep valley. The DC-3 began to circle. After an initial, "Oh, Lord, not here," I realized this was Atar. The plane taxied to a stop and the door opened, like opening a furnace door in a steel mill. Facing us was a wooden sign in English:

WELCOME TO ATAR
CAPITAL OF MAURETANIA
Alt. 747 feet Temp. 135 degrees

Several GIs in the local weather monitor unit were standing around watching the plane unload. They cheered as the two other Navy officers and I disembarked. As one said, here are our replacements, the Navy is taking over! Well, it was at least 500 miles in any direction to any body of water.

The Americans were part of a weather detachment, also air rescue as necessary. No, their life wasn't entirely dull. A favorite sport was hunting gazelle. The GIs informed us that gazelles will run exactly as fast as the pursuers can go in their jeeps, up to sixty miles an hour cross-country. A harrowing thought.

Atar was a small garrison town of French Colonial troops. In the French colonial town square was a simple cement road marker showing: "DAKAR - 1,000

KM" on one side, and "MARRAKECH - 2000 KM" on the other. Not far from Atar was a small native market town of about ten square blocks of one-story row houses. Back in Atar I visited the city hall, which was also the capital of that desert province. At city hall I called on the French military office, and was promptly invited to dine at the "popotte" or officers' mess. I gladly accepted. What a hard-bitten bunch of expatriates! Some had been in Atar for four years. The differences between Pétain and De Gaulle were really rather less important than the concerns of day-to-day living were for these professional soldiers in the desert. But I, as an American with some knowledge of French and France, was a curiosity to them. Under the colonial military system, the officers frequently stay with their selected colonial troops throughout their careers. In fact, companies and even battalions are sometimes named after the particular *Coloniaux*, the colonial officers in charge. Absent any other gift I could give for the occasion, I ceremoniously pulled out five one-dollar bills, which were well accepted and obviously went much further here than at home.

I walked back the two blocks to the garrison building to rejoin my group. We slept in the open in a courtyard in our skivvies under a near-full moon. No insects. No breeze. Nothing was heard except the sonorous snoring of the two Senegalese guards staying with us. These six-foot-plus tribesmen were impressive, with yard-long bayonets affixed to their ancient and well cared for rifles.

The DC-3 took off promptly the next morning, droning lazily over a varied desert topography with no sign of human or any other presence from horizon to horizon. Finally, we saw a settlement. The plane circled down to the airstrip at Tindouf whose very name is associated with romantic visions of Foreign Legion fame. Tindouf, with a castle-like structure in the middle of the town, was impressive, but the heat was worse than any blast furnace. All I wanted to do was cover up and not move; every bit of fresh air simply seared the skin. I crept somehow into a shaded doorway with a Moorish decor and just stood there gasping for air. How could anyone or anything live here?

After what seemed like hours, we were back on the plane taking off northward. It was not long before we were crossing mountains and suddenly, like a line drawn across the earth, the ground below became green. We were flying over the fabulous Agadir valley, a highly fertile area known for its fruit, particularly its oranges. Soon we landed in Marrakech, a modern French colonial city with a large separate Arab quarter. A staff car drove us to the Mamounian Hotel, a magnificent Moorish style, tiled wall, luxury hostelry, slightly down at the heels, but still so lovely that I doubted I could ever afford it as a civilian.

The contrast between this place and Atar and Tindouf, not to mention the towns in Brazil, was overwhelming. Unfortunately, we didn't have time or energy for sightseeing in Marrakech. The C-47 we were now on took off early the next morning. The next stop was, again, a jarring contrast. The stop was the major U.S. air base near Oran, bustling with GI activity. The swarms of fighter planes were garish in their war paint graphics. On closer look, the artistry was indeed graphic. They showed enlarged and virtually functioning parts of the female anatomy with names to match, a few as mild as "Dripping Daisy," emblazoned over and around the noses of the planes. And it was a GI lunch in the regular Quonset Hut mess hall, where we were given a square, compartmented tin plate, GI issue knife and spoon (no forks). In the serving line, mashed potatoes were slopped onto the applesauce, salad was covered with a scoop of ice cream, meat was graced by butter and honey meant for the bread which was under the salad.

CHAPTER 6

ITALY AND CORSICA...

I reached Algiers' Maison Blanche airfield Friday, July 23, 1943. Upon debarking I called OSS headquarters as I had been instructed to do. The man's voice that answered the phone had a record of my name and expected arrival time, and said that "Rudy" was on his way to meet me, to call for me in person, and to watch for him at the main arrival area. It was not long before I saw Winnacker waving at me from across the driveway. We gathered up the two duffel bags, travel stained and pummeled, and drove to the OSS headquarters building, the Villa Sineti, a handsome suburban villa with an exotic if unkempt garden now largely a parking lot for jeeps and a motley collection of requisitioned civilian cars. The ten-day Odyssey was over; time to get to work.

•••

Rudy Winnacker had been working alone, frantically doing what he could to help OSS people and the military planning officers they were working with in the Theater to complete details of last-minute preparations for the invasion of Sicily. The more he did, the more was requested of him. We had the weekend, daytime and late into the night, to sort out the collection of materials I had brought along. It included everything from strategic surveys to cartographic materials, political who's who to city and town maps and lists of government buildings, road and rail facilities, bridges, communications centers, factories, power plants, and, of course, on the railroads.

By Monday morning we were in business, supplying background data for proposals on bombing targets for Col. Ed Glavin, the OSS Theater Commander, to take to Allied military strategy meetings. We had data for possible landing points for infiltration operations for the major OSS groups, the French SI (secret intelligence) and SO (special operations), and for Italian SI on Sicily and the Lipari Islands.

Sicily was a disappointment for the OSS because no agent operations were in place when Allied troops arrived. Donovan was in the Theater for the actual landings, which began July 10, the week before my arrival. One story had it that the first OSS person to land on Sicily was Donovan himself— he accompanied the first wave of troops ashore.

The OSS groups in Algiers improvised a good deal due to the newness of the mission and to the need to fit in and sell OSS resources to the military commands.

Some senior military officers had the "what have you done for me today?" attitude. Not knowing about OSS activity in the days prior to the North African landings, and unsure of the role of intelligence in general (OSS in particular) some key military commanders and staff officers threatened to "throw the OSS out of the Theater". They wanted to use the allocations of personnel and materiel for more "cutting edge" purposes. Yet here was Donovan asking them for more support, for planes and boats for OSS to infiltrate agents into Italy and France.

The situation was actually further along than the pre-landings failure in Sicily would indicate. The OSS mission was to penetrate France and Italy from bases in North Africa, using whatever human and materiel resources could be found locally, and there were plenty, particularly towards France. The objectives in each case were: make contact with local resistance groups inside the country; identify them and their key members; provide them with communications, training and materiel; and develop coordinated action between them and other groups and Allied military headquarters. First, OSS wanted the local groups to obtain and report reliable military information on the location, identity, and movement of enemy forces. This meant separating rumor from observation, identifying the sources, and taking all the steps necessary in organizing increasingly reliable information from inside. Following that would be preparations for underground warfare, to impede the movement or action of enemy troops.

•••

The OSS program to penetrate Metropolitan France had already been started by Henry Hyde, a brilliant and eclectic New York lawyer. Hyde had been brought up in France and was now Chief of French SI in the Mediterranean Theater. The coastline of southern France was relatively open, which made getting into France from the south far easier than by crossing the Channel in the north. On the Channel coast, the Germans had defenses in depth and they were then massing equipment for their Operation SEA LION, the name for Hitler's plan to invade the British Isles. Actually, two distinct OSS agent networks had already begun to report to Algiers from inside France. They were kept separate as there was concern that one had been penetrated by the Germans and was being "played back" under German control. There had already been successful airdrops to the Resistance over large areas of France.

Then there came a dramatic development. A French submarine had escaped the German attack on the Toulon naval base when the Germans took over the rest of unoccupied "Vichy" France after our landings in North Africa, and had made itself available for agent operations. This remarkable story is about the submarine *Casabianca* and its daring Captain, Jean l'Herminier.

The *Casabianca* was a 1,500 ton vessel, reasonably modern with a complement of eighty-five that had been interned in the French naval base at Toulon, near Marseilles, when the French front collapsed and the Germans occupied France but left southern France "unoccupied." The German armistice command first decided to use the French navy to defend against any Allied landing on the French coast. The *Casabianca* was among several naval units whose refitting had been approved by the German/Italian Armistice Commission so that it could be sent out to duty in the French colonies, in this case Madagascar. Commanded by Captain Jean l'Herminier, the *Casabianca* was nearly ready to put out to sea when the Allied landings in North Africa hit on November 8, 1942. The French Navy commanders at the Toulon base had meanwhile passed the word among themselves to be ready to scuttle every ship should the Germans order them into action against the Allies. Despite this, l'Herminier had managed to scrounge enough fuel oil so that his tanks were virtually full even though the fuel gauges showed near empty. He also had smuggled extra rations on board and such other preparations he felt he could make without being noticed, so that he would be ready to take off should the occasion present itself.

At dawn, November 27, without warning, German planes attacked the naval base, in an effort to prevent any French units from defecting to North Africa. l'Herminier immediately ordered the sub to cast off and made it across the inner harbor as the German planes began to bomb. The *Casabianca* submerged right outside the breakwater and "felt" its way down the winding estuary for two hours, Toulon being some 15 miles from the open sea. In this range the submarine was blind and had no functioning radio because the Germans had ordered it removed. The gyrocompass was damaged. The sonar was questionable. The new propellers that had been mounted months ago had never been calibrated. How many revolutions meant what speed? And, of course, this was before any French vessels had radar.

l'Herminier finally had to surface so the crew could get the sub's bearings. Rising to periscope height, they found to their dismay that in their haste to leave they had not removed the copper cover over the periscope. A junior officer volunteered to go out on the half-submerged deck and knock off the cover, understanding that he would stay out in case of German air attack. He was successful in clearing the periscope and the *Casabianca* headed for North Africa still submerged. When they surfaced again, expecting to be some 15 miles off the North African shore, they found they were within a mile of Cape Matifou, the entrance to Algiers harbor. They came up in the midst of a flotilla of British destroyers on maneuvers, none of which had detected them! Under the threatening guns that the British promptly aimed at them, the crew quickly broke out their largest French flag. Signals began to flash. At this all the crews who were reading the signals broke out in cheers, and the destroyers escorted the sub into Algiers harbor. Within three weeks of arriving in Algiers, the *Casabianca* was ready to land its first secret agent mission for the OSS, French SI operation PEARL HARBOR, on the west coast of Corsica.

•••

The OSS program to penetrate Italy was wracked by controversy from the start. Two groups formed, frequently in competition and sometimes not even in contact with each other, The operating heads of the Italian SI Division included a number of bright and active Sicilian-Americans, some with "Mafia" ties, others not. The mission in Algiers was headed by Vincent Scamporino, a lawyer in New York City specializing in labor practice and Biagio Maximilian Corvo, a young journalist from Bridgeport, Connecticut. They felt they should concentrate on collecting political and personality data and on working through pre-war or exiled or still available Sicilian and Italian anti-fascist political leaders who might return to Italy after the war and have an influence on future political alignments in Italy. They were not prepared for the assignment thrown at them to give immediate support to military tactical operations. The fact was, however, that OSS had to earn its place in the Theater by providing significant tactical support for military operations before it could obtain support for its more strategic programs. The result was that there were no tactical missions in place inside Sicily when the landings took place.

The misunderstanding in Sicily angered Donovan, and he ordered immediate priority to organizing across-the-lines reconnaissance missions. He appointed a new chief for Sicily, Lt. Col. Guido Pantaleone, a respected corporate lawyer from Cleveland, who was working in the SO (Special Operations) Italy group. "Pants" was easy to work with and personally popular among his colleagues. We briefed him as well as we could on whatever intelligence data we had collected that could be useful to him in staging tactical missions. He went to Sicily, got things going, and personally led one of the first reconnaissance missions. Unfortunately, the mission misfired. Everyone escaped except "Pants" who was captured by the Germans and never heard from again. It turned out he was the highest-ranking U.S. officer to be captured in Sicily. In fairness, there was little time to do much in Sicily from North Africa and no hands-on experience in military support work in penetrating enemy lines. The rest of OSS learned from the mistakes.

For example, after Sicily there was an attempted landing on Sardinia. This was the first use of an American PT boat from the famous U.S. Navy Motor Torpedo Squadron ("RON") 15, but the PT boat as yet had no radar. Radar did not reach the Squadron until late fall 1943. The Italian SI escort officers did not know the coast and had not adequately plotted and silhouetted the features of the landing pinpoint to help recognize the landscape of the area in the moonless night on which PT operations were run. Four agents were put into a rubber dinghy to paddle themselves to shore, paying out a long line back to the PT boat as they went. It was agreed that after the line stopped paying out, which would mean the craft had reached shore, the escort officers on the PT boat would wait twenty minutes, then pull in the dinghy and take off. As it happened, the group landed not at the pinpoint but several miles away, at the foot of high bluffs which were hard to scale and which made exit from the beach near-impossible in the black of night. By the time the agents realized this, they saw to their dismay the dinghy being pulled out to sea, leaving them stranded.

•••

The next Mediterranean Theater target was the Italian mainland itself. With Italian SI bogged down with Sicily and the offshore islands, a new unit was formed in Algiers for penetrating southern Italy and giving direct support to the Military. Designated OSS Fifth Army Detachment, it was composed of operations people from SI and SO and appropriate support elements like Communications and logistics. The OSS Fifth Army Detachment was to carry the brunt of military support intelligence missions into Italy and up the entire length of that hapless country for the entire campaign.

There were also some interesting special assignment groups and people in and out of the OSS Algiers headquarters, with strange and unusual operations. One was headed by John Shaheen, a flamboyant international oil investor and free-lancer, whose operation was to kidnap or subvert the Italian Navy's deputy Chief of Operations as the key to the surrender of the Italian Navy. Shaheen was aided by Mike Burke of University of Pennsylvania All-American football fame and "Jumping Joe" Savoldi, from the professional football world. Then there was Douglas Fairbanks Jr. leading a team that used PT boats along the Italian coast to drag helium-filled balloons festooned with metal foil, the "chaff" to fool radar beams, giving German radar the impression that sizable naval vessels were passing by. Although it was not an OSS operation, Allied personnel regarded it as such. Frank Schoonmaker, the wine expert, who had been given the task of developing clandestine operations inside Spain, headed another operation. When I met him in Algiers he had just been sprung from political prison in Spain, as the result of what others said was a deliberate tip-off to the Spanish police from the U.S. Embassy. It was no secret that U.S. Ambassador Carleton Hayes openly opposed any secret operations by OSS or anyone that might upset his position as Ambassador in "neutral" Spain.

Morale was generally high at Algiers. Everyone was overworked and developing new, imaginative ways of doing things. For R&A, there were new tasks shaping up, for example, obtaining published and research data on France, its coast and geographic grids, and data on new and undiscovered resources built to defend the coast against landings. There was the task of collecting serial numbers of specific types of captured German military equipment. This was already being done, but on a haphazard basis, by Army units on the Tunisian front in going over captured "Afrika Korps" materiel. The point was to read serial numbers from captured tanks and certain models of trucks or their transmissions, and to accompany this with interrogations of prisoners-of-war about how long the tank or truck had been in action, that is, in the hands of troops. This would give an idea of how new it was. Combining data on dates of manufacture with actual delivery dates could give an estimate of tank or truck production. This was especially useful if identifiable drops in production could subsequently be checked against strategic bombing missions against German factories, meaning to see when bombing raids on German industry actually caused a drop in German production, as a guide to future repeat bombings.

The four other members of the R&A team whom Winnacker had requested along with me finally arrived two months later. In late August, after a harrowing trip. The OSS Travel office had arranged for them to wait for transportation at a military base in Virginia. They waited for over a week, and then spent fourteen days and nights crossing the ocean on an LST, a round-bottomed Landing Ship for Tanks. These LSTs were notorious for their "30-30 minutes," meaning a 30-degree roll to each side within a minute's time. All the team members required several days' rest; one of the team, sociologist Fred Fales, had been so seasick the entire trip that he needed extended hospitalization.

Algiers has a beautiful location with a harbor like the playing field of a huge amphitheater. I was billeted in an apartment house on the Chemin des Crêtes, the "route of the crests." It was like living in one of the top row seats behind the goal line at a major football stadium. Algiers was spread out below us. Every evening was foggy. Every day was cloudless and dry. The Zannetacci family owned and ran the place and did our laundry and took care of our things with attention bordering on affection. Wayne Nelson, now an operations officer, was sent to Algiers with Fifth Army Detachment and became a housemate. Also DeWitt Clinton, a distant relative of the New York Governor who built the Erie Canal, and French lieutenant Georges LeNen, of pre-Landings fame. Clinton was born in southern France of an American mother who was an expatriate living near the Riviera. He had been educated at home, and then had taken up commercial fishing as an apprentice. This stocky redhead with patched teeth had reached the U.S. about the time the Germans broke into France in 1940. The OSS recruited him in 1942 because of his knowledge of the southern French coast.

My first air raid: German planes made several direct air attacks on Algiers. It was sensational to see the spread of the black-out, the sweep of the searchlights, the anti-aircraft tracer fire, and one German plane downed in flames at sea. It was so spectacular that one night I was tempted to go out on the balcony to get a better view; I was humbled the next morning to see the chards of AA fire in two-inch pieces on the roof. Any one of those pieces could have been lethal.

On several weekends I had the use of a decrepit but operating '34 Ford convertible. I do not remember where it came from, only that it was a faded tan color, with red leather seats from which the red dye came off on the seat of my pants. Several of us piled into the Ford on a Sunday in August and drove west on the coastal road towards Cherchell where some attractive beach resorts were.

At the "Mirabella," I met Madeleine and Andrée, two pretty teenagers. I drove up behind them and thought at first they were naked. Well, they were nearly so, with near-flesh colored, minimal suits that anticipated the bikini by more than a decade. Phone number 680-50. Invited there to dinner. Charming house on the coast. Brought some supplies from the PX. Dancing to phonograph music on a large concrete deck built out over the Mediterranean. One haunting song Madeleine identified for me was a poem by Verlaine. "The lengthening shadows of autumn pierce my heart with pangs of loneliness..." Prescience? These were the very words later used by the BBC as code signals to call the French Resistance to action at the time of the Normandy landings.

After several weeks, knowing I was shortly to leave for Corsica, I invited Madeleine out on a date. I had gone to some effort to make reservations at a fancy black-market restaurant, followed by the theater. But Mama interceded. What were my intentions, she asked? Oops. I had forgotten about this aspect of Continental etiquette. I should have asked Mama along on that first date. As she said, she cannot have her daughter seen going out with a foreign sailor. It was the first time I felt the strain of living my cover.

•••

Donovan persisted in his uphill fight to convince the Theater Commanders that OSS needed access to several specially equipped bombers to use in parachuting agents behind the lines and to PT boats to land agents along the coast line. Donovan called Wayne Nelson to help, as though Nelson were still active as an aide to Donovan, forgetting that Donovan had released him to become an SI operations officer. Nelson came in to see me one day. He was putting together a brief for Donovan to take before the Theater Command, and needed some documents, just documents, to prepare what would look like a detailed briefing dossier. Just something we could spare for now. Well, we had a strategic survey of Bulgaria that would serve for this purpose. Wayne inserted bookmarks at several randomly selected pages. I hated to think that Donovan's briefing material included this bookmarked Bulgarian survey. I never knew for sure.

OSS did have access to bombers to parachute agents into Italy, Southern France, Yugoslavia and even as far as Slovakia. Naval support was obtained less by high-level mandates than by dealing directly with RON 15 and with African Coastal Forces, a British SOE Maritime unit set up specifically to work the Channel coast and the Mediterranean shore. We OSS people learned from them most of what we came to know about landing and retrieving agents by boat from enemy shore.

A degree of competition developed between air drop landings and maritime landings as the preferred means to place agents into their target territories. While the OSS parachute training unit, set up near Algiers and headed by Lucius "Luke"

Rucker, was unsurpassed, jumping was still a traumatic experience for some of the agents who were recruited. After all, many of these agents were lawyers, engineers, teachers, or former businessmen and government officials who were not too athletic by nature although willing. Airdrops were not always accurate. In contrast, landing from a boat, clean and dry on shore at the exact pinpoint, had its attractions. Italy was, after all, mostly coastline. This maritime landing potential in Italy lent attraction to our moving on to Corsica, helping liberate it, and then using it as an advance base.

Also, Rudy Winnacker echoed Gen. Donovan's guidelines that we R&A people become involved in other people's operations to help them do their jobs better, and that we also support the development of OSS resources to collect and analyze information. I began to work with teams making plans for landings on Sardinia and Corsica.

•••

The landings in Italy at Salerno, south of Naples, on September 8, 1943 pushed the OSS into far greater military effort than Sicily had months before. Some agents had been parachuted into Italy and were in place and reporting intelligence by radio and by back-and-forth line crossings before the landings. An initial British-American landing probe from Sicily onto the toe of Italy grew slowly. After Mussolini was forced out in July 1943, the Italian population was stirred up and it was not difficult to find Italians volunteering to be agents or to go on line-crossing missions. Once on the mainland, the OSS Fifth Army Detachment plunged into activity building upon good popular support for the Allied cause among the population. A headquarters and a training base were set up at Caserta and staff moved up from Algiers. Close liaison was kept with Fifth Army Headquarters whose key staff officers increasingly came to rely on and ask for OSS information, both agent reports and intelligence analyses.

After the Italian landings were consolidated, later in September, Winnacker returned to the U.S. and H. Stuart Hughes became senior R&A man in the Theater. The high caliber of OSS people building up around the Algiers headquarters was impressive. I recall coming onto an impassioned argument between Peter Mero and Henry Hyde. Mero was our brilliant Communications chief, as knowledgeable in modern technology as he was in European mannerisms, essential for appreciating traffic from secret agents in the field. He was a former ITT engineer who had come to the U.S. and a commission in the Signal Corps from senior positions with ITT in Hungary and Austria. He and Hyde were arguing at the tops of their lungs on the balcony of Villa Sineti, our headquarters building. The verbal exchange began in English and when this was too confining they sprinkled in German words, finally finishing in French, the richness of which allows direct insults without causing hard feelings.

At one point, I remember thinking that war brought unusual combinations of people together. Henry Hyde worked closely with Stuart Hughes. Hyde's father, James Hazen Hyde, had virtually been forced into exile from the U.S. for alleged stock market manipulation in 1930, by order of the U.S. Supreme Court then headed by Chief Justice Charles Evans Hughes, Stuart's grandfather.

The island of Corsica opened up. A day after the Allied landing at Salerno on September 9, a radio message was received from Ajaccio, the capital of Corsica, announcing that the population had liberated itself, that collaborators had been jailed but that there was uncertainty about what the 80,000 Italian troops on Corsica would do. Donovan obtained Theater approval to send a mission to Corsica. Casting about among available OSS people, he spotted Carleton Coon, Arab and Mid-East scholar, who happened to be in Algiers en route to Cairo. Donovan preempted him to delay his trip a few weeks and to form and head a preliminary exploratory mission to Corsica. Coon took along a team, including some Americans of Corsican ancestry who happened to be in Algiers, and some personnel from Communications and from the Operational Groups (OG). If the situation was favorable, there would be a composite OSS mission sent to Corsica, including SI and SO specialists, and the OSS-trained OG. These were the uniformed "hyphenated-American commandos," of which Italian, French, and Norwegian OG units were formed.

Sardinia was next. Donovan tapped Serge Obolensky to head a team that would parachute in and talk the Italians there into surrendering. Obolensky, a tall, aristocratic man of great charm and courage, had been a social fixture in New York and was now a lieutenant colonel paratrooper in SO. I helped him assemble the briefing plans: the best place to land, the approach from there to Cagliari, the capital city, the probable military headquarters, air intelligence photos, and street scenes from the files. I included the location of Italian military units in so far as we knew, the airfields and possible air strength, and any data we had on names, ranks, and attitudes of military leaders. In the middle of our briefing, Obolensky, with extra heavy Russian accent applied for the occasion and perhaps to relieve the tension, rose and went to the map table saying, "Giff me map, giff me picture (air reconnaissance photos)." He studied the material; all that was missing, I thought, was a monocle. "Ah, I will jump here!" He pointed to the alternative landing point that appealed to him most. The mission of four men went off as planned, and upon landing he skillfully bamboozled the Italian command in Sardinia into requesting inclusion in the Armistice signed with Italy and to offering their cooperation with the West in everything short of military re-involvement. He also secured the release of the ill-fated OSS team that had been captured off the narrow shore below the high bluffs on the western coast.

• • •

Coon returned to Algiers within two weeks and advised that a permanent mission to set up a forward base on Corsica should be authorized for the earliest possible dispatch. He left most of the members of his preliminary mission in Corsica to make arrangements for more OG commandos and for a forward field headquarters.

The situation in Corsica was that most of the five divisions (80,000 men) of the Italian Army had opted for neutrality and repatriation at least to Sardinia. The Germans were holding on to the flat east coast of Corsica and were evacuating the remains of their "Afrika Korps" northward and over the island of Elba to the Italian mainland. Regardless of any other factors, Corsica appeared to offer us the potential of a secure base that was virtually within sight of the Italian coast, and, as regards the Salerno landings, some four hundred miles behind German lines. As soon as the Germans left Corsica, the place would be wide open for us to use.

Corsica actually liberated itself. As soon as word of the invasion of Italy reached Corsica, the Gaullist groups, mostly the middle class, the business people, took preemptive action. They rounded up the Vichy-collaborationist sympathizers and set up an autonomous regime for the island. Part of their motivation was to beat the

Communists to the punch. There was an active Communist party on the island that hoped to monopolize the future of the Resistance there. Happily, the Communists were more talk than action. Our activities on Corsica would be among a friendly and supportive population.

Coon's report was convincing. I worked with DeWitt Clinton who was designated by Henry Hyde of French SI, and Lt. Col. Russell Livermore, a New York investment advisor who was commander of the Italian OGs, to make detailed plans. Also designated to Corsica were a Navy lieutenant from the OSS Maritime Unit, an Annapolis graduate, and Lieutenant LeNen. Out of deference to Clinton and his ancestors' role in the Erie Canal, the code name CANAL was assigned. Donovan personally approved the proposal, and it became a matter of transport, of how to get to Corsica. We arranged a deal with the French Navy to go on a re-commissioned French destroyer, the *Fortuné*, that had just been released from internment in Alexandria harbor, and that was to escort an LST to Corsica, carrying among other things radar for Corsican air defense. The first group to come with me were Clinton from SI, Marine 1st Lieutenant "Pinkie" Harris, a demolitions expert from SO, and French Major Paulo Guisti, of a prominent Corsican family. We were to be followed by other OSS people representing Communications, and services. As R&A man, one of my primary targets was gathering serial numbers from German equipment and, since Corsica was part of Metropolitan France, to see what other documentary information I could gather on the French mainland. The full company of Italian OGs would come on their own shortly, as would liaison people from the Fifth Army Detachment who would use the strategic location of Corsica for Italian operations.

September 27, 1943 in the late afternoon we boarded the unimpressive and, in fact, shabby French destroyer *Fortuné*, of some 1,800 tons displacement, I believe, and joined up with LST 79, which was carrying new radar equipment to be installed on Corsica..

Once at sea, we began to realize that by accompanying the LST we were limiting our speed to the LST's maximum of ten knots. At that rate it would be a two-night trip in contested if not outright enemy waters. I was by then Navy Lieutenant Junior Grade and I smiled to myself when I realized that that extra little half-stripe probably led the French to defer to me as senior American officer present. I was welcomed on the *passerelle*, the bridge whose rusty binnacle compass was questionable even to layman's eyes like mine. The only other navigation aids I could see were French Navy charts and a couple of battered pairs of field glasses.

I have four strong remembrances of this trip:

The hammocks in the sleeping quarters head the list. Once I got the hang of the one assigned to me (no pun intended), I found a hammock to be the perfect sleeping environment. The world could pitch and yaw around me; I was as if suspended in space.

Second, the officers' dining table in the wardroom was made of pegboard. You put your plate down and held it in place with four pegs, the same with your glass. This way, your plate and cup or glass was steady despite the pitching and rolling of the ship. Incidentally, looking around the wardroom I saw the walls were lined with small pictures of French military personalities. One picture was discreetly covered by a small French flag. I lifted up the corner and found that it was a picture of discredited Vichy chief Marshal Pètain.

Third, my "naval command" experience came in for a severe test. On the second morning, we sighted land through the fog off to starboard. It seemed to be islands, not the southern tip of the Bay of Ajaccio. Or, what did I think? Somewhat incredulous that I was being asked, I studiously viewed the charts on the bridge and came away with a purely horseback statement that it seemed to me we were seeing islands off the northwest tip of Sardinia called the Iles Asinaires. As it turned out, I was right, and was amused at the compliments I got on my navigation. We had the rest of the day to sail to reach Ajaccio.

Finally, there was the "action stations" call. An Italian fishing trawler was sighted early in the morning and the *Fortuné*'s captain asked my OK for something I didn't understand except that it obviously involved the Italian sea-going tug that had appeared on our port quarter. Suddenly, he veered the destroyer away from the LST and charged at the new target. Were the guns still spiked from internment, I wondered? When we came near the trawler, we saw the crew of four already lined up with life jackets on, expecting the inevitable. After some bilingual megaphoned palaver, two crewmen of the destroyer were put on the Italian boat, which followed us to Corsica at ten knots. My first Navy "action," I thought with a faint smile.

The morning was clear and sunny when we sailed into the beautiful Bay of Ajaccio and tied up at the main dock. I got off and was waiting for our OSS people in Corsica to meet us when suddenly an armada of German planes flew overhead. This was accompanied by sporadic anti-aircraft fire. I ducked under a balcony of a nearby building and peered out cautiously. Five or six of the planes had been shot down and were tumbling out of the sky in flames. It turned out they were new German guided glider bombs with their own motors that flared fiery exhaust. They were not shot down at all but on their final guided run for the target. They headed for and hit the LST and sank it, with the much-needed anti-aircraft radar still on board.

The German radio that night boasted of new secret German weapons. One of these weapons was the guided aerial torpedo. Swarms of these, the radio said, had bombed the city of Ajaccio in Corsica, causing major damage to warships in the harbor and defense installations ashore. Despite the relatively tranquil look of Corsica, we were deep in a combat zone.

In Ajaccio we were billeted in the annex of the Hôtel des Etrangers, a small, charming hotel building owned and run by an active Résistance leader in the Maquis. Martin Baretti made us welcome. His wife Carol, a British actress, had arrived in Corsica at age nineteen on a theater group tour, met Martin, and never left Corsica. She was for some years honorary British consul in Ajaccio. Using our mainland French Francs that had been supplied to us by the OSS Special Funds people, we paid cash for everything and in effect bought what we needed at about one-fourth of its listed price, even less after haggling. Baretti became our purchasing agent. We bought three cars, a Renault Viva Grand Sport limousine, and a couple of Peugeot 403 sedans, both former Ajaccio taxis. All had been dismantled and literally hidden in pieces from the Italian occupation authorities. Reassembled, they served us well and proved to me that tire sizes on a car do not need to match.

•••

The Germans held the East Coast of Corsica, which is relatively flat its entire length, and used this as a main road to evacuate the remains of the Afrika Korps northward from Tunisia through Sardinia to Corsica and then over the twenty-five miles of water to the Italian mainland. Our OGs tried to recruit Corsicans to generate missions to interdict the Germans but there was little they could do. The Corsicans were bitterly anti-Italian and really did not know the Germans who, at any rate, seemed to be leaving on their own as rapidly as they could. One mission ran head-on into German tanks; three OGs were killed, Lt. Gordon, the team leader, and Master Sergeants Grasso and Maselli, both demolitions experts. The confrontation was in a mountainous town near Lèvie in the center of the island. The villagers there prepared a loving burial site for the bodies. Sadly this ran afoul of U.S. military regulations regarding cemeteries for U.S. servicemen. According to regulations, a minimum of twenty bodies is required to establish a U.S. military cemetery. Some months later, a U.S. graves registration unit came by. They disinterred and removed the bodies, much to the regret of the villagers.

October 3, 1943: Reports reached us that morning in Ajaccio from Corsican contacts in the north. They reported that the Germans were about to evacuate Bastia, the city on the northeast coast closest to the Italian mainland. A group of us took off for Bastia that morning. Among us were Marine lieutenant "Pinkie" Harris, an OSS/SO demolitions expert, DeWitt Clinton of French SI, and two Corsicans, Alex "The Shirt" Pozzo di Borgo, a close Corsican Maquis contact, and French Major Paulo Giusti, a native Corsican who was invaluable to us in facilitating our stay in Corsica. He knew or was related to "everyone," and had "connections" which are the essence of Corsican life. A note on Pozzo di Borgo: He always wore a white shirt, from which came the nickname, and he was a descendant of a former foreign minister of Czarist Russia, in the days when government officials were hired without regard to nationality.

We took off for Bastia in the Renault six-passenger limousine, first to Corte, and then northeastward on the direct stretch towards Bastia, only to find the bridges and culverts blown. On many of them, the terrain was shallow enough so that we could drive down the bank and maneuver across or ford the stream if there was water. As we approached nearer the coast, the culverts were too deep for the Renault. We backtracked to the north and approached Bastia again from the West, across the Col de Teghime. There we found that the French colonial troops, the famous Moroccan Goumiers, with their long flowing brown and gray striped robes, were just taking off down the slopes with their weird chants and cheers, making their final attack in darkness on German outposts below. The Germans withdrew in haste as the Goumiers, six-foot-plus desert warriors of legendary ferocity, screamed down the mountain-sides towards the last defenders. With the bridges out and thousands of Italian soldiers left behind in limbo by the Germans, we steered the clumsy Renault down a goat trail and reached a big cemetery near the coast five miles south of Bastia. The car was ruined by rocks we hit going down the goat trail. We slept in the hulk a few hours, and were awakened at dawn by a massive American air raid on Bastia, which no one knew had been scheduled or apparently thought to call off.

We pulled our things together in a duffel bag we found in the car, sliced off a slab of the Corsican prosciutto ham that the Shirt had thoughtfully brought along, on a slice of the round loaf of Corsican bread he had also brought. We locked the doors of the Renault in silent tribute to its having gotten us this far, and headed north on foot along the highway. For a while we walked along with French colonial troopers moving north to enter the city, and found an Italian army unit lining the road looking on, like spectators at a construction project. Behind the Italians was a small motor pool of their jeeps and trucks. Giusti winked at us, passed his hand across the major's stripes on his French uniform, and pulled out a mimeographed official requisition form he had picked up in Ajaccio. He approached an Italian officer with numerous stripes and stars on his collar, and solemnly handed him the paper, pointing to a four-by-four truck next to the officer. The Italian saluted, barked some orders at his men, and they promptly cleared their materials out of the truck, started the engine, and drove it up to where we were. We climbed in; Guisti saluted; the Italians saluted, and we were off to Bastia.

We entered Bastia on the shore road past the cathedral and towards the Citadelle, a fort on a moderate elevation above the Old Port just beyond it. We passed columns of parked German equipment left behind. Thanks to "Pinkie" Harris we tried to be a little scientific about checking cars and tanks for booby traps. There did not seem to be any. Each of us appropriated an Italian jeep that the Germans had left behind on the streets. These were small FIAT four door convertibles, stripped down except for an essential item of accessory: a brass manual horn built into the dashboard, complete with black rubber honker. I asked some of the stray Italian soldiers to climb into some of the tanks, in case they were booby-trapped, and to read serial number off the tank transmissions. I told them where the numbers were, and gave them cigarettes for their trouble. Harris was horrified at this casual approach to bomb disposal.

So, here I was at the "front," in the *maquis*. My excitement at this was somewhat dampened when I met an American lady war correspondent in khaki uniform who had just flown up from the island of Pantelleria. She was the first American to land on that island and so she had accepted the Italian commandant's Beretta .38 pistol in surrender. It was Helen Kirkpatrick, a tall, striking lady reporter for the Chicago Daily News. Once I recovered from the feeling of resenting a woman invading my moment of glory, I admired her for her courage and enterprise. As I have ever since.

There were numerous tales of shrewdness verging on heroism among the population. One that I personally investigated involved the main electric power plant for Bastia and the nearby gas works. Despite German intentions to blow them both up, when the demolitions squad arrived to set explosives, the manager emotionally pleaded with them not to blow up the plant because it would surely set off the gas in the nearby storage tanks. This would, he said, lead to such a powerful explosion that hundreds of homes still occupied by civilians would be destroyed with much accompanying loss of innocent lives. The Germans appeared to relent, and instead set their mines under the gas tanks themselves. Before midnight the Corsican manager let the gas out of the tanks so that when the mines went off they merely bent the metal of the nearest empty storage tank. This saved both the power plant and the gas works; in a few days sheet metal workers had the storage tank repaired, and restored both power and gas to the city.

•••

As we anticipated, Corsica became a highly effective maritime operations base. Looking eastward from Bastia, you can see Elba clearly on the horizon, and the island of Capraia north of it. With the battle lines on the mainland just north of Naples, we were looking at enemy held territory three hundred miles behind enemy lines.

We had a remarkable array of resources for our work. For transport, the British Royal Navy's African Coastal Forces unit arrived in Bastia and volunteered their services. This remarkable group of sailors and former fishermen, capable in all types of ships from destroyers to dinghies, was a part of the Royal Navy reserves, formed specifically to do maritime infiltrations in the Mediterranean. They became our maritime collaborators, and had three Vospors, eighty-foot British gunboats, as their mainstays. More than that, they were our mentors, since we had no OSS Maritime Unit specialists of our own present.

There were no Maritime Unit people in Corsica except for one man. He was a regular U.S. Navy lieutenant who had bad personal problems. A graduate of Annapolis, he found himself frustrated at being assigned to OSS and to irregular units at that. For him, it was no place to start a regular Navy career, and he had formally requested return to the Navy and out of OSS. Furthermore he was a newlywed, and was irritated not to have had a single letter from his new bride since leaving the States. On about his second day in Corsica, a packet of some fifty V-Mail letters from his bride reached him; she had written virtually every day. In remorse, he shut himself into his room for the better part of two days and wrote some twenty V-Mail letters in return, back-dating them so that his lack of writing would not be noticed. In less than a week his orders to return to Navy auspices arrived and he took off on the next transport plane to Algiers, not even bothering to say good-by.

We frequently commented that the British taught us all we knew. They literally taught us the fine points of landing "bodies" on the Italian and French shores using rubber dinghies. They taught us how to cope with phosphorescence in the water and how landing on open beaches in the dark of the moon was preferable to landing in hilly spots where observers might look down on us without our seeing them.

British Major Andrew Croft of SOE, a tall, angular cavalry type showed us camouflage techniques on the dinghies we used for landings. British Lt. Cdr. Patrick Whinney of SIS and the African Coastal Forces added their data on pinpoint landing sites. We had an informal working agreement: We would pool information on landing points; we would coordinate dates of missions and the boats used; we would indicate the nature of the mission and the number of people involved. Identities of personnel, meaning agents, and targets or missions would be kept private. Where appropriate, we welcomed their sending individual personnel along as pilots or maritime operations experts. So, within the bounds of keeping individual operational security, we had a remarkable cooperation of otherwise rival services.

The pioneering American Navy Motor Torpedo Boat Squadron 15, known as RON-15, arrived in mid-October and November, moving up from its bases first in North Africa then on Sicily. Newly equipped with radar, these sleek seventy-seven foot boats from the Higgins yards in New Orleans had their own mission to interdict enemy coastal shipping. We made our first contacts with them in what became an effective partnership to land and retrieve agent operations in Italy and up to southern France.

In mid-October, we were joined by five Italian MAS boats, stranded by events at the Italian Navy base on the island of Maddalena just off northeastern Sardinia. The officers and crews, the elite of the Italian Navy, eight boats in all, volunteered to join the Allied cause. These remarkable boats were shorter than the American PTs, fifty-five feet compared to seventy-seven. They were, as a result, slightly more maneuverable and with greater speed but, as we learned later, not a good place to have a squeamish stomach in a choppy Mediterranean storm. Each boat had twin screws, each shaft powered by an 18-cylinder Isotta Fraschini motor, no larger than a six cylinder auto engine because three cylinders worked off the same bend in the crankshaft; a masterpiece of Italian engineering. They were also able to maintain headway at walking speed on the pair of silenced four-cylinder FIAT auxiliary engines.

I visited Maddalena a week later, on October 22, on my way to Naples on an American PT boat, the 208. My mission was to meet Sherman Kent who had just arrived to inspect the R&A structure in the Mediterranean Theater as part of his activities following Winnacker's departure. I was also asked by our Communications people to carry cipher material and deliver it to the Commo people in Naples so that we from Corsica could open direct communications with the OSS Fifth Army Detachment people who had just reached Naples.

In Maddalena, a British Coastal Forces officer told me the story of how they had arranged for five Italian MAS boats to volunteer to join us. He was there when an agreement was reached with the local Royal Italian naval command that the boats would be under our orders, meaning those of the British "African Coastal Forces" unit, but that they would not be put into a position of having to fire on their own countrymen.

The agreement was accompanied by some strange twists. Reportedly the British ordered a formal inspection of the Italians, boats and personnel. All the boats were spruced up and the Italian officers and crews were formally lined up for inspection before their moored boats. Each boat complement, its two officers and crew of eight, saluted smartly when the British inspection team approached, except for two Italian crewmen who, at the "salute" command, unthinkingly stretched out their right arms in the fascist salute.

The five boats selected took off for Bastia, Corsica, their crews amazed to make a service trip on their own power. The Italian Navy was so short of fuel that service trips were out. The MAS boats were tied bow to stern and towed to sea by charcoal burning tugs, then turned loose for brief sorties, then towed back by the tug.

That night, on PT-208, we went on to Naples. It was a clear and moonless night. Excited about the long quiet ride on the PT, I volunteered to "take the con," to steer for one shift. It was exhilarating, three Packard engines purring below, a calm sea and nothing in sight. I was mesmerized. I lined the bow up with a star. Well, at the end of my watch we were a good ways off course, but not irreparably. We simply approached Naples around the south of Capri instead of from the north. I felt pretty sheepish, though. Just because I wore a Navy uniform didn't mean I knew how to navigate a vessel.

In Naples I found our new headquarters and duly exchanged the sensitive Communications materials I was carrying. I met Sherman Kent and the R&A people accompanying the Fifth Army Detachment. Kent would come to Corsica the following week. He rode with me in a taxi back to the port. The driver was in typical style careening the little three-seat FIAT through the streets and Kent, conservative despite his cowboy swagger, was concerned for his life. He was yelling at the driver in his best Italian: *"Piano, piano,* you bug-eared son of a bitch, *piano!"* The driver took it as a compliment, since "piano" means softly. He beamed and went even faster.

At the port, the U.S. Army Military Police began harassing the PT boat officers and me because we were out of uniform. We had all exchanged uniform pieces with the British RAF as we liked their flying jackets, or we had bought Italian boots, or were wearing the black flannel CPO shirts. I took leave of Kent and joined the PT boat officers, only to find three other OSS people there. One was John Shaheen who was then a Lt. Commander. The other two were key members of his special project group: Lt. j.g. Michael Burke and "Jumping" Joe Savoldi, former football star now in the somewhat ad-libbed uniform of a civilian attached to U.S. military forces.

The MPs became increasingly unfriendly and we took off on the PT Boat before they could arrest us. Shaheen urged the PT boat captain, Lt. Torrance, to head for Capri which the Germans had abandoned and which had probably not yet seen an Allied officer. We zoomed into Capri harbor in late afternoon and found that there were indeed no Germans or Fascist Italian military there. In fact, we were greeted with flowers and wine. We were driven up to the main square in a huge open tourist car. At the square we saw the main hotel marquee sign was being over-painted from "Deutsch-Italienischer Offiziersklub" to "British-American Officers Club." It did not take long for the Italians to adapt to circumstances.

After dark, we saw Naples across the bay being hit by a major German air attack. It was incredible to be a spectator fifteen miles away watching the wall of anti-aircraft tracers, the searchlights, and at least two German planes apparently shot down. We returned to Bastia the next morning. Shaheen and his team looked over our Corsica set-up approvingly, then talked their way onto an Air Force plane heading back to Algiers.

•••

My first task in Corsica was to send back data on captured or abandoned German equipment. Then I went around the island to see what additional information I could bring in. By luck, the local French Navy command had a copy of the map grid that tied Corsica into the European cartographic grid. These grids were prime military map guides for artillery and apparently remained the best maps of their type until they were made obsolete by radar and later by satellite navigation systems.

I worked closely with the SI and OG people. I set up an intelligence library with data and maps that I had brought with me. We pooled our resources. Albert Materazzi of the OG, a professional Army Map Service expert, set new standards for us by introducing techniques new to us, such as silhouetting coastal pinpoints from elevation maps to guide the missions landing on the Italian coast.

I helped the OGs plan missions onto the mainland. They set up observation posts on the islands off the Italian coast. I helped plan the mission to take over Capraia on October 19, going in a British Vospor motor torpedo boat, the MMS 116. I went along on take-over of the island of Gorgona opposite Livorno and the raid on Pianosa just south of Elba where we went to rescue an American pilot. We coordinated our operational schedule with the British ACF without going into details of the nature or destination of our respective missions. We agreed on a policy that used the Italian boats for trips not involving the movement of our Italian agents, in case of any untrustworthy Italian crewmen. For guerrilla actions like the openly uniformed OGs, we did not hesitate to use the MAS boats. For missions sensitive to security details, that is, not to risk the presence of outsiders that might identify individual agents, we used the American PT boats.

The original landing on Gorgona had its comic opera aspects. I had pulled together whatever I could find on the island, its topography, the town, other means of access or escape from the island, the roads or paths on the island, location of power plant and telephone central, the administrator's house, navy semaphore, and post office. Basically Gorgona was an agricultural penal colony. The island consisted of two hills like crude bosoms, the cleavage towards the mainland. A small town nestled uncomfortably in the cleavage. Its population was perhaps two hundred, mostly prison staff and their families. The telephone had an open line to the

Livorno City exchange that was twelve miles away on the mainland. I gave myself the job of finding the telephone switchboard as quickly as possible to cut off phone contact.

Lt. Col. Russell Livermore personally headed the mission, along with some ten OGs, all of course in Army field uniforms. I mention this because my Navy gear was black, black shirt, black pants, and black cap. The MAS boat commanded by Italian lieutenant Cosulich nosed its way slowly into the harbor among the fishing boats most of which were like overgrown dinghies. It was around 11:30 of a calm moonless night, after an hour and forty-five minute rapid trip at some 25 knots. The OGs took off for their assigned designations, starting with the coast guard station and the town offices. I located the small shed with the telephone switchboard. I started to tear the fuses out of the circuits to stop all calls, but hesitated to damage other lines as this might be detected from the mainland. Leaving one man to guard the station, I climbed up the hill to join others in the main castle-like house, which served as the penal colony center.

All the prisoners, perhaps seventy men, were lined up and briefly interviewed to be sure there were no political prisoners. The answers were almost musical in their near-innocence. What are you charged with, the prisoner was asked. They all replied "*allegato*" meaning "*alleged*"— burglary, or rape, or theft, meaning that they were falsely accused. None of the prisoners caught on that they should have expressed hate for Mussolini or Fascism to win anything from us. The place was jumping with fleas and reeked of plumbing inadequacies, to put it mildly. We worked our way back to the harbor. It was fiercely cold and I had a throbbing headache from incipient flu. A man came up to me in a dark uniform, an Italian Navy *Capo* or chief. He was administratively in charge of everything on the island except the prison. Seeing my dark uniform, he assumed I was the blackshirt secret policeman. On behalf of the people on the island, he had a gift for the commendatore, pointing to the silver lieutenant colonel leaf on Livermore's shoulders. He handed me a small package wrapped in folded over white paper which he opened carefully. It contained eight white fishy objects which I recognized as squid, a delicacy of the whole area, obviously freshly caught. This was too good to miss. I approached Livermore formally, saluted, then announced that the people of the island had a gift for the Colonel, and held out the squid. To say that he reacted unenthusiastically is an understatement, except that he did have the sense of humor to laugh heartily at the situation. It did however leave me with the problem of translating his expletive into a diplomatic word of thanks and hopes for long lasting American-Italian friendship.

The OGs observation posts on Gorgona and Capraia were largely to serve the Army Air Force. They watched for low-flying German planes that might try to use the shadow of the islands to hide from Corsica's radar detection until they could make a surprise attack on the U.S. airbase at Borgo just south of Bastia. An Air Force radarman was stationed with portable equipment on Capraia with our OGs. There were at least two instances where this made the difference between a surprise attack and those extra few minutes of scrambling time that the Capraia operation afforded people at the Borgo airfield.

In turn, we OSS helped the Navy units, the PTs and the British gunboats. The OG spotters on the Observation Posts could observe German coastal shipping which the Germans increasingly relied on as roads and railroads on the mainland were increasingly subject to Allied air attack. For several weeks, information was supplemented by one of our agents, Robert L. Pomeroy, a former American newsman active in Italy, whom we stationed on top of Monte Cappani, the highest point on Elba, where he had a clear view of Porto Ferraio, the main port.

One evening in late October, all spotters confirmed German convoy activity. Based on the reports, Captain Norman Dickinson RN, the British Senior Officer Inshore Squadron (the coordinator of naval activities for us all) called a meeting of unit officers and decided to initiate a coordinated attack. American PTs with their radar would be the eyes and ears. If a large vessel like a freighter or a destroyer were encountered, the PTs with their torpedoes would attack. In case of barges or the so-called flat-bottomed "F-Lighters" or landing craft, the British gunboats would go in with their cannon. I went along on the leading British motor gunboat to help identify shoreline silhouettes as a supplement to their navigation inshore. What happened was a demonstration of British nerves and dedication that I will never forget.

We were at sea for some two hours heading towards the Italian coast north of Elba. At midnight we encountered part of the German convoy and came head-on against a German F-Lighter carrying, we estimated, over a hundred German army troops. The British Vospors were in a line, moving snake-like towards the F-Lighter. When it turned back towards the mainland the British in utter silence formed an arc to the south of it and bore into within a hundred yards. I ducked behind the tarpaulin wondering if anyone was going to open fire or did these crazy Brits intend to ram the German boat? Suddenly the Lieutenant who was captain of the boat said very quietly: "Carry on." The forward cannon of the Vospors all came to life at once with shattering effect on the F-Lighter. The 88-millimeter cannon on its top deck literally blew straight into the air taking the bodies of its crew along. Next, the ammunition on the doomed ship went up. The Vospors turned away to the south. The rest of the German convoy apparently turned back northward. One of the PT's radar warned of a larger vessel approaching the area, possibly a destroyer. We turned and headed back to Bastia, a successful mission. No, no efforts to retrieve survivors were deemed advisable.

•••

We took over a house overlooking Bastia on the winding road up the mountain side called the Route de St. Florent. The house was owned by a representative of a French steamship company who was pleased to have us maintain and then repair the house. It was four stories, two stories above road level and two downstairs. Our sleeping quarters, facing the bay. It was drafty and cold, yet comfortable. We had two maids, Annette who cooked and served, and her aunt who cleaned. They had a time getting used to American food, but they could do wonders with powdered eggs, including bartering them for local chickens, langoustes, venison and port. One night Donovan came to dinner. Annette was all flustered, confiding to me that she had a uniform that she had borrowed for the occasion, but she had no perfume. Absent any PX, all I had was some Aqua Velva, which I offered her. Sure enough, its characteristic odor wafted amply about the dinner table as she served.

The crews of the U.S. PT boats, and others, found the Florida Bar near the port. They instructed the giggling bar girl to mix a special drink, this *avec* (with) that, *avec* that—mixing bad local brandy with cedratine liqueur and a local sweet Muscatel wine, and reportedly some French Scotch, or was it alcohol from the torpedo tubes? It became famous as the "*Bastia Avec Avec*."

At Christmas there was entertainment from a glee club that the local airmen assembled. In the middle of the evening, we were called to our OSS house.

A message had been received from John Shaheen in Naples at the OSS Fifth Army headquarters asking us to pick up an agent "immediately" at a given pinpoint on the Italian coast south of Elba. The weather was stormy and we had two landings backlogged and didn't appreciate being treated like taxi drivers on call on short notice. Two evenings later, the weather let up and there was a boat available. We went to the pinpoint and found a dozen Italians, all calling themselves "Ammiraglio" or "Commendatore" or "Ingeniere," titles of status. It turned out that they indeed included senior Italian Navy personnel, among them the deputy chief of staff of the Italian Navy and the engineers who designed the latest Italian navy magnetic torpedo. This part of Shaheen's operations had succeeded.

•••

On Sunday, February 20 I was made duty officer as our CO, Lt. Col. Russell Livermore, was procuring supplies in Algiers. The responsibility of leadership would have normally fallen to Major Nathaniel "Bo" Wentworth, but he was in Ile Rousse. Lt. Albert Materazzi, the OG intelligence officer, was sick in the hospital. Our Communications man brought me a message from emergency equipment on "O.P.2," which was Capraia. Germans had landed, raided and blown up the OG unit's shelter destroying the equipment and invaluable radar set. Fortunately, the personnel were safe and had hidden out on the rough mountain side. They needed new communications, signal plans as well as the new radar set. I ordered a new commo pack made ready, called the Army Air base at Borgo to give the A-2 the news and to ask for his readying the replacement radar, which he told me would be ready right after lunch. I called British Navy Captain Norman Dickinson to prepare a boat for our use. After several failed attempts, I finally reached Wentworth at Ile Rousse and he encouraged my actions and ordered me to take the mission. This seemed quite a defining moment. I still envisioned myself as a simple research man, not one who would actually command a unit that could potentially engage combat with the enemy.

It took several hours for A-2 to ready the new radar, but I finally got it and met with Lt. Iapelli, the Italian officer whose boat, MAS 546, was designated to take me and the crew to Carpraia. Capt. Dickinson ordered his operations officer, Lt. Charles Buist, to accompany us. We cast off at dusk.

At cruising speed in the MAS it took little over forty-five minutes to get near Capraia. I suggested approaching from the north to then round the southern tip of the island. The harbor with its small, inverted-L shaped breakwater and enclosed fishing port was on the southeastern coast facing the mainland. Seeing no activity we crept in at near-silent speed on the auxiliary engines, hugging the shore as the OG's message had indicated that mines, possibly acoustic-type, were probable and would be in deeper water. We landed successfully. I radioed our OG team on our FM handy-talkie and was surprised and irked that there was no response. I dispatched one member of the crew to take an islander along and call the Americans while we off-loaded the equipment.

In short order, some of the OGs appeared. They had not received any word of my coming, and told me another boat with British officers on board had been in earlier but strangely, it seemed to them, had not had any supplies for them. They were glad to get what I brought because this would put them back in business. It seemed odd to me that another boat would have gone to Capraia without Capt. Dickinson telling me about it before I left.

This was a communications misunderstanding. We had very good, in fact unusual, international camaraderie in Corsica between and among British SIS and SOE, American military and air units, the local French authorities, and the various parts of OSS. The Capraia operation was ours, American OSS, and there was tacit understanding that the British would not go there without clearing with us. With my taking so long to obtain the new radar set, a British boat had gone out to reconnoiter the island in daylight.

Our delivery on Capraia now complete, we cast off for the return trip. Again, I told the helmsman to hold near the shore, as I feared mines more than grounding. The boat was caught by the wind and nudged too close to the breakwater to suit me. I didn't dare order a change in the engines because a backfire might set off an acoustic mine. Still, I heard Iapelli to my surprise order the main engines on "half ahead," meaning engaging at half power to maintain headway…mines or no mines. It was the last thing I would remember.

CHAPTER 7

RECOVERY . . .

I awoke in a stone building I recognized as being part of the chapel of the local nuns. It was clear something major had happened. With ironic humor I recall saying to myself, now what would the hero in the movies do at a time like this? Obviously ask about the others: *"Como sono gli alteri?"* I ventured. *"Tutti bene, tutti bene,"* the sister replied. That bothered me. If all the others were all right, why was I the only one bunged up? I was half-conscious and in shock. I had no feeling in my left leg. The OGs had brought some morphine from their medical kits. I recalled I had been on the bridge of the boat at the left, Iapelli in the middle, Buist to starboard. We must have triggered a mine, but the details would come later.

I learned that Patrick Whinney had arrived with a British team that approached Capraia offshore on an American Air Force air-sea rescue boat, the ARB 402, which had reached Bastia only a few days before. The ARB's were like PT boats but less powerful and with a large cabin as sickbay midships. The OGs contacted some fishermen who rowed out in their wooden boats so as not set off any remaining mines. Whinney explained what had happened, that a mine had detonated to starboard. Several of us had been blown into the water and rescued by the fishermen. Whinney said he wanted to get us off using only wooden rowboats. His men, the OG's, and the fishermen were building appropriate stretchers out of wood to help in this. I remember much movement but I was sedated.

It was daylight when we reached Bastia. Capt. Dickinson was there to greet us with his gruff British "I say, Old Karlow, blow up all my boats, will you?" and he patted me on the shoulder. I was taken north of Bastia to a tent-city field hospital for two days. There was alarm because, while in the polluted harbor water, a form of gas gangrene had set in and was spreading up my leg. I was flown in an Air Evacuation plane to Cagliari, Sardinia where the U.S. had a military hospital that was in a former TB sanitarium with huge windows and balconies. The surgeon, Dr. Lippard, a serious and conscientious man, actually a pediatric surgeon in civil life, explained to me that my left knee was smashed and at best I would have a stiff leg, but with the gangrene spreading he had to recommend amputation.

By the time I began to come to, it was my birthday and the nurses had a cake for me. I asked what would happen to replace my leg. Shouldn't muscles or nerves be tapped in some way before what's left of my leg heals? Neither Dr. Lippard nor his two assistants, Drs. Bougie and Lin, had any idea. No one on the staff knew either. No one had even seen an artificial leg.

•••

Penicillin was the new wonder drug. The first thing the doctors did when I arrived at the military hospital in Cagliari was put me on penicillin. I may have been one of the first patients to get penicillin in the Mediterranean Theater, judging by the fuss that seemed to be made over me. It was ordered flown in for me; I have no idea by whom. The pilot who brought it came in to the hospital specially to my room to meet me. Apparently the penicillin did the trick. The gas gangrene was eliminated and the slow process of healing begun.

I started to assess what I would no longer be able to do without a left leg above the knee. Tennis was probably out. Walking up stairs? No idea. Probably not foot-over-foot without a knee, but one step at a time. Auto driving? The left leg works only the clutch; I ought to be able to pump a clutch pedal. Dancing? Worth a try. Why not? Swimming? Probably not with any artificial leg, or what? I couldn't imagine swimming with a so-called "wooden leg." Swim without one? Why not? A nurse showed me an aging copy of LIFE magazine with a picture of an older man wearing an artificial leg properly called a prosthesis, made of what looked like aluminum with leather straps. What were artificial legs made of?

I gained strength rapidly. As the winter weather abated, the nurses could wheel my bed out onto one of the broad balconies that were a feature on each of the four floors of the relatively modern tuberculosis sanitarium that the U.S. military took over to make into a major but underused field hospital. On April 1, 1944 I was flown on a medical evacuation plane to the Army hospital in Bizerte, Tunisia. A fat medical dossier, carefully compiled, was entrusted to me by the Army doctors, to be turned over to Navy medical authorities. I looked through it. It was full of charts, ward records, and pictures. Two weeks later, when I arrived on a stretcher by LST at the Navy Base Hospital in Oran, Algeria, I learned that somewhere, somehow the dossier had disappeared. It was never found.

The Navy medical staff at Oran started a new medical record on me based on my recounting what had happened and on all the medical terms I could remember bearing on my case. One question recurred. What ship was I on? What command? I began to realize that I had been on an Italian flag naval vessel that had no visible direct U.S. Navy affiliation, and where I was the only U.S. Navy person on board, and without formal orders at that. What a rigmarole that could set off if some administrative type tried to straighten out the record. I thought my "license to steal" Navy orders would cover me in a broad sense, but I had no copy with me. I said I would write for a copy. Did I have specific mission orders? Was I in combat? I slipped successfully back into the safety of "intelligence mission" jargon and the question did not come up again. I was surprised and almost relieved when Commodore Yates, the hospital commandant, came to my room one evening with the nurse who was his date, and stayed just long enough to pin the Purple Heart medal on my pajama jacket. The citation only said "enemy action."

"So you're in intelligence...What part, ONI?" he asked.

"No, OSS." I said, but he had not heard of it and asked if the unit was part of the Navy? I informed him that we reported to the Joint Chiefs of Staff. He looked puzzled.

"Sounds just like intelligence," he rejoined with a smile. He said he wouldn't ask any more questions, but added "a good luck, son" patting me on the shoulder before leaving with the nurse. The medal seemed to legitimize things for me. I didn't need to go into detail but at least I didn't worry about charges of "misconduct."

Mail reached me from family, from Livermore and Wentworth in Corsica, and from OSS colleagues. To my complete surprise, Lou Robbins, a near classmate from college, who was a lieutenant on a cruiser that had stopped in Oran, somehow heard that I was in the hospital, came by to see me. At night my leg was put into traction with weights across the foot of the bed to help the healing process. In short order a traction device was rigged up so that I could have the proper traction on during the day. The portable brace-like apparatus was clumsy but would make it possible for me to move about. I had to learn to walk on crutches. But first I had to get up out of bed. What a crazy sensation that first time, to get up and be completely off balance without the weight of the missing leg and without a leg to respond to reflex actions, and with the one remaining leg weakened from being bed-ridden for two months! But what a joy to be free of bed-pans.

Early May I went on board the Navy Hospital ship *Refuge*, a converted passenger liner on its maiden voyage for the Navy. It was carrying basically "well" passengers, to break in the staff with an easy first trip. The first night out in the Mediterranean was the hardest. All the lights were on, inside and on deck, and floodlights illuminated the Red Cross markings on the white hull. The Germans were known for ignoring such markings. More than that, movies were shown in the open on the afterdeck. Many of us could not help a feeling of near panic. The ships' complement could not understand why the patients didn't seem to like the movie. Most of us had been conditioned to blackouts and the change was just too sudden. Our nerves were too much on edge to accept lights at night at sea in a war zone.

I had made friends with Joe Crisanti, a Lieutenant j.g. like me. He was a great extroverted Chicago lawyer whose left leg was mangled when, as a gunner on a Navy oil tanker, he had been blown over the side and down on the concrete pier in an air raid on Naples harbor. Joe walked with a limp using only a cane for balance. It gave him a dapper air. He took me under his wing and helped me get settled on board the *Refuge*. We reached the ward where we were both assigned, and I looked on with amazement as Joe went right up to the ward nurse, obviously freshly commissioned, and asked her to go light on the mayonnaise when she brought up our club sandwiches. When the nurse protested that she should not leave her post on the ward, Joe told her confidently that he would watch the ward for her in her absence. She went off, duly returned with two sandwiches — and caught hell from the senior nurse the next day. There was a lot of this gentle horseplay to lighten the trip.

After passing Gibraltar, we had a relaxed two-week journey. The ship was diverted from Philadelphia, as originally scheduled, to Charleston, South Carolina. When we sailed into the Charleston harbor, easily half the staff and passengers on board who, like me, had never been to the deep South were shocked. Huge whitewashed signs were painted on the warehouses: WHITES ONLY, NO BLACKS. We tied up and the first people on board were Red Cross ladies bringing, of all things, cola drinks. Thanks, but no, we were craving plain fresh milk.

I hit a problem at Charleston because the hospital had few patients. We were the only combat patients and received extra attention because of it. Or at least this is what I concluded on my second night there. I was as usual strapped into the bed so as to keep my stump, the amputated leg, in traction. A young woman entered my room, one of the ward assistants. She stroked my forehead and in her melodious Southern accent asked me in a whisper if I wanted company. The prospects danced in my head but so did the problems: She sat in the chair and removed her jeans, then wriggled up on my bed and began to tug at my traction straps. She didn't know how to release them and I couldn't help much in my tied-down position. She put her jeans back on and as she was leaving I wondered whether indeed this amputation business would make problems for me that I had not anticipated. Silly thought: No traction, action.

There was a major problem in that the commandant was reluctant to release me to go to the newly established prosthetics center in Philadelphia that the Navy had just set up, regardless of Navy instructions ordering all amputee patients to be treated there. No way, the commandant said, I'd leave for there only when I was fully healed. I made a phone call to Florence Smith in Washington. Two weeks later, orders came through and I reached Philadelphia by Navy plane on June 11. My mother and sister were on hand to meet me and, once they were over the shock of my injury (and of the terrible "butch" haircut I got in Charleston), they gave me full moral support, which was invaluable.

Their real shock had been at my sister's apartment in Washington one evening back in March, when a dour looking Navy officer in uniform had knocked, stood there and then asked to come in. He announced somberly to my mother and sister that I had been severely injured, but he had no details. He was a chaplain and asked if he could lead them in prayer, well meant, but not the way to break this kind of news to my not-very-formal-religion-type mother or sister. My mother at once called Florence Smith who provided details for her within a day or two when they became available through OSS channels.

At the Philadelphia Naval Hospital I was treated by an outstanding group of surgeons, Donald T. Jones, orthopedic surgeon and Milton DuPertuis, plastic surgeon, by specialists and by the new chief prosthetist, Basil "Bill" Peters. The Army and the Navy had fought over Peters to gain his services. It seems that Peters had once suggested an improved knee joint for President Franklin D. Roosevelt's full-length braces. After Pearl Harbor, the Army had drafted him but Admiral MacIntyre, the Navy Surgeon General, heard about it and ordered Peters pulled out of Army boot camp and commissioned into Navy as Hospital Corps officer.

•••

I was determined not to be handicapped or "disabled" in the formal vernacular. The medical team, with the continuing ministrations of Bill Peters, made this wish possible. I can say in gratitude that, once fitted and released, I have been inconvenienced, but have only rarely felt myself "handicapped" in my reasonably active life. This may be only a matter of semantics but to me there is a definite distinction in terms.

Early in August, the Chief Surgeon at Philadelphia, Capt. Schaar, came by my room to ask me, since my personnel record showed I spoke French, if I would go see a French Navy officer who had just arrived, a double amputee, who spoke little English and who would appreciate company. I grabbed my crutches and went right up to his room. Turning into his room, I saw a rather frail hawk-nosed man surrounded by traction and handgrip equipment on and over his bed. A handsome lady in a smart, dark blue shirt-and-skirt uniform that I did not recognize sat by his bed. On the wall there was a picture of a submarine with its full complement taken in a formal picture, and under it the traditional French sailors' hat ribbon marked "*Casabianca.*" I said in amazement, "But you're l'Herminier!" "*Mais, vous me connaissez?*" Of course I knew him but had never met him.

Here was Capt. Jean l'Herminier and his wife, Madeleine, whom the French had commissioned an ensign in the French WAVES to accompany and take care of him. He was delighted to hear I worked for Donovan and assumed I had been assigned to keep contact with him. It began a long friendship. Bill Peters and the medical team were challenged by the reconstructive surgery needed for this type of double disarticulation. First, a platform was built so that he could sit upright in bed and while operating a wheelchair. Then, using the platform to mount prostheses, they let him begin walking on short legs, graduating to longer ones as he regained his balance. The results were that l'Herminier walked out of the hospital two years later, stiff-legged and with canes, but at least minimally ambulatory. As he specified with his great good humor, he just wanted to be five centimeters taller than his wife.

My own new leg arrived in October 1944, literally a World War I model that still was the U.S. military issue. It was made all of wood, heavy to the point of clumsiness, with an articulated ankle joint that I found prone to make a clanking sound when I was walking, and with a clumsy knee stop with a leather check strap to keep the knee from swinging freely. I was self-conscious over the loud slap-slap noise of the knee joint. The knee had a leather check strap that frequently needed adjustment so most of the time the knee was completely free-swinging, like a pendulum. This made for a clumsy walking gait. The thigh had a cup-shaped socket that I had to put on over two or three thick cotton stump socks. A two-inch stainless steel hinge at the hip held the leg onto a three-inch wide leather belt strapped around my waist designed to keep the leg on and straight. It was just as uncomfortable as it sounds.

Although clumsy at first, I eventually learned to walk and even to get back into ballroom dancing. Some young women from the local USO service club came by once a week to work with patients wanting to learn to dance again. They were good sports because we fell down once or twice, and I'm sure it is not pleasant to be kicked in the shins by a stray artificial leg. Whoever you were, girls, my eternal thanks!

By this time I began to realize that prosthetics was a much-neglected profession, one that seemed to attract an assorted spectrum of practitioners, whether MDs or craftsmen, ranging from carpenters at one end, to gadgeteers at the other. Only a few specialists that I met in New York and Philadelphia seemed adequately informed of or sensitive to the needs of the customers, meaning the amputees whom they served.

Peters was one of the exceptions. I was one of his first patients at the Naval Hospital and he tried his new designs out on me and on a number of his other patients. He had a gruff but effective way to get at his patients' problems and set them right. Even after the war, when he started his own private practice in Philadelphia, the most difficult cases in the area were referred to him by surgeons who knew of him, and by the Veterans Administration and the insurance companies.

I kept in touch with Peters. In the late 1940s, he used me as a guinea pig before the National Research Council. He was showing new designs for above-knee limbs, specifically for reshaping and redesigning the socket so it would be held on by air pressure, the so-called suction socket. This would eliminate the need for that restrictive belt around the waist, and make it possible to slide into a movie seat, because the foot and the whole leg can be turned outward.

Being a guinea pig had its problems. I remember one time in Washington I was on center stage before a group of the National Research Council's sub-committee on prosthetic appliances. There I was in those black bathing trunks while a doctor was lecturing about the dangers of "negative pressure" on my suction socket. He warned that excess pressure over 3 pounds, or was it 14 pounds, might cause the blood vessels in the patient's stump to break down. I felt none of the symptoms he was describing and I thought his warnings were far fetched at best. I thought for a moment to contradict the doctor right there on the stage, but figured the normal progress of scientific reporting would benefit more by my keeping quiet for once in my life. In a few months the subject of "negative pressure" disappeared, never to show again.

My main problem was atrophy. I could tell I was steadily losing volume in the stump of my leg. It was visibly getting thinner and requiring another and yet another stump socks, as many as four at a time, to keep any kind of hold on the leg. By 1948 Peters had designed his version of a shaped socket with contours that matched the shape of the four main muscle channels in the thigh. The Veterans Administration called this approach a quadrilateral socket. Peters went on from this with his "musculature" socket, as he called it. With his modified quadrilateral design, my thigh began to gain in size and weight, quite remarkably adding up to two inches in circumference measured at the top of the stump in just a few weeks.

Then Peters put me on the suction socket design. He sealed off the open bottom of the quadrilateral socket design leaving only a hole near the end with a removable screw-insert valve. He showed me how to use a surgical stockinette to pull my stump fully into the socket to remove the stockinette itself and all the air that could readily be exhausted, and how to seal the opening with the valve. This meant that air pressure kept the leg on me, and the restrictive waist belt was no longer necessary.

What a relief it was to take that belt off and no longer to feel like being in a harness! Yet what a problem it was to learn to keep my balance all over again. My leg and hip muscles developed and stabilized. I did so well on that design that, before the end of 1949, I took off for an overseas job in Germany, coming back to visit Peters just once a year for a check-up.

●●●

Donovan wrote me a most encouraging letter in October 1944, shortly before I was released from the hospital. I returned to Washington on the train. On Monday, November 6, 1944, I walked without a cane into OSS headquarters. Florence Smith spotted me and there was a warm welcome. Suddenly I realized that the man at my side was Donovan himself. He had come out of his office just long enough to greet me and to say that he was glad to see me, that there was still a lot of work he wanted me to do and to let him know when I was ready. I guess the elapsed time in all of this was thirty-two seconds, but his presence and words made all the difference in the world to me. Speak of instant rehabilitation! I tried to hide the tears in my eyes. They were tears of pride.

●●●

I returned to work at the Washington headquarters Monday, December 11, and reported to Duncan Lee, then head of the Secretariat, Donovan's personal staff. Lee, a reddish-haired, soft-spoken Southern lawyer, patiently showed me the work that he and the two other members of the Secretariat were doing. Before papers went to Donovan, our job was to complete the staff work; to be sure everything needed was there. When papers came out of Donovan's office, our job was to decipher his handwriting where necessary and to see that whatever he had decided or instructed was indeed carried out or communicated. Finally, and if possible, we should see how often we could anticipate his actions and reactions and do the necessary staff work before he even saw the original of the subject at hand. Lee left government shortly after I arrived there.

Donovan's habit of reading omnivorously was an effective way for him to keep on top of the sprawling, throbbing number of worldwide activities in which OSS was now engaged. There was the successful support to the cross-Channel landings in Europe in June, which was followed by the highly commended direct support by the resistance forces built up by OSS to the U.S. forces that landed in August in southern France. In about three weeks, American troops had blitzed up from the Riviera to the German border. The activities of the underground in France and Italy had created major obstacles to enemy troop movements that had exceeded all expectations. Further, there were ongoing activities in "neutral" countries like Switzerland, Spain, Turkey, and Thailand (where the King himself was a key member of the underground). The OSS began penetrations into Germany itself, also into Greece. There was active combat in Burma, under Colonel Carl Eifler and the famous Detachment 101 with its Kachin tribesmen that kept the Japanese from reaching the Indian Ocean. At the same time bases had been established in India and were being opened in China.

Sometimes there were light touches. Walter Mansfield was a lawyer from the Donovan Leisure office who served as Marine lt. colonel administrative officer for the new OSS base in Kunming, China. He received a routine personnel cable from the OSS support base in Calcutta, asking if he would want a WAC on his T/O, meaning a woman soldier in his organization. He replied, "Yes if she brings her slot with her." Donovan flared up when he read this and fired off a cable to Mansfield deploring what he termed childish salaciousness in what were historic documents, namely the file of OSS cables that he knew would be archival material some day.

What about planning for the future? The war was winding down in Germany, and Donovan was busy drafting a comprehensive proposal for the position of a national intelligence agency in peacetime. By the end of November 1944, a copy had been sent to the President and eleven copies of a slightly fuller version had been sent by hand to the Secretaries of State, Army, and Navy, and to the Directors of the FBI and of the Budget Bureau, among others. Donovan's initiative reignited the inter-agency turf warfare around Washington, and it flared into a raging fire. There was a momentary reprieve. The Germans staged a mass attack at the Battle of the Bulge in December that was stopped short of it main target, Antwerp. This was Germany's last charge. Any remaining ability by Nazi Germany to make future assaults was being sapped away by the air war in the West and by Russian advances in the East. The Germans had literally been driven out of any pre-World War II USSR territory. France was lost to the Germans. U.S. troops were entering the western edge of Germany proper. Italy was virtually lost. In the Pacific, the Japanese were being driven back. Came New Year's Day 1944-45 and with it the hope that this year, 1945, would be the year for the war to be won.

Early in February we were shocked to read in the newspapers all about Donovan's recommendations. The paper that he worked so hard to write, and sent out so carefully only to ten selected top government officials a few weeks before had been leaked prematurely to the Chicago Tribune. The information, put all out of context, was spread all over the front page under the banner headlines: "NEW DEAL PLANS SUPER-SPY SYSTEM" and "DONOVAN PLANS POSTWAR GESTAPO."

Who leaked it? Given the turf battles in Washington, it could have been any one of the addressees. Donovan was bitterly disappointed and we all shared in the shock of this gross and incredible security violation. War is vicious, but turf war, in some ways, can be just as deadly.

A new load of work began for the OSS Secretariat. A growing volume of manuscripts for books and magazine articles by and/or about OSS and its activities had to be screened for release and publication. OSS had become a sexy subject for reporters, for serious writers, and particularly for fiction writers. Donovan had mixed feelings. He wanted OSS exploits to be known, but security and timing worried him. We understood his ambiguous signals; encourage subtly, but release charily. As an early rule of thumb, if we could recognize any specific operation by name or by description in the drafts of the books we were reviewing, we should seek a rewrite to conceal or fictionalize identifiable details. We could see the handwriting on the wall. Press stories and books would grow and become a flood, and we would be like the King who ordered the tides to halt. We frequently sought only to delay some items until the end of the war would change the basic rules for releasing information. By this time, Duncan Lee had returned to civilian life, and our ranks in the Secretariat had thinned to two others and myself.

In the meanwhile, both the European and Pacific Wars were continuing to wind down rapidly. The OSS efforts to accept the early surrender of the German forces in northern Italy, the fruit of careful efforts by Allen Dulles working out of Switzerland, were turned down by Roosevelt and Churchill in favor of continuing the war in Europe until an unconditional surrender by Nazi Germany was achieved. The collapse of Germany came quickly thereafter. In Japan, the dropping of the atom bombs finally ended the militarists' tight hold on that country.

Although the wind had been taken out of Donovan's sails by the leaked article in the Chicago Tribune, he sought ways to maintain contact with members of the OSS. He once asked me to see about ways to keep a registry of key people who were leaving OSS and their military services, and to find a way to set up a mail center for keeping an informal "on call" reserve together. I began to build a roster on some rudimentary manual punch cards and would try to interview or collect exit reports on as many names as I could or thought appropriate. I had some help on this from Mike Burke, who had been active with the Shaheen operation in the Mediterranean and who afterward had parachuted into France before D-Day. Burke went to work for CBS in New York, and, after great effort, was able to get "Post Office Box 109," Donovan's code number in OSS somewhere in a Long Island post office. Donovan was pleased with this. I suggested designating an informal committee to nominate, screen, and in general refine this list. Donovan felt it was too early since he was chary of anyone finding out that he was involved with such a "continuity"—his word—effort, and suggested I keep things going on my own for awhile. I called it the "Continuity File" and maintained it for some time.

CHAPTER 8

PEACETIME INTELLIGENCE...

The end came quickly for the OSS, on less than two weeks' notice. V-J Day was August 14. President Truman had already named commissions to dismantle the wartime apparatus. "Get the boys home" was the word of the day. Donovan thought he would have time for an orderly rearrangement to peacetime circumstances. He feared the pell-mell demobilization that began almost immediately. He sensed clearly that the end of the war did not mean the coming of peace. Also, he realized he was not being consulted about the future of the OSS or any future intelligence agency. He chaired a series of internal meetings on function, staff, and budget reduction, and began to make public statements about the needs for peacetime intelligence work, without him, he emphasized, as he was returning to civilian life.

On the weekend of September 20, 1945, a letter arrived for Donovan from Truman acknowledging his capable leadership of the OSS and stressing the need to "conserve those resources and skills developed within your organization." The letter continued, stating that "...the peacetime intelligence services...are being erected on the foundation of the facilities and resources mobilized through the Office of Strategic Services..." and that the OSS was to close by October 1, 1945.

Many OSS people in Washington or returning from the field were already leaving for civilian life. The disclosure of a final date increased the level of personnel departures to a stampede. OSS went out not with a roar nor with a whimper but with a slosh as of water escaping from a dam whose gates had been opened for the water to flow out in all directions.

• • •

October 1, 1945. What a topsy-turvy time! I could not imagine simply shutting down an intelligence service without replacing it. But then, the Armed Forces had just been "unified." This turned out to mean that the two forces, Army and Navy, had been "unified" into three forces, the Army, Navy, and Air Force. And for the OSS, Truman had said it was important to build on its foundations for a future peacetime service. But today OSS was in two parts, the Research & Analysis and Presentations branches were assigned to the State Department, and the operational elements to the War Department in a new entity called the Strategic Services Unit, or SSU.

I reviewed my own status and plans. I was asked to stay on in the Director's office of the SSU at what was then good rank and good pay. I checked with the Navy Personnel authorities because of my status as a Lieutenant (Retired). It did amuse me at my age of twenty-four to see myself listed as "retired." The Navy offered me a promotion to Lieutenant Commander if I would stay active in the Navy for six more months, but no one could say for sure where my assignment would be. It might very well be in the Navy Department. My fascination with intelligence won out. I decided to request the Navy to return me to civilian status, and accept the position with SSU, to continue on the Director's secretariat.

•••

The job of the SSU was to liquidate the operational intelligence functions not needed in peacetime. Although the time period was not specified, it was assumed to be two years. Yet this was qualified. SSU was not to be integrated into G-2 or any other part of military intelligence. There were still high-level discussions about a new central intelligence structure and about the parts of SSU that would be appropriately held intact for it.

Brigadier General John Magruder was named head of SSU. Here was a man of great wisdom and charm, tall, slender, with a warm smile. I had heard that he had had a highly controversial career because of his views on China when he was an observer there in 1941. When the war broke out, he had attained the rank of Brigadier General, a rank he still held at war's end. Advocacy of an independent intelligence structure did not bring the proper rewards to an officer of his stature. Magruder welcomed me on his staff, told me of his conviction of the importance of a new intelligence structure, which he wanted soon. In a light touch, he warned me that he had no middle initial, yet almost everyone writing him assigned him one. Usually, it was John J., with John A. as runner-up. He noted I did not use my first name, and made it a point to call me "Serge P."

Magruder retired shortly, and was replaced by Major General (now back to his "permanent" rank of Lieutenant Colonel) William W. Quinn as Director. Quinn was the highly successful former G-2 for the invasion in southern France by the Seventh Army. He became one of the OSS' most satisfied customers because of the effectiveness of the intelligence and of the intensity of the Resistance in France. This had made possible the rapid sweep through southeastern France in time to join at the German border the armies moving eastward from the Normandy landings.

By attrition, I became chief of the Secretariat which by then meant my being personal aide to Quinn who was an effective military officer in a highly difficult political situation. I recall his first weekly staff meeting, a practice continued from Donovan's OSS days. The activity heads had assembled as usual before the Director entered. When he did, we all rose. Quinn strode in, greeted this with a smile, and told us all that he appreciated the gesture, but that he was now back to permanent lieutenant colonel, not general, nor was he Donovan. So please… no stand-up reception.

By that time, I was working mostly on arranging de-briefings for leading returnees, and keeping up with (or down to) the dwindling personnel rosters of the various SSU elements. Mostly this included the SI, SO, and Morale Operations staffs which were all demobilizing and yet still supporting active overseas bases in Europe, mainly Germany, and in Southeast Asia. In addition, I became involved in handling the voluminous files being sent back from abroad and which required an archiving policy.

On one April day, as I was leaving the building at the end of the day, Quinn came up to me with a sly smile to tell me he had a great job for me. He wanted me to prepare a report on the OSS activities in World War II. Would I please get at this as soon as I could clear my desk, and confer, first of all, with Donovan. Quinn knew I was still in weekly contact with Donovan, mostly helping him find documents incident to OSS operations that should be in the historical archives that Donovan was beginning to assemble from his personal papers that had been transferred to the Donovan, Leisure law offices in New York.

The situation was complicated. There were two major hurdles to overcome. The first had to do with Donovan. Donovan had always had a historian, originally Wallace R. Deuel who was head of the Chicago Daily News foreign correspondents when the war broke out and whom I had come to know well. At the end of the war, there was a formal History Project with a sizable staff headed by Professor Conyers Read of the University of Pennsylvania, a respected historian and educator. The Project included among its distinguished members several people of stature, such as the well-known writer and *New Yorker* editor, Geoffrey Hellman. They insisted on editorial independence. Their approach was to interview people as close to the events as possible, even overseas, to catch the substance and flavor of the activities just completed. Editing and evaluation of the stories would come later.

Donovan reviewed some of the drafts and abruptly closed down the History Project. He felt the incoming material was "too much like Drew Pearson" in its breathless and on-the-scene tempo, overlooking in his eyes the background and significance of the OSS activities that were being described. He did not want a scholarly history; he had in mind something more like a "war report." I thought this would be a good title to use, and outlined my preliminary ideas. I started with the premise that the report should be Donovan's. We would review the enabling documents on origins and administrative development of OSS, use regular or monthly reports, as well as mission and activity reports from abroad. In the process we would involve as many senior and representative field people as we could to draft and comment on the various sections. Above all, I wanted to find and recruit a senior editor and an appropriate small working staff. I wondered if Donovan would accept me, specifically the path I proposed to take to record an adequate record of the OSS. After a lengthy interview and a vivid description of what he found missing in the previous effort, he welcomed my approach and promised his full cooperation.

I called Rudy Winnacker and others of my R&A friends who were historians by profession to ask for suggestions. Winnacker summed up the historian's view— great opportunity, don't look for an editor, do it all yourself. No way, I thought. This was far too much for me. My task was to get it done, not to do it myself.

Professor and Mrs. Conyers Read invited me to dinner in their gracious Georgetown house. Dr. Read was somewhat appalled to realize that he, a leading historian, had been taken off the task and replaced by a relatively junior non-historian bureaucrat. He had learned the power of turf-warfare around the OSS, not to mention its perpetuation in the pages of an official history. I told him my ideas of going to a "war report" formula, and not calling it a "history" in order to mollify the turf warriors. He graciously offered his help in reviewing any of the work he and his group had done, then grumblingly said, "All right, Peter, as a historian, I can say only that you write it and I'll attack it."

Through a mutual friend, I renewed acquaintance with Kermit Roosevelt, grandson of President Theodore Roosevelt, and a remarkable combination of scholar, diplomat and operator. I found that our approaches would coincide and that he had the drive and ability to do the job. Roosevelt had come to Donovan's attention early in OSS days through a graduate school paper he had written on policy implications that made World War II unavoidable. Donovan recruited him in 1942 virtually via mail. Roosevelt had been active for OSS in Turkey and the Middle East. In August 1946, I nominated him to be Chief Historian of the war report on a consultant basis. Quinn approved.

Roosevelt plunged into the job and began making an outline that was to become the table of contents. He made an effort to allocate as much space in the War Report to each element of OSS as was commensurate to our evaluation of the particular element's contribution to one of two criteria: either (1) to winning the war and saving U.S. lives, or (2) to setting a model for activity in a future permanent intelligence agency. Meanwhile, I was organizing office space and recruiting researchers and support personnel. My main concern was working out ready access to the wide array of documents that we needed to review and use. We had superb help on this from Mrs. Charlotte Gilbert, the librarian for the Operations archives. She established a standard routing practice for bringing to our attention any new reports reaching her facilities, and she helped us set a pattern for permanently categorizing and filing OSS documents that would then be ready for permanent archives after we completed the project.

The next hurdle was the need for approval of those to whom Bill Quinn reported in the War Department; soon to be renamed the Defense Department. Here the turf war seemed to come to a head. A number of senior officials, civilian and military, simply wanted no record left of the activities of that civilian-dominated intelligence agency, as though, like ancient Carthage, its name and the initials OSS could be ploughed under. Kim Roosevelt, as Chief Historian, helped, and, as Quinn commented, it simply has to be difficult to close down an office headed by a real, live Roosevelt, even if of the Oyster Bay variety and not of the Hyde Park strain. Actually, the Joint Chiefs of Staff turned down the idea of a permanent record of the OSS. It took General Eisenhower as Chairman of the Joint Chiefs to overrule their decision. The official authorization to prepare a "War Report of the Activities of the Office of Strategic Services" came in a memorandum from Admiral Leahy dated July 26, 1946, when I was already nearly three months into the work.

I shared an office with Kim Roosevelt for several weeks and was surprised to overhear, when he was talking on the phone, how often he had to spell out his name. I asked him why it people had difficulty spelling "Roosevelt." He replied with a smile that he didn't mind spelling the name, he resented people telling him how to pronounce it, "Ruh-sevelt."

Finding suitable people to help with the history of OSS was a harrowing and exhausting job. Among the staff I recruited was Wayne Nelson, who after Corsica had served in French SI operations with the Seventh Army up through southern France. His extensive knowledge of OSS from working as Donovan's aide and as an operations man in one of the most successful Theaters of operation, and his limitless photographic memory of papers, places, and events were all invaluable. John Hulley, who had served in England, handled European operations, and Major Emily Shek, one of the earliest Womens' Army Corps (WAC) officers to be commissioned, pulled together much of the India and Burma data.

We were able to snag a number of senior people on their return from abroad or prior to their leaving OSS. These people included Whitney Shepardson, the head of SI Branch who was generous with his time, despite his involvement in closing and yet maintaining key personnel and functions. He briefed us on developments related to SI. Kay Halle was the spark plug behind the development of Morale Operations (MO); writer and historian Walter Lord contributed on Europe; newsman Edward J. Michelson added material on the Middle East; labor lawyer Gary Van Arkel on the Labor Section; Colonel (later Major General) William R. "Ray" Peers on Detachment 101 in Burma; author Edmund Taylor on Thailand, and businessman William J. Wilkinson Jr. on India/Southeast Asia; these among many others. Their input added dimension and depth to the end product.

We faced some major limitations. First of all, time constraints. Could we finish by summer 1947 since SSU was to be liquidated by then? Documents were still flowing in from individual OSS offices as they were moved, reduced, or closed, and from abroad. But some of the major bases, like those in Germany and in Asia were in full operation with only limited time and interest for weeding out files of past operations. Significant documents from the White House and from the offices of the military chiefs and the directors of State Department and FBI offices were still being collected. For example, by June 1947 we still were coming upon some essential documents illustrating various ideas on allocation of intelligence functions at top levels of government. Of necessity we had to stop considering new document accessions after June 1947.

Second, we had size constraints. We could not list too many names of participants, no matter how deserving. We decided not to mention names at all, except in recording the early days of OSS where individuals played unique roles in bringing the first elements of the organization together. There was also the added effort of meeting arbitrary security considerations. The entire manuscript had to be typed without error, one original and three carbons, and the used carbon paper had to be preserved and turned over periodically to Joint Security Control for destruction.

By early 1947, SSU was shrinking fast as the demobilization program progressed. When the top floor of the Administration Building became available, we were moved there. This made life easier for us because we were frequently called in to answer requests by outsiders and by departing staff concerning declassifying documents on particular OSS activities and operations.

Roosevelt left in June on his pre-scheduled Near East assignment. The Report had been outlined and the work scheduled, most of it in final form. His direct contributions, the overviews, philosophic considerations about OSS and intelligence work were completed. His contribution was invaluable and it was a pleasure to work with him. The Report simply could not have been done without him. I admit I had a few moments of near-panic, as some drafts were not yet complete, and I, myself, had to re-do certain sections after Roosevelt left, particularly on the Far East, that did not meet the standards we had set. One of the problems was that material from the Far East was still trickling in as we were trying to wrap up the manuscript. Mary Louise Olsen was invaluable in going after the most glaring omissions and patching separate accounts together. Our editors Maryette Coxe and Delia Pleasants pitched in unselfishly. Our two full-time typists, Gladys Lane and Charlene Olsen, outdid themselves.

There was, however, one major unfinished detail. We envisaged three volumes: The first for developments in the U.S. in organizing and operating the COI and OSS; the second on overseas operations; the third a volume consisting of exhibits, originals or photo-copies of basic documents bearing on the organization and its operations. There was also to be a fourth volume, separate from the others, actually only a collection of papers, on subjects that should not be included, because the activities were continuing and could expose otherwise clandestine contacts or information still requiring close security protection. For example, any reference to UL-TRA or code-breaking or certain types of possibly continuing counter-intelligence cases, or sensitive subjects like the use of drugs for currency where this was unavoidable were not included in the first three volumes of the Report. This fourth volume, actually no more than a few file jackets, was never published and to my knowledge was destroyed and never entered the archives.

Donovan added a written foreword when he accepted the manuscript of the Report:

> *"I feel that this War Report presents a well-rounded study of the first comprehensive organization for intelligence and unorthodox warfare in the history of the United States ."*

By this time we were the last employees of the SSU and the last occupants of the former OSS Administration Building, which gave us an odd feeling of anachronism and unreality. Is this how it ends? With some pride, relief, and exhaustion I signed the cover memo transmitting the manuscript to the Joint Chiefs of Staff:

> *"The project to prepare a War Report of the activities of the Office of Strategic Services was assigned to me by SSU Special Order 57...The security classification of the Report is subject to determination by Joint Security Control...The bulk of the source material for the Report has been assembled in the files...and integrated into the OSS Archives which, after 1 July 1947, were transferred to the jurisdiction of the Central Intelligence Group."*

> *(Signed) Serge Peter Karlow*
> *Executive Officer for History Project.*

What would come of it? There was a snag during the last few weeks when I asked whether the Report would be typeset? If so, why did we have to work so hard to hand in spotless and error-free typed pages? No information was ever provided, not even whether or not the Report would be published at all. The Joint Security Control officer, for want of any other instructions, insisted on a perfect typed submission. Still, I know it was promptly typeset since I saw page proofs on the first volume while still checking documents into the Archives.

•••

As for my choices, I considered dropping government work and returning to school to get an advanced degree, as many of my contemporaries were doing. There was also the new GI Bill that covered much of the tuition cost. And yet, I was not of a mind to take my eyes off whatever shape or form an organized intelligence operation would have in the future. The Central Intelligence Group (C.I.G.) had formed by this time, the result of all sorts of involved high-level compromises. One thing was clear, Donovan was to have no part of it. Some former colleagues who were already in the C.I.G. urged me to come aboard. My initial inquiries led me to William G. Tharp, a major just getting out of the military service who was on the administrative staff that was building up the C.I.G. I called on him. He had once served under General Quinn and was most cordial. He gave me a set of forms to fill out, an elaborated version of the four-page Personal History Statement I had filled out for the COI, the OSS, and for the Navy. This time it was called Form 47 and was eight pages long. Tharp did mention that my having been in the OSS might create some problems because the C.I.G. was in no way carrying over functions or people from "the old place." It hardly sounded to me like a stirring recruitment pitch.

One theme kept recurring in my mind as a lesson from OSS days: technology and equipment. Lessons from the British impressed me. The way they had thought ahead to set up "African Coastal Forces" to operate maritime landings in the Mediterranean without knowing what kinds of boats or craft they would be operating, whether rowboats or motor launches, but appreciating the expanse and importance of coastlines in the Mediterranean. They were ready and had experience from cross-Channel probes and maneuvers, even down to how to paint the rubber craft for landings to reduce detection at night. When it came to maritime operations, they taught us all we knew. Also, how to prepare and use false identity documents and authorization stamps; silenced and disguised handguns, booby traps, and underwater limpets (to sabotage ships in the harbor); audio surveillance equipment, and deception and psychological warfare techniques. Now, here we were, the United States, the greatest technological inventing and producing country of them all, and we had relied so much throughout World War II on British equipment! Could not, or should not, we take steps to anticipate our own needs and possibilities in equipment? I wrote a short paper on this and passed it to some friends already in C.I.G. It met ready acceptance. I was invited to join and set up a special equipment staff that would review World War II developments in equipment and new technological developments from wartime work. In addition, I would canvass or draft a wish list of equipment for future operations. What a challenge!

I submitted a formal application and completed the Personal History Statement Form, taking them in to Tharp in person. Security clearance, he told me officiously, would take a few months but he would be in touch with me. I relished the vacation time. I took several trips to Philadelphia to improve the leg fit, and spent a week in Williamsburg with my mother to decompress and practice walking, and walking well, on my new leg. Just before Labor Day, I had a call from Tharp asking me to come in to see him. He told me with an air of sharing a deep confidence that my case had been "a hard one" to review, as he put it, "because you were so close to the Old Man." Meaning Donovan. "But," he continued. "We have looked you over, and we think you'll be all right."

My first reaction was to get up and walk out, but I was too numb with surprise and disgust to get on my feet. Or foot, as the case was. Two weeks later I was in the Central Intelligence Group.

I came to work in the newly organized Central Intelligence Agency after the Labor Day weekend in 1947. The "front office" headquarters was in the former OSS buildings at 25th and E streets, the old Public Health Service complex. The operating offices were scattered around downtown Washington and in the near suburbs in various rented or temporary buildings.

An office was ready for me in one of the row of four "Tempos," those monotonous sand colored two-story "temporary" buildings, designated by letters of the alphabet, that had been planted on numerous parking lots or parklands in Washington since Pearl Harbor. They had served their purpose well, to accommodate the suddenly swollen Washington wartime bureaucracy, but now, just two years after the war's end, they were already eyesores.

The "I", "J", "K", and "L" buildings were in a beautiful location, like a stage set for a movie on life in the Washington government. They stretched in a tree-shaded line behind the Lincoln Memorial along the south bank of the Reflecting Pool. Surrounded by an eight-foot high chain link fence, the four buildings were arranged like overgrown railroad coaches, end on end with a corridor down the middle and offices on each side. At predictable intervals there were breaks, wide points in the corridors where the rest rooms were located, or the stairwells for access between the two floors.

Each building had a single entrance manned by a guard to check building access passes. Visitors were routed to a separate entrance on the front of the buildings, that is, the side facing the Reflecting Pool. There, receptionists were on duty to announce visitors and call people in the destination offices to send down an escort who would take them to their appointments.

Cars with reserved parking space stickers were admitted to the single-lane driveway behind the buildings where a column of angle-parking spaces was provided. These spaces were at a premium and soon became a prime status symbol.

• • •

The startup of CIA was very different from the early days of both COI and then OSS. Back in 1941, and especially after Pearl Harbor, there was a crisis atmosphere in the Washington bureaucracy. Actions were taken and new structures created, then made to fit into the overall structure. When President Roosevelt created COI with a one-page memorandum, then continued and expanded it into OSS, high-level bureaucratic concern in official Washington quickly built up over the new civilian-run national intelligence organization. Its vaguely worded mandate washed over existing jurisdictional lines. The new structure grew like Topsy and there was the need to feel that something was getting done took precedence over doubts about what it would do and, more than that, who should control it?

There were no such doubts in the general public's mind, shaken as it was by the shock and excitement accompanying the outbreak of war: After all, the romantic glow about secret intelligence and psychological warfare, and sabotage and guerrilla operations, were the stuff of current novels and mystery stories. In summary, after the Pearl Harbor attack, the imperatives of being at war and the rapidity with which Donovan built up the OSS left critics in the anti-Franklin D. Roosevelt press and in the established government agencies—Army, Navy, State Department, Bureau of the Budget, Treasury, and FBI— far behind.

The new organization had high morale and a spirit of enthusiasm and experimentation, even if at the expense of administrative order and management detail. The OSS was an exciting place to work. In contrast, intelligence in the peacetime military services had long been considered a sideline job, not one to further careers for any upwardly mobile and ambitious officer. It was felt that assignment to G-2 in the Army and ONI in the Navy would leave career officers stranded in staff jobs, and backroom staff at that.

When Donovan's people began to arrive on the scene, they turned out to be university presidents, deans, department heads, professors and assistant professors, mostly holding one or more doctoral degrees; generally tops in their fields. They joined engineers, scientists, bankers, and businessmen of standing in their respective professions. They brought with them the disciplines and techniques of academic work, plus an element of scientific business management. At first they met scorn and open resistance from military officers. Just what do civilians, academics and businessmen know about military intelligence?

CHAPTER 9

START THREE...

In short order the newcomers redefined the very concept of intelligence into that of a strategic study — geographic, structural, social, economic, resources, transport, political, psychological, military, and health — with military only a piece of the overall study. This comprehensive redefinition of intelligence was one of the greatest contributions of Donovan's activities to the war effort. It revolutionized the structure of intelligence research and analysis to support national military and strategic policy-making. Donovan's people also galvanized psychological warfare and para-military activities, but the changes were not as relatively deep.

Then in 1947, open suspicion and distrust of CIA both at official levels and in the press, came to a head. The popular post-war demobilization mentality, to "get the boys home" and dismantle the wartime superstructure as rapidly as possible, underscored a growing feeling of skepticism in influential segments of public opinion: Wasn't the war over? Were those wartime functions really still needed?

Within the Government, an open effort began to expunge Donovan's wartime influence from the new peacetime central intelligence organization. Donovan represented the continuation of an independent and free wheeling function. The public concerns whipped up by the anti-Truman press, about such things as a "Post-war Gestapo," fell on fertile ground. Should an all-powerful intelligence service be allowed to happen again, anywhere in the world, in our lifetime?

Actually, this quickly became a meaningless question because, despite SSU's mandate to liquidate OSS, sizable parts of the old OSS organization were still hard at work in key areas abroad, both in Europe and in the Far East. For them, the Cold War was already a reality, although it had not yet been named or openly defined. Inevitably, as the nature of the Cold War became clearer, these overseas OSS installations became the nucleus for CIA overseas operations.

As a result, two conflicting sets of reactions developed within the new organization. There were the newcomers to intelligence, many of them newly retired military officers assigned to keep themselves informed on what was going on in the new agency, and to keep some sort of control over it. And, among the carry-overs from the OSS, they ranged from dedicated activity heads down to support personnel. What they shared was the inability to turn themselves away from their part of the national wartime intelligence effort that they still considered vital to the nation in the qualified peacetime to come. There were others who stayed on because they might have trouble adjusting to the slower pace of peacetime work. Among all was an air of defensiveness, a feeling for the need to tend the flame, to keep intact the activities that the general public seemed to ignore or vastly undervalue, or reject out-of-hand.

World events soon made the difference: the Cold War was beginning. In Greece in 1947 there was the dramatic attempt by the militant Communist party to take over the country by force. In Italy, a disciplined Communist Party threatened to overrun the scheduled national elections of 1948. Communist movements toppled coalition governments in Romania and Bulgaria. Churchill used the term "Iron Curtain" for the first time in his speech at Westminster College in June 1948; the Soviet Union had become the enemy, and international communism was all over the world.

President Truman soon came to realize that a centralized intelligence organization was needed, with a collection capability and the necessary analysis resources to keep up with the world situation. This led to what was in effect the continuation and further development of what OSS had been doing in the fields of secret intelligence and the accompanying counter-intelligence function. This became the new Office of Special Operations (SO or OSO) in the Central Intelligence Group. Later under CIA it was euphemistically named Deputy Directorate for Plans (DD/P). It was at times referred to as SI (secret intelligence) or FI (foreign intelligence) activity. Despite the open continuation of so many OSS activities, the official and public sensitivity about Donovan led to strenuous but uphill efforts by the chiefs of the new activities to disclaim any connection between the former OSS and the new CIG/CIA.

But Truman needed more in order to mount suitable counter-actions to the worldwide activity of the Soviet Union and its communist allies in other countries. By summer of 1947 he had approved establishment of an office to carry out psychological and political warfare, going as far as morale operations, sabotage, and possibly paramilitary activity. Obviously this was left as vague and general as possible. Frank Wisner, a brilliant former OSS officer involved in Balkan operations, was named its head. It was at first given the innocent name of Office of Policy Coordination (OPC), physically located in the State Department, but was combined into the new CIA under Gen. Bedell Smith in 1950. It was merged into the CIA as PP (psychological and political activity) Staff.

•••

I started in the Central Intelligence Group after Thanksgiving in 1947.

My job was called "Special Equipment Staff." I began by making a formal presentation to Col. Donald C. Galloway, the chief of Operations, and his Senior Management staff at one of the weekly meetings. I said I was driven by the continued use in our operations of goose quills to froth out traces of secret inks on pieces of paper, a technology that was known as far back as the Middle Ages. I balked at agents having to learn Morse Code at a time when new developments in equipment miniaturized communications and made it user-friendly beyond our fondest wishes. I planned to go over new and continuing equipment requirements with each of the area and activity chiefs.

At the same time I would meet with technical people and assess what new developments and items of hardware were becoming available that might facilitate operations or make possible newer, broader activities. The result should be the outlines of an equipment development program. The group, I noticed, reacted positively when I seemed to criticize wartime OSS efforts, such as relying too much on British equipment for World War II operations. There were only a few questions, mainly on budget matters. It was suggested that the budget for my activity be included in funds allocated to the technical services staff that was left over from OSS. I agreed with this as I thought that this was the very element that stood to gain the most from my activities.

Looking around at the people attending the staff meeting, I saw more new faces present than there were old, meaning ex-OSS people. Most of the newcomers were newly retired colonels from the Army or Air Force. I wondered to myself if they had been appointed more to watch over and restrain the activities of the new agency than to mobilize and promote its activity. Perhaps the group thought my function would offer each with another way to stay informed and maintain control. Anyway, the group endorsed my mission, and I was in business.

After the staff meeting a medium size, somewhat pudgy, pinch-faced man with thinning reddish hair introduced himself. He was ex-Colonel Sheffield Edwards, newly designated chief of the Security Office. He wanted to say that, in his opinion, the use of machinery was a matter of major importance for the future of intelligence since human beings, with the best of intentions, were fallible and so often unreliable as sources of intelligence. I had never thought of machines as replacing humans, only making their work more effective.

I had similar meetings with most of the other newly designated chiefs, and came to realize that I faced a difficult situation. I would have to balance making a realistic list of the expressed "needs" for equipment with equally realistic information on new developments, and how they might be useful. Put another way, I had to define what we needed, and what new and potentially useful technology had been developed in the war, and since. Also, how to keep potential users informed of the latest developments.

This turned out to present some practical organizational problems. With the end of OSS most of the bright and imaginative equipment design and research people had gone back to their civilian pursuits. The people who were left behind and were now in charge felt challenged by my entry on the scene, even to the point of being reluctant to show me what they had available. The fact was there was not all that much new and applicable for circumstances short of "Hot War." Also, in-house development activity had stopped with the end of OSS two years before, while science and technology unleashed by the War was bringing out an increasing stream of revolutionary new products and ideas.

There had been three streams of equipment development in OSS: In COMMO, the Communications Division, which included surveillance equipment because of its electronics component; in Cover and Documentation, which was concerned with producing what I called "stage props", items to gain access to denied areas through verifying cover stories including fake personal identity documents and designing concealment devices for agent operations; and in Research and Development, which mainly concerned sabotage items and weapons-related tools for irregular warfare.

In the COMMO area, technology was moving with dizzying speed from vacuum tubes to solid state components leading onward from transistors to integrated circuits, each step opening new frontiers of possibilities for new functions and greater miniaturization. In OSS we used to joke about planting a microphone in the olive of a martini to overhear conversations. Even before 1950, only a few years later, it was becoming possible to put an entire recorder into that olive. It was obvious that communications between secret agents in denied areas would take new shapes that we could only dimly imagine. COMMO accepted the overall responsibility for audio equipment for surveillance, although this was a sideline to their mission of operating secure international communications, I quickly developed cordial relations with the key people in COMMO.

My headaches were in the rest of the equipment field. Joseph R. Lears was the chief of what was left over from two OSS divisions: The Cover and Documentation Division (C&D) and Research and Development Division (RDD). C&D's work on operational "stage-props" brought together information on how to penetrate and survive in a denied area; for example, how to cope with Nazi German controls over civilian life, both in Germany and in the occupied territories. This involved assembling the equipment and techniques to make the necessary reproductions and forgeries so that an agent sent into a Nazi-controlled area could pass security checkpoints. I remembered from 1943 in Algiers the only resource we had was a British outfit which helped us with falsified French or Italian identity documents and the appropriate rubber stamps and seals required to validate them, as well as papers and other items to support an agent's cover story.

There was a problem in this for OSS in that we wanted to keep our operations distinct from British operations and out from under British control. This was sometimes not easy to do because to get support for cover and documentation it was necessary to give the technical people some details about the agent for whom documents are needed, and the operation of which he is to be a part.

RDD presented a challenge in that no one had had a clear picture of what would be needed for sabotage operations when World War II broke out, and therefore what should be developed by way of new and concealed weapons and explosive devices. There were some ingenious new items in this field, but they came out of vague ideas of what might be useful, since there was so little direct experience in guerrilla warfare and its needs.

There was *BEANO*, a baseball-shaped hand grenade that was easier to throw than the traditional standard pineapple-shaped grenades. I could see how a round ball shape could be thrown more accurately, but I never saw any record of their actual use.

WHO ME? was the name for a stink bomb in a small tube like that used for trip-sized toothpaste. Squeezed out of its tube, it could quickly empty a meeting room. It was used in the Far East on at least two or three reported incidents.

A number of plastic explosives, firing devices and delays were used effectively in Europe and Asia. *CLAM* was an explosive with magnets that were to be hung on trucks or automobiles. Similarly *LIMPIT* and *PINUP GIRL* were explosives for use on ships. *CLAM*, *LIMPITS*, and *PINUP* were largely British developments. An American original was *BLACK JOE*; a high explosive disguised to look like a lump of coal and intended to be thrown into the coal hopper of a steam locomotive. When shoveled into the boiler, the locomotive would be blown up. They were deliberately not used: In Europe, both resistance forces and air force bombers were told not to destroy locomotives: They would be too valuable for our forces when once we landed in France or Italy.

At war's end Lears was a lieutenant colonel running a small air base in Florida that was used as a test area for RDD. He was moved to Washington and by attrition became the head of what was left of the dwindling divisions. Requests for equipment and support kept coming in from the overseas installations, mainly for cameras and film for document copying, enough to keep a skeleton force going. There were also requests for identity document reproductions and for equipment to make validating stamps and seals. Lears had a supply of German MINOX cameras, the tiny Latvian-made "spy cameras" that took remarkable pictures particularly of documents close-up. There were models of concealment devices and letter-drop housings, but they required finishing and camouflaging before use. I told Lears that I wanted to help him develop his services for the future. While we were personally congenial, I realized that he regarded me not as a partner but as a threat. I probably could not have avoided this under the circumstances, as I was busy with contacting the customers while he was still sorting out what was left over from OSS days. I decided to go ahead in defining the current "wants" or "needs," and then share with him whatever information I came up with on how these needs could be met.

The initial results of my surveys were not impressive. They were modest at best, and were almost entirely reactions from World War II days and, as the RDD technicians said, they were hardly targets for "research," not to mention "development," but rather for adaptation and ingenuity. For example:

How to send hand-written messages electronically and securely, on miniaturized equipment. "Miniaturized" generally meant no larger than two packs of cigarettes end-on-end. This was one of the early and more persistent requirements that I gleaned. This reflected the anxiety of World War II officers wanting to get away from the need to use dot-and-dash and encoded messages on their agent communications. There was work being done along these lines, using principles of the old wire-bound "Telautograph" system. An electronic device to do this was produced commercially in the 1950s, called the Electro-Writer. It was used on private-wire or in telephone-line form by retail stores to take inventory, or in wireless-radio form by bus and train dispatchers to check on baggage or rolling stock. It was quickly overtaken by further developments in technology.

How to "bug" the Soviet Ambassador's car while it is parked in a public garage, for example, in the heart of Ankara, Turkey and you have no more than five minutes' uninterrupted access to the car. In subsequent discussions about this, we extended the access time to ten minutes. I assumed that the FBI must have some good equipment, and started the wheels turning through a painfully slow and reluctant liaison process via the Security Office to meet with FBI technical experts.

The meeting was a disappointment although interesting in pointing up the contrast in approach between the FBI and intelligence. First of all, access is not much of a problem for the FBI, where a flash of a badge immediately elicits voluntary cooperation from garage keepers, or hotel people, or anyone who could help. We had to explain why we only had ten minutes access to the Ambassador's car. It seemed that FBI efforts to place listening devices into a target automobile could be done at a far more leisurely pace and with a full team of installers and audio specialists on hand to help. At any rate, the equipment they showed was still based on vacuum tubes and some transistors. They gave me no indication that they had anything newer or better. I suggested periodic contact between bureau and agency technical experts, but nothing ever came of this. It was my first taste of how restricted any collaboration was between the two organizations. Apparently any communication between CIA and the FBI had to channel via our Security Office to the office of FBI Director J. Edgar Hoover. I found this hard to believe; there must be more business of mutual concern between the two agencies than this slender channel would allow.

Developing photographic film without a darkroom. There was a clumsy item with a name like "Unifix," a one-step developer commercially available and somewhat adapted to what was assumed to be usability in the field. It involved a long intestine-like tube, looking like an elongated condom. The idea was to work in a darkened room or basement, draw the undeveloped film into the intestine, then seal the end with a clamp and pour a solution into the open end and let it soak. After a period of time, the film would be developed and could be extracted and exposed to light. The fluid in the intestine posed a major disposal problem in an urban setting. It could not be poured down a toilet as it would blacken the porcelain.

New on the market were Polaroid cameras, and I called the company and arranged a visit. I took Lears with me to Boston, where a Polaroid technician listened to our deliberately vague outline of our needs. He showed us a black box into which one would place undeveloped film in its cassette and thread it into the works along with a new special Polaroid film. Close the door, press a button, count to ten and out comes the newly developed film and a transparency of copies of the pictures. This might have a use in the field but after a little more hum and haw, the technician realized that we were talking of more rudimentary conditions than this box allowed. He suggested that we consider a simple field expedient by tacking the lead of an undeveloped film onto a table. The chemicals packets from a roll of Polaroid film, the messy instant-copy type then on the market, would be extracted in darkened room. The undeveloped film would be run between the fingers while holding the mashed packets of the chemicals. Ten seconds later the lights would be turned on and *voilá*, there would be the developed film, and the messy fingers would not be too difficult to clean up. Actually, this was tried successfully, but it was a pretty sloppy way of doing things, even for a field expedient.

Adapting or making identity documents for agents: This was the most frequent requirement expressed, especially from the personnel operating in Germany and Austria. The use of authorization papers and personal identity documents was common practice in most European countries and was developed by the Nazis and carried further by the Soviets in controlling virtually every aspect of civilian life. In wartime there could be frequent exceptions to what would be considered "normal" activity, due to drafts into labor or military service, or subsequent war damage and dislocation. Now, with the Cold War stabilizing conditions, the role of civilian controls became even more important. I was surprised to find that no one in the operating divisions or in the technical staff was doing much to study this system and how to live with it.

Secret writing and secret inks were far more in use than I had expected. The techniques for their use seemed medieval to me. Leaving aside the chemicals used, application was all important so as not to leave wet spots on the paper or pressure marks that could give away the writing itself. Then there was the need to "steam" the prepared paper to fluff up the texture and delete any pressure lines. It was the stuff of traditional spy novels and, like it or not, it was still needed. I asked how "secure" our chemical formulations were, and was informed by the technicians that, properly used, even a minute dilution of blood or lemon juice could be quite secure, while the "best" secret ink could be detected if applied amateurishly. I found few operations officers going to the field were given instruction in using secret inks. In making my rounds of the operating divisions, I did attract some attention to this subject.

• • •

I was called in on three problems of security policy that came up due to developments in equipment and techniques.

The first had to do with copy equipment. The 3M company, makers of Scotch Tape and myriad other consumer and office products, sent sales representatives to show off the new "Thermofax" desk-top copy machines. Immediately the question in CIA was what the presence of these machines would do to security, particularly if anyone could simply make copies of any and every document circulating in the office, regardless of its security classification. My interest was in another direction: The 3M machines used a waxy, heat sensitive paper. Could we use sheets of this paper and, for example, insert them into someone's files so that information on other paper in those files would transfer itself to the 3M paper, which could be secretly removed and retrieved the next day? It turned out that 3M was concerned about this problem and working hard to eliminate any "travel" of text onto or off their "Thermofax" paper.

Another subject was hypnotism. A serious demonstration was held at one of the weekly staff meetings to let a Mr. Backster of Chicago, an expert in hypnotism, show how he would put every CIA man going overseas under his hypnotic spell. Once hypnotized, a man could memorize "an entire volume of the Encyclopedia Britannica" and, when de-hypnotized, would have no memory of having been hypnotized. Then, upon arriving at his destination, presumably Moscow, the man could listen to the station chief playing a tape with Mr. Backster's voice reciting the hypnotism formula. The man would immediately go into hypnotic trance and recite, presumably, that volume of the encyclopedia. To demonstrate, Mr. Backster had with him a red-haired young man who looked like a sleepwalker and went into and out of hypnotism at a syllable of Mr. Backster's voice. Asked my opinion, I was highly skeptical of the whole thing and particularly of Mr. Backster, and suggested we consult people at the University of North Carolina where a Professor J.B. Rhyne was doing experiments in extra-sensory perception which were often reported in the news in those days. Col. Lyle T. Shannon, a tall, slender redheaded officer who acted as chief of Services, was particularly fascinated by this. I believe that the group voted to give Mr. Backster a $200,000 research grant after all, and I have no memory of or interest in what came of it.

The third proposal was adopted. It had to do with the polygraph, a machine that measures changes in blood pressure, respiration rate, and amount of perspiration as an indicator, described as an "infallible" indicator, of a subject's telling the truth. This so-called "Lie Detector" was fully endorsed by FBI Director J. Edgar Hoover as a standard instrument to be used on all staff personnel as well as operational people. Again, it was demonstrated with staged trick exhibits like in a circus sideshow, like guessing the cards in a hand or verifying a birth date. Basically, this machine offered a way to limit human participation in judgment of veracity of an agent or on information. The results could be unquestionably relied upon by the entire intelligence community. Indeed, the use of the polygraph was made mandatory by all intelligence and security agencies, across the board.

•••

By 1949 the Cold War had become intense in Europe, and our people in Germany and Austria called on Washington for technical support. The particular demand was for help in getting agents across the border into the Iron Curtain countries, mainly East Germany, Czechoslovakia, Hungary and Poland, and in surer ways of communicating with them. I finally spent the better part of several weeks studying this problem and concentrating on what was called for here.

It soon became clear what we were up against. We were facing the machinery and practices that constituted the communist way to exercise official controls over every aspect of civilian life. They followed a pattern that with minor changes was replicated in each of the "peoples' democratic republics."

Leave aside passports for international travel that were given out only to those government officials or trusted individuals usually on official business for the state. Even here there were some special wrinkles, separating diplomatic passports from special passports or some form of fragmentary "passport" good for one limited trip to one destination and immediate direct return.

The basic document was the identity card or internal *Pasport* as it was named in the Soviet Union. Without this card, one could be arrested immediately and without question, and jailed or sentenced to exile or death without hearing. This meant that an individual literally did not exist without the government's attesting to his existence by issuing the identity card. The cards soon became passport-like booklets, with pages for personal data, the inevitable passport-type picture, residence information and room for the confirming rubber-stamp imprint by the local police precinct; work permit and employer attestation as well as confirmation by the local labor union, and special privileges such as a driver's license, access to a restricted area like along a national border, and need for special medical treatment or attention such as veterans' disability allowance.

In East Germany this document was in a gray-green cloth cover and called *Deutscher Personalausweis* or DPA; in Czechoslovakia it had a bright red cover and was called *Obçanski Prukaz* or OP. Each document had serial numbers keyed into its point of origin by town or county or police precinct. There were often serial numbers or added key numbers particularly for restricted areas near the Berlin border or near military installations.

Lears took me over to the print shop to show me how documents were forged, or, as he said in high good humor, "How we make new originals." As a professional pressman he liked quality work. The trouble was, the "originals" of which his people were to make "new" copies were of shoddy quality work. I was more than just surprised to see some of the originals sent in from Frankfurt and Berlin and compare them with the "new originals." You could tell the difference across the room, what with more glossy finish, brighter print, not even a near match to the paper stock not to mention the cover cloth or the staples. Lears explained they had a hard time obtaining samples of originals, as they could only get them through the Immigration and Naturalization Service and could not tear up or mar the documents as INS felt it was committed some day to return them to their owners. I went at once to the operating division, and two weeks later, Berlin sent in a bundle of twenty DPAs. At this Leers commented that technically the documents were not all alike, some darker and some with more marked watermarks. His people could make a "new original," then it was up to the operations officer to get his agent by with them. The people in the operating division strongly took exception to this, and by all principles of common sense I agreed with them.

At the next weekly senior staff meeting, I reported that document reproduction problems were holding back the development of agent penetrations into the Iron Curtain countries. I outlined my theory that we were facing a systematic effort to control civilian life in communist countries through an involved system of serial-numbered identity documents. We must break this code barrier, and I had the promise of cooperation from the chief of the European Division, Richard Helms, a regular participant in these meetings, to help me resolve the hold-up. At this, Leers deprecated the seriousness of the problem, and as proof presented Col. Galloway with a false driver's license, made out to Galloway in his "operational" name, which was "Dennis C. Grayson."

Galloway seemed pleased, turned the card over, saw the space for his signature, and promptly signed it "Donald C. Galloway." He noted his error, grinned, tore the card up and tossed it aside, and the subject of operational support to the field through better document forgery was about to be dropped. At this, Helms protested that his people needed more help as a priority matter, as their ability to send anything but low-level agents into the Eastern Bloc was at stake. Galloway suggested that Lears personally visit our people in Germany and Austria and assess needs at first hand.

The trip was disastrous for Lears. Frankfurt headquarters told him that they were considering starting a facility of their own to do technical aids work there on the spot. Karlsruhe base complained about the unsuitability of document reproductions sent them from Washington. Munich wanted better secret inks for communications through the mails, reported that the East German police used more sophisticated chemicals than were being issued by Washington. Vienna had started to use a local forger, absent any support from Washington, but was concerned about possible security implications.

The final straw came after Lears' return. He had promised the Berlin base to make some concealment devices to use as letter drops, in the form of individual bricks. To confirm the order, Lears cabled Berlin to double-check the color and texture of the bricks needed. This was summer of 1949 and Berlin was still a massive pile of bricks of all kinds, and rubble and debris left over from bombing and block-to-block warfare, with the main streets and some of the larger side streets just barely cleared for traffic. Peter S., the Berlin base chief, sent a fiery cable in to Helms, then Division Chief in Washington, stating that Lears was either stalling or inept, and decrying the futility of dealing with Lears in the face of the crying need for agent support services. As conditions settled down, controls became more widely applied, and without more sophisticated support there would be no more than low-level in-and-out operations.

Helms called me in to discuss the situation. He liked my outline of the Soviet control system at the meeting. He said it was the first logical rationale he had ever heard that described what we were up against, and that outlined a starting point to an organized agent support resource. This might very well hold the key to mounting effective agent operations across the Iron Curtain. He invited me to join the European (EE) Division. He wanted me to go to Germany to organize and be in charge of providing the needed services and facilities to support agent operations for both German and Austrian installations. He proposed to keep me and my activities strictly within EE Division. This was so that he could assign personnel (the bureaucratic term was "personnel slots") and funding to the enterprise laterally within Germany until we were fully in business. Also, it was so that I would not to be held back by any obstacles thrown up by the technical people. I should work with them and draw from them whatever they could produce, and otherwise see about what would be necessary to procure or produce any needed materials locally. In Helms' typical direct way, it was a straight pitch to me to do a job, to work out the details as we went along, but mainly, to get things done. It was fairly close to a carte blanche.

It was a challenge I could not turn down. My new assignment was announced in September 1949; I was to leave for Germany before the end of the year. I could now concentrate on building my own ideas into reality.

I wrote a final report on the Special Equipment Staff, since the function was terminated with my reassignment. I described the SES modestly enough as a useful initial step to improve communications between the users of equipment and its designers. I reaffirmed the importance of keeping the operating divisions up-to-date on technical equipment matters, particularly with so many new devices and concepts becoming available as a result of World War II, and cited my move into the Eastern Europe Division as a logical step in this direction. In bureaucrateze, this worked out to something much stuffier, like having demonstrated the continuing need for providing to operations people the practical information they require on modern equipment and its technical capabilities. There was the corresponding need to give the technical specialists better feedback on new and more sophisticated post-war operational requirements brought on by the Cold War. This was somewhat self-serving, but the extent of what still was left to do was illustrated for me quite dramatically in a three-day operations course given by the Office of Training.

I signed up for this as it offered a refresher course for operations officers with assignments to go abroad. It included a problem that went along these lines: How to recruit an Argentine art expert to spot Nazi war treasures smuggled out of Germany, get him out to a training base in Uruguay, train and brief him, and return him to Argentina with proper communications and control. The training people thought I spent far too much time on the details of moving the agent across borders, and obtaining exfiltration papers and cover story for him. I seized on his name in the problem that happened to be "de Duarte." Since "de Duarte" was Evita Peron's name, I developed a fancy scenario by hypothesizing his having access to high-placed relations as sources of cover and documentation. Finally, the training officer cut me short by saying, "Never mind the details, he'll be able to get out of the country all right, and back in for that matter. Don't worry about that, it's not important to the problem." I made strong and explicit comments on this in the course post-mortem. I said that we must not disregard these operational details, particularly not in a formal program of the Office of Training. I was given only a mediocre grade for the course, needless to say.

Lears seemed relieved at the prospect of having me out of his hair. I believe he figured he could control my work in Germany because I would have to come to him for help, and he felt comfortable with this. He became supportive, almost paternal in helping me in my preparations. Actually I liked Lears as a person but, from my point of view, he was way over his depth in a job that had grown far too big for him, and he did not see my efforts as helping him survive in this period of change. In turn, I thought I was helping him, and certainly intended to, at least for a while. Then I was appalled at finding him trying to cover up for the deficiencies in his program by taking on the role of pitchman for gadgets. I bumped into him one day in one of the operating division offices showing off a pair of cheap Japanese miniature cameras, the kind that you could win in a gumball machine on the boardwalk at Coney Island. He was asking operations officers if they thought devices like that could be useful. The answers he got generally were a non-committal yes, if they work. At this point, Lears would pull out a World War II Minox camera and point out that these had been available in his catalog for some time yet very few people had asked for any. He in effect told his potential customers that they were either inept or lazy. At least, that was the impression he gave. I assured my new colleagues that I was not working for Lears but for the operating division, and that I was coming over personally to organize a new technical support program in the field.

I was surprised and delighted at how smoothly things fell into line for me, the best indication of how badly the services that I proposed were needed. To review some of the main requirements:

Identity documents: Lears had several ladies on his staff, researchers keeping files on these. The ladies were very helpful to me, in fact they were delighted that someone was using their services. The files were slim; for all of Eastern Europe there were perhaps fifty useful exemplars, all of which were on loan from the Immigration and Naturalization Service — in case the original bearers should ever want the documents back. Why would they want them back? The only answer I got was the famous Washington aphorism that there may not be a reason for it, it's just policy. I set up a new document identification system to make it possible to find documents by type and by point of issue, the basic criteria for documenting a cover story for an agent.

I arbitrarily defined of documents:

International travel documents, true "Passports" in Western terms, but in communist countries issued only to governmental or officially approved and trusted travelers and then usually only for very limited periods or destinations, like "one trip" or "three months."

Personal identity papers, the communist internal passport that each adult person had to carry at all times, to certify that the bearer was indeed who he claimed to be, where he was supposed to be, and doing what he was expected to do. These small booklets with up to twenty pages contained the inevitable identification picture and utilized various shades of cover material, paper stock, proper and usually sloppy watermarking or tinting, with staples that rusted in predictable ways, glues and grommets to seal in the pictures, serial numbers and issue numbers frequently keyed to each other, and an array of rubber stamp imprints to certify every entry that are the joy of the policemen, border guards and customs functionaries.

Residence registrations issued by local police authorities. Any change of residence requires prior police approval and appropriate de-registration from the old address and subsequent re-registration at the new address. The interval for moving, sometimes a few months' duration, was an excellent window for backing up an agent's cover story.

Labor or work permit or employee identification, usually issued by employers or municipalities. Again, a change of jobs required de-registering and re-registering, as with the residence permit.

Labor union membership, issued by union or municipal authorities. Again, there were employers' organizations, or both.

Driver's permits. A surprisingly small percentage of the local population of Eastern Europe had auto licenses, but many had motor cycle authorization.

The remaining categories were for club memberships, certification for access to restricted areas such as along the borders or near defense installations, which required frequent or regular renewal, or special veterans' disability and hospitalization entitlements.

For communications purposes, the new DI system let us short-hand a document's description by something like "EG (East Germany)—2 (identity document)—B (second issue)— 5 (identified variation, like off-color paper)— Goerlitz (point of issue, either by name or using a number code)—Dresden (place of intended use)—carpenter (occupation)— M25 (sex and age)." On receiving this and checking the files, we could come back with the nearest alternative, like "2B4-Liegnitz-mason-M45 -brown-balding."

Printing and reproduction was obviously in trouble, as the operating division people in the field were openly critical of the output. It was not hard to see why. The reproduced documents, meaning the forgeries or "new originals" made by the printers in Washington, were simply too good. The paper was too shiny, the inks too bold, the colors too strong, and the print too exact. It was hard for American craftsmen to put out an inferior product. The pressmen pointed out to me that ideally the European stations should go out and procure European paper stock and inks and whatnot and send them back, but no division had expressed any interest in or expertise for doing this. And there the matter rested, on dead center.

The same applied to printing for the psychological warfare people. Underground newsletters and leaflets were not appropriate in Eastern Europe when printed on modern coated paper. I looked in wonder at one membership booklet for a notional underground East German anti-communist organization called "Victims of Fascism." Technically, the quality of the shiny booklets put the U.S. Passport to shame. They were simply too good for the purpose for which they were made. No organization in post-war Europe, particularly an allegedly under-cover one, would have such expensive membership cards.

Secret writing is a field to which I have never been a devotee, despite the long and romantic history of secret inks. The chemicals used and their concentration, or rather their dilution, seemed to me often less important than the skill and care with which the writing was applied. The best tool to write with secret inks may well have been the goose quill pen, to whose period in history I relegate this whole field. True, minute dilutions of blood, urine, or aspirin could if properly applied pass the scrutiny of many checkpoints or censorship offices, particularly if manned by poorly trained personnel. This led some of the secret ink chemists in Washington to confide to me their belief that perhaps operations officers were too clumsy to learn this tricky craft, or too lazy to teach it to their agents. Whatever, this technical tool did little to improve relations between the Washington-based technical people and the division people in the field.

Microdots also come to my mind as being in the category of art form. In the heyday of photography, a page of text could in expert hands be reduced to the size of a typewriter dot or period. Then, with clever use of penpoint or razor blade, the microdot could be excised from the developed film and tucked in the letter under one of the typed periods. Lears still thought that case officers should take the time to learn microdot as a technique, and teach it to their "best agents." Again, it seemed to me that this was a technique whose time had passed.

Other devices like concealment sleeves for letter-drops, hollowed pencils to hide photo film, weapons like concealed blades and metal files, were left over from OSS days. Obviously any camouflage for them would have to be made where used.

Audio surveillance equipment would be part of my technical mandate but would be manned by Communications Division people already on the scene. I learned that both Berlin and Vienna had active programs going already.

My most immediate challenge was to develop good rapport with my new colleagues in EE Division. They were a widely and wildly assorted bunch who lived and loved their work and whose camaraderie I came to treasure.

There were administrative formalities. I resigned for cover purposes from CIA and became an employee of the Department of the Army, later Department of Defense. I was assigned a pseudonym and a cover story and given emergency phone numbers. As a test I called one of the numbers and was pleased to find that the person who answered recognized my name with plausibly little hesitation, and took a message, which I duly received in buckslip form the next day. I changed all my charge accounts and bank accounts appropriately.

An operational name was to be assigned to my new activity, and Lears suggested using one of the technical project names allocated to him. The name was *OCHRE*. I took strong exception to this, since pronouncing it sounded like clearing one's throat, and the dictionary definition alone was a final turnoff — "A yellow fecal material..." I went myself to the central registry people. They assigned me what became the final name; it was *TOPAZ*. Actually, the psychological warfare people on their own named their part of the effort *CARAT* and my overall activities *MODEL*. What's in a name? The next name on the roster to be assigned after *TOPAZ* was *ULTRA*, which was issued to the operation that handled the drug and behavior business that had such problems later.

The final details were in the travel arrangements. The travel office took advantage of the slow point in the travel season to book passage for me on the *Ile de France*, a ship famed for serving the best meals on the French Line if not on any transatlantic liner of the day. I had Christmas in New York with my mother and family friends, and took off for Europe on December 28, 1949.

CHAPTER 10

TOOLS OF THE TRADE...

The *Ile de France* over New Year's — it sounded like a glamorous prospect. Those were the days when transatlantic travel was still predominantly by sea, and it was possible for government employees to book passage on foreign liners. The ship was the pride of the French Lines, and offered luxurious amenities. It boasted that First Class passengers on the ship could request any menu dishes they desired, and it would be served to them for dinner that evening. I took advantage of this only once, requesting a baked Alaska. It was delicious. Unfortunately rough seas plagued the whole crossing and consequently the dining rooms were noticeably under-populated. Although my stomach was fairly seasick proof, I did notice the steady pitching of the ship as it nosed into storm-level head winds, and frequently saw blue water pouring over the bow as it plunged into the waves.

New Year's Eve on board was not quite what I expected. I joined in with two State Department officers and an American couple in their early 50s with Pepsi Cola. We decided to meet in black tie at the main bar at six thirty. There were not many people, and only few of them were dressed in tuxes or cocktail dresses or other than business clothes. Before we could share a second round of drinks, the stewards ushered us into the Theater for "the concert." This turned out to be a solo performance by Wyaceszlaw Malkucynski, the most prominent pianist interpreter of Chopin at the time. After a lengthy and flowery introduction in English and then French by the social director, Maestro M plunged into Chopin head-first, rendered resounding if funereal pieces magnificently for over an hour, ending with the Polonaise, whose melodious passages sounded almost like jazz in comparison to the classical pieces. Then came a reception in the main lounge decorated with elaborate flowers. Cold sober, we went to the main dining salon about eleven. "Champagne," we called, but inexorably more splendid hors d'oeuvres arrived, along with a sweet aperitif wine. Near eleven thirty some workmen appeared with a step ladder, set it up under the massive gold clock over the main entrance, and moved the hands ahead the requisite nightly one hour, a normal procedure on an eastbound sailing. That made the time already twelve thirty, when the ship's captain arose and gave a speech in Franglish that was touching, and endless. Several of us had the same idea at the same time: Let's go down to Tourist Class and see if things were livelier there. They were. A good jazz ensemble was playing current French popular tunes — the Edith Piaf and Charles Trenêt variety — and also extra young men were needed and appreciated. I met two delightful young French girls, both actresses, sisters living in

Paris, with the story book names of Solange and Desirée. I visited them in Paris one evening the following week, when I spent several days, "delay on route" there.

•••

I reached Paris on Tuesday, January 2. At the suggestion of my State Department fellow passengers, I changed my hotel reservations to the Hotel France et Choiseuil, near the Embassy on rue Meurice. The hotel consisted of a charming group of small three and four story buildings around a cobblestone courtyard. I dutifully called on my CIA colleagues. I particularly came to know Barney Bland and his wife Carolyn, both of whom I had known casually in Washington. Over lunch one day, Barney noted that I spoke reasonably accent-less French, and asked me if I would be willing to come in from Germany for a few days at a time to handle some Paris-based agent operations for him. I had no idea whether or how this would work out, nor on schedules, either his or mine, but told him I would be delighted at any excuse to come to Paris, particularly some that would give me paid weekends in Paris. The main operation he had in mind on which to use me was codenamed *UNHOLY*.

One day I took the train from Paris to Rouen, to visit French Navy Captain Jean l'Herminier and his wife Madeleine. Their house was near a badly damaged part of the city, and in fact had been damaged itself. The damaged third story was not rebuilt but had been made the roof of the house. All around them, reconstruction had begun and life was returning to normal. The special wheelchair that Bill Peters had designed for him was in daily use, and l'Herminier would circulate around the house adeptly, as small ramps were built to cope with uneven floor levels. His book about his adventures on submarine *Casabianca* had just been published, and he gave me a copy with a typically flowery French dedication:

> *"To my dear friend, Peter Karlow, Lt. USNR, the story of the campaign of "Casabianca" for the liberation of Corsica. He was one of the first to start preparations for the great landings in Provence, bringing in American Navy speedboats. In the course of a raid on the little island of Capraya, to maintain control there, his speedboat was struck by a mine in an acoustic mine field. After long time in the water, he was rescued and transported to Cagliari where his left leg was amputated above the knee. Through a happy coincidence he and I were sent for healing and limb fitting to the same Naval Hospital in Philadelphia, where he never missed a chance to visit and comfort us, my wife and me, and lavish his attention on us."*

> *With all my affectionate memories.*
> *J. l'Herminier, Captain First Rank,*
> *French Navy*
> *Rouen, the 6. January 1950.*

Back to Paris and on to Germany, on Sunday night, January 7, 1950. I looked forward to the train. I was to ride on the vaunted Orient Express, but its fame did not live up to what I encountered at the Gare St. Lazard. I had not expected the sight of so motley a collection of rolling stock — old wooden Wagon Lits cars from all over, and with destination signs from Bucharest to Belgrade. Even though I am a railroad buff, the prospect of a night on this was not appealing.

"*Karlsruhe, Eine Stunde!*." The gruff voice of the conductor and the heavy scent of onion on his breath woke me from a night's fitful dozing. As I came to I realized that it was not all a bad dream. I was indeed on the Orient Express, or rather on a rattling wood and brass sided 1930s model sleeping car that had somehow survived the war, still bearing the brass letters "Wagons Lits". I curled up fully dressed in an upper berth of an overheated four-bed compartment, which I had to myself. It was three in the morning and pitch black outside. That the conductor had barged into the sleeping compartment to wake me was not the style I might have expected from seeing movie versions of life on Orient Express trains, but it got the job done. I remembered that the train was due in Karlsruhe at four in the morning. And that I had somehow worked the compartment window open from the top to let in some cool January air. It was a mistake as the cool air was heavy with coal fueled steam engine smoke, and I felt as if my throat was coated with coal dust. As the train began to slow down amid a plethora of high-pitched European train whistles I realized that I had arrived in Germany — Sunday January 8, 1950 and the war was less than five years ago. I had a fleeting thought of breakfast, a prospect that seemed somehow remote at the moment.

Everything somehow seemed remote.

The train finally screeched to a stop, and I wrestled my three pieces of luggage and a bulky duffel bag down the coach corridor and onto the platform with no help from the conductor. Come to think of it, he was nowhere in sight to give a hand. No hand, no tip. Nor was there anyone else on the virtually lightless platform of the huge but roofless railroad station, except for four men in heavy coats who had also arrived on the train. They seemed to know where they were going, and went. The air was raw and cold and wet with a slight drizzle of dirty would-be snow. There was ample bomb damage visible, overhead and to each side, but the track area and several platforms had been swept clear of rubble. At the head of the track, the locomotive was wheezing and smoking, and its fireman and a pair of oilers or uncouplers were doing whatever they were doing silently and stolidly. I realized the station was a T-headed design, where the train pulls in to the dead-end at the head of the platform and the locomotive is uncoupled. Another locomotive is attached to the erstwhile rear of the train, and takes it on the next leg of its journey.

That high-pitched whistle sounded again, this time from way out on the platform. The wagon couplings chattered as the train started moving slowly out into the night, minus the uncoupled locomotive still panting on the track near me. I noticed as the coaches were moving away that the outside destination sign on my coach said "Budapest," a reminder that life and the railroads go on despite iron curtains or other political games. Still, I could have cried when I saw the last of the train head off Eastward leaving me behind feeling stranded on the dark platform with four unwieldy pieces of luggage at my feet.

I went over and asked one of the railroad workers where I could find a telephone. His answer, near-phonetically, was something like "*Uh. Dess wuzzy'ney.*" It was my first brush with Hessian, the German dialect of the area. There was a light in what I guessed was the stationmaster's office some hundred yards away and, happily, I spotted an abandoned pushcart in front of it. I took the one suitcase with my valuables, left the other three on the open platform, rushed over to appropriate the pushcart, came back for my other luggage, and got back to the station master's office. I asked the sleepy watchman inside if I could use the *Telefon*. Wrong; I should have said *Apparat*. I put a pack of cigarettes before him on his desk. Again wrong. He grumpfed, saw the cigarette pack, and brightened up. He put down the slab of bread he was chewing, dialed the number I gave him, and, with a crooked smile, handed me the phone. I did not yet understand the cigarette economy. One or two cigarettes would have been plenty. A full pack was equal to about ten dollars, and traded freely.

After a number of rings, a sleepy American voice answered. No, he did not know my name, but he would call "the major" and tell him I was at the Bahnhof, and I should stay at the stationmaster's office. Easily a long hour later, as dawn was breaking, a black four-door German Opel sedan finally pulled up, driven by an American soldier. We loaded the luggage and drove through streets still heavy with bomb damage along rows of three and four story barracks-like concrete buildings to what was "our" headquarters.

Up a flight of stairs to the duty officer's office, where Major Jim Carini, whom I knew from Washington, greeted me. Carini offered me a cup of poor coffee, and told me he knew I was coming and was glad to see me. Oh, well, I thought, bristling for a moment. If he knew I was coming, and I knew he knew because Bland in Paris had cabled my itinerary, why couldn't someone have met me at the station? No, don't expect anything and you're never disappointed. Anyway, I was tired and irritable but the coffee was warm even if the reception was, well, understated. The driver took me to the hotel across from the railroad station where I was given a large, comfortable room, and promptly flopped down for a final bit of sleep. Not to be: There it was, louder and louder, the sound of Germans going to work, their hobnailed boots walking in step as though they were marching, an eerie sound.

It took a bit of effort and some sense of humor to get used to life in Germany and life in the U.S. military. I was to have total immersion in both at the same time. Looking back on it, I realize how much competent support and help I received from the German administrative staff at the time.

First, though, the administrative work I had to do, the adventure in setting up a new organization and assembling personnel and preparing the necessary physical facilities in the confusion of Occupied West Germany, was a strange experience. First of all, this involved learning to live with the idiosyncrasies of dealing with U.S. military procedures. Then, there was winning support from the various parts of the intelligence structure (the initials CIA were never used) who did not easily communicate with each other. A short summary will give a picture of the structure of ad hoc arrangements by which we operated.

The intelligence part of the German Mission (OSO) was in Karlsruhe, headed by Gordon Stewart, soft-voiced person who turned out to be easy to get along with. His high forehead, large but even features emphasized solidity and thoughtfulness, some of the manners of a church man or a professor. You quickly realized he was a man of a high intelligence and good humor that belied any impression of stuffiness. He had a breadth of knowledge of Germany from pre-Hitler days, a clear view of his mission, and a gentle but forceful way of leading a very diverse assemblage of staff people. Stewart became for me a sensible leader, a strong supporter, a valuable advisor, and, along with his wife Peggy, warm personal friends.

His deputy was Lt. Col. Lou Kubler, a big, gruff type with a heart of gold whose background included serving in the New Jersey State Police criminal laboratory at the time of the Lindbergh kidnapping. This background made him sympathetic to my technical oriented mission. Kubler was of invaluable help with higher-level Army military housekeeping authorities. He was able to get housing for office space and for my laboratory, also automobiles, special passes, access to military warehouses, and exemptions from numerous "normal" military inspection and reporting procedures. I would start in Karlsruhe but the center of action was to be Frankfurt, which was some three hours north on the Autobahn super highway. Frankfurt was becoming the center, the headquarters of the U.S. military occupation of Germany. Within two years OSO moved to Frankfurt and formed a composite German Mission headquarters, headed by Lt. Gen. Lucian K. Truscott, Jr. In World War II, Truscott had been the commander of the Southern French landings in 1944, a military operation that used, in fact, relied on as never before, OSS-produced intelligence and para-military support from the myriad Resistance operations set up for the purpose.

The psychological warfare part (OPC) had already been set up in Frankfurt. Several OPC units were already in business. Interrogators were active at refugee reception centers like Oberursel, north of Frankfurt. Operations officers were working with refugee political personalities who had ties into East Germany, Poland and Czechoslovakia.

Again, everything fell in place for me remarkably smoothly. My function gave promise of filling a number of immediate operational needs, and I had full cooperation and backing from both OSO and OPC—probably one of the first, or few, activities to have this joint backing. From the OSO side, Stewart provided five or six people who were linguists in German, Czech, and Polish to handle document intelligence, plus administrative slots for a secretary, the motor pool, and procurement and services. From OPC, in the person of Roland D., a very strong supporter, came the initiative to recruit from among the personnel of the Army's Civil Censorship unit, and the money to procure equipment. Roland was easy to work with, but did enjoy keeping an air of mystery around in that we never knew when he would appear or even where to reach him directly instead of through another OPC office. Roland's impact was great: Particularly important was the first-rate printing equipment we acquired. German technology had deeply influenced printing and graphics in Eastern European countries literally from the days of Gutenberg. For our work, a core of German equipment including presses and binding units was indispensable to do leaflets or documents.

It was a lucky coincidence that the Army had just decided to end its Civil Censorship unit. We in effect took over several of its remaining personnel including three experienced printers, two chemists for secret ink work and such others as experts on packaging and model making who could make concealment devices.

These personnel acquisitions involved me in a comic but potentially sticky negotiation. Civil Censorship had been headquartered in Frankfurt at 44 Feldbergstrasse, a four-story corner apartment house that far exceeded our needs. Inside its entrance was a large double living room which was used as a military officers' club, the "Club 44", complete with glass brick semi-circular bar, and antlers and other hunt regalia on the walls plus beer mugs as decor. On my first official "call" on the Frankfurt Military Post, the Post Commander, a full colonel, asked me point-blank, since I was taking over Civil Censorship assets, was I going to keep that outrageous "Club 44" going? Ten minutes later, the Deputy Post Commander, a lieutenant-colonel, got right to the point with me: He hoped that as a contribution to Post life I would keep that Club 44 going unchanged. For the record, the matter solved itself in a few months. The major and the captain who were the last heads of the Censorship unit both reached the end of their military terms and returned to the U.S.

We found suitable buildings in Hoechst, outside of Frankfurt and, when they were ready, moved there, abandoning "Club 44" and its building. Ironically, electricians installed new fluorescent lights at 44 Feldbergstrasse three weeks before we moved out; they had been on order for some time and no one had thought to cancel the order. Another detail: Checking out of the building meant accounting for every item of furniture on the inventory. I saw some of the Germans from the Military Post Housing unit take a wooden chair and smash it into pieces. They explained to me that instead of "one chair damaged" we then had "five chairs incomplete." It helped meet the quota of inventoried furniture for which we had to account. This was obviously a practiced and effective way to deal with Military Occupation housing inventories. I guess the American taxpayer was ultimately billed for all the costs.

Setting up what became TAD, the Technical Aids Detachment, took less than a year's time. A blueprint was pulled together for refitting our headquarters in Hoechst, some ten miles outside Frankfurt. The buildings were four adjoining three story brick tenements, three apartment houses that had been for employees' living quarters and a fourth separate building in a dismal industrial compound that was the center of activity for the former I.G. Farben complex. The buildings were in a miserable smog-ridden section of town, but inconspicuous. Dummy entrances and unloading platforms were built on the front, the street side of the main building. We used them every now and then to bring in or remove some openly innocuous items, just in case anyone was trying to observe us. There was the headquarters building, two plant buildings, and a separate building for special projects. All windows were barred and gates sealed or made for a guard to watch. There were some smaller outbuildings for basic auto maintenance equipment and, in our prime, for a semi-trailer with village-sized electric generator scrounged from some disbanded Army unit.

Given TAD's expanded mandate, that is, to provide support for OSO and OPC, I set out an organization plan along military lines. My "G-1" was planning, mainly my deputy, Dr. Allen Gold, a high-strung ulcerous mad-chemist type without whose competence despite his histrionics we could not have designed the facility, or selected and installed the equipment. He also maintained the "work order" system that I designed. We called the system the ANVO, as in "accept no verbal order." Every request for service was given an ANVO number. This way we could keep track of the nature of the job, the customer, the date due, the estimate of work hours required, and problems encountered. There were over 1200 ANVOs in our three years of operation.

My "G-2" was intelligence, the documents collection and analysis group. I started this group in Karlsruhe with Wesley Parcells, who was among those assigned to me by Stewart from the OSO group. Parcells gave a first impression of a most serious and studious researcher, but this belied his organizational ability, his diligence and energy, and his unfailing good humor. Whereas Washington's files contained 50 exemplars of the essential personal identity documents from East Bloc countries, Karlsruhe's files were massive, with several crates of documents waiting to be processed. The drawers and hoppers full of documents, I guess over two thousand prototypes, had been taken from refugees when they checked in to the reception centers that were established for them throughout West Germany. Why were not more exemplars sent to Washington? Parcells reflected the view of our German staff—What's the use, they don't know what to do with them anyway. Indeed I was shown some atrociously bad — or rather, too good — copies of documents sent in from Washington, and unusable.

We rearranged all the items in the files to make them accessible; to correspond to the filing system, the DI, document intelligence system, that I had designed back in Washington. Working days and late into the evenings, I was delighted to see that we had a workable set of files taking shape within two weeks. The results exceeded my expectations by far. We soon were able not just to meet requests from the operations officers for personal papers by areas of operation and agents' occupations, but to make suggestions to the case officers for other and perhaps more suitable cover stories. The word got around quickly; within a year we were supporting the German Mission as well as that in Vienna and had requests from London and Ankara as well.

By that time I had named Parcells chief of intelligence and head of German work. For Poland I had John Kopera, a competent Polish linguist with operations training and a good feel for cover building, and for Czechoslovakia the two "Z's," John Zinski and John Zarek, Czech speakers with some operations training, the latter three sent over from Washington. They quickly became experts in the documents, controls, and customs of their respective areas, and traveled frequently to the operating bases.

My "G-3" was production, mainly printing: My OPC contact, under Paul Szego. Roland still had a close-to-the vest air about him that at first worried me. Instead, it turned out he just wanted to make sure that his project requirements, in a time crunch, would meet their production deadlines. He turned over all technical contacts and assets he had developed. Essentially, he had screened and arranged to take over a number of the technical specialists from the U.S. Army's recently terminated Civil Censorship office, all corporals and sergeants with some time still to serve in the military. They turned out to be a remarkable collection of talents—compositors, pressmen, practical mechanics, chemists and photographers. All were challenged by the task of forgery and making printed products not traceable to any but German nationality. We divided the group into Printing, Chemicals, Photo, and Special Projects.

All new personnel had to be security checked in Washington, but were put to work on a provisional basis. Once, in a briefing on TAD that I gave, I humorously expressed my wonder at this array of talent being available in one place and speculated that, had they not been drafted into the Army, they surely would have used their talents as high-paid technicians for the Mafia. Actually, we lost only one person to the Security checks, and this one was a shock to all of us. He was part-American Indian, former Army sharpshooter with a World War II record reflected in a chestful of combat decorations, but who somehow had been in a restaurant workers union back home in Phoenix that made its way onto the Attorney-General's list. I protested all I could, as he was a very popular man in our group, but in the end had to order him back to the U.S. We helped him arrange to marry his attractive German fiancée, and gave them an appropriate send-off party, which turned out to be happy for him and a good morale setter for the group.

My "G-4" was services and procurement. More on this later.

In February 1951, just one year after my arrival, we officially "launched" the shop. Lou Kubler, Mike Ray and I met to go over a checklist of what still had to be done. We were set up and working. The buildings were useable. Over 30 good personnel were at hand and productive. Effective communications were established through personal visits with the operating bases in Berlin and Munich and points in-between through my visits and those of the unit; in short, we were under way and open for business. We needed a military detachment designation to be fully registered on the Post. My being a retired Navy officer helped lend this authenticity. A detachment number had been assigned by the Army. Kubler wanted to use the name "Signal Service Detachment" something that was neutral and non-descriptive, a designation actually already used by some other units as an innocuous cover name. I held out for "Technical Aids Detachment". So, as appropriate to the ad hoc or field expedient nature of this whole undertaking, we christened the new shop right there on the spot, a EUCOM (European Command) entity in good standing, named TAD for short, with me as retired U.S. Navy Lieutenant as Commanding Officer.

••••

My mandate was expanded to include supporting the work of the SR Division, the operating Division whose mission was to penetrate the Soviet Union and cope with Soviet penetrations into Germany and Austria. The center of SR activity in Germany was in the Munich area. The Division's technical equipment and documents specialist, John Parker, toured the German Mission with me in September 1950 to find the best location for the services that the Division's operations would need. Having seen the paucity of support available from Washington, he was prepared to recommend setting up a separate shop in Munich. First, however, he visited me at TAD, thought it was exactly what the Division needed, and announced that he wanted to send his assistant over to work on Russian matters at TAD. "And," he added, looking at me as if he had just had a great original idea, "You should marry her."

Her name was Elizabeth Rausch, known as Libby. She arrived in March 1951. On one of our first dates she wore flat gold earrings with the monogram "ER." To make conversation, I asked why she had no middle initial. Her answer was that her parents always thought that the "R" would be her middle initial. They were correct. It was love at first sight and we became engaged in late August on a weekend in Salzburg, Austria where we attended the annual folk music festival there. We married in Paris in May 1952, which involved a bit of corner cutting and the invaluable help of Barney and Carolyn Bland. Since neither Lib nor I were living in France, we had to establish residence, which of course was the Blands' apartment on rue Jean Giraudoux, near the Etoile. A small arrangement with the concierge in the apartment house backstopped this. Then came the eleven steps of French bureaucracy, including waiving the banns, registering with the local mayors, obtaining the license and the accompanying social security papers. I spent a few days in Paris and Carolyn Bland went with me through the ministries. I had both Lib's and my passports, and after the first office stop Carolyn realized with a deep blush that the French officials thought she was my bride-to-be. At each stop her blush was so winning no one ever checked Lib's passport picture. It sure speeded things up to have the "bride" there, if only in convincing proxy.

Lib didn't really see why we had to get married in Paris, except that getting married in Paris seemed like a fun idea to me. And, why did we have to wait until May, except that was the best time to visit Corsica where we would go on our honeymoon? Looking back on it, I am glad she was tolerant enough to marry me at all.

••••

All this administrative detail in organizing TAD should not hide the fact that we were called into ongoing projects well before we were set up in Hoechst. I had hardly been in Germany three months before my audio surveillance man and I were asked to participate personally in an operation in Austria involving what was hoped to be a trap to catch a Russian officer who had indicated he wanted to defect. A safe house had been rented in Grieskirchen, a small Austrian town roughly half way between Munich and Vienna. It was in the American sector of Austria but near the border with the Soviet sector. We bugged living room, bedroom and bath and set up observation rooms through one-way mirrors. I was to be ready to identify and copy personal identity documents or any other papers the defector might have. Given the short time we had, the house would have served its purpose well if indeed the would-be defector could have been lured to a rendezvous there with his girl friend. Unfortunately, it did not work out. It was, nonetheless, a first for me in that we technical people participated directly in an ongoing operation. It set the pattern for much of our technical support thereafter.

In the next three years, TAD was involved in over 300 operational support requests. Some were exotic for their times and broke new ground. One example, was a plan to steal a Soviet MIG.

The U.S. Air Force formally and at the highest level placed a requirement on CIA and in turn on the German Mission to procure a Soviet MIG fighter plane of the latest design. This activity was designated a top priority request. When I first heard of the project, I was highly skeptical of its advisability if not feasibility. TAD was asked to construct a mock cockpit of this new and yet unknown plane. We were asked to build a full-sized model based on information the case officers had collected from interrogations of pilots, guards, and technicians who had been in or near locations around the Soviet military airfields near East Berlin where some believed this type of plane was based. The model began to take shape in our "special devices" workshop. It was not easy to create from such vague descriptions, even with the help of Air Force technical experts. At one stage, for instance, we had conflicting data on two levers down on the floor to the right of the pilot's seat. The conflicting information was that one lever was to raise or lower the wheels, while the other lever worked the ejection seat mechanism in case the pilot had to bail out. There was a point when we could not be sure which did what. Having the model provided an excellent base on which to focus questions for future intelligence collection.

We were also asked to produce a silenced Luger pistol that would be effective in firing silently yet able to penetrate the cotton padded winterized uniform of airport runway guards. Our technical device man, a serious tinkerer, called me one day to demonstrate his progress. He had lengthened the barrel of a Luger and silenced it, and he wanted to demonstrate to me what he had done. We went into one of the small bedrooms of the fourth house of our office complex where he had his workshop. He clamped the Luger into a workbench clamp, aimed to fire endwise into a long wooden box like a dog coffin, as I called it, filled with cotton batting which weapons people use for testing pistols. He had built it for the occasion, extra long, perhaps seven feet long, and packed extra tight with cotton waste and old pillows. The gun was fired; the clap of sound was not as loud as expected, bearable even within the room, which was in itself remarkable. But, the barrel lengthening had made the gun's muzzle velocity far higher than specifications. The bullet went through the entire batten-filled dog-coffin lengthwise, burst out the other end, and went deep into the plaster of the wall behind. The next day I cabled the technical shop in Washington that our Luger conversion met the specs and was sufficient.

The reply was that it couldn't be done, at least not on the equipment we had. Would we please send them the Luger for them to test? Yes, we answered, as soon as the operation is over.

At this point, there were two potential pilot recruits, a Czech and a Pole, picked and in training for the pilot's job. Apparently both passed a "final" exam involving begin taken to a British airfield in northern Germany and instructed to get into a jet neither had ever seen, a British Vampire and start it ready for takeoff within two minutes, or whatever the specific time parameter was. We began to prepare cover documents for both, working with Parker and other case officers on a plausible story for their new identifies, which strained our credulity. How can you come up with a cover story for someone who may be caught stealing a Soviet warplane?

At this point also, General Walter Bedell Smith, the Director of Central Intelligence, called the project officers to Washington to review the project. John Parker attended to represent the technical equipment aspects. General Smith reportedly asked only one question: Where were the pilots trained? The answer was at a US Air Force base in West Germany. After all where else could you get jet plane training in Germany at the time? Smith hit the ceiling, canceled the operation on the grounds that training a pilot at a US military base to steal a Soviet warplane from a Soviet air base could be an act of war. My reaction was that someone in the Air Force should have made that judgment before placing the requirement on CIA in the first place. Parker was more direct; after all the investment of energy and skill that he had made, he felt drained and let down and resigned from the Agency on the spot as, I believe, did some other case officers associated with the operation.

Oh, the Luger: We sent it to Technical Services in Washington. They tested it and came back to us with their evaluation: We were just plain lucky, they said, to have produced a "true" barrel. It was damning with faint praise, but I was pleased. The fact remained that the weapon worked. The fact also was that I used competition with Washington as an incentive for TAD people to do better work. This competitive spirit was effective for our work in Germany but not the best way to develop team playing between us in Germany and the technical service people in Washington.

The variable rust license plate; The Berlin Base asked us for altered East German auto license plates. We duly changed the numbers, prepared a proper registration certificate to match, and since it was not sure whether the car on which they were to be used was in good shape or old, our chemists conjured up a bag of rust treated so that it could be rubbed on the license plate until the appropriate level of rustiness was reached.

Flooding the identity card system: Our information on the Czech *Obcanski Prukaz* basic identity document was so extensive, and our varieties of reproductions, or "new originals," so good, I proposed that we prepare kits complete with stamps and seals so that Czechs could fill out their own documents if we could infilter them into Czechoslovakia. This might well destabilize the identity card system that was so basic to Soviet control over civilian populations. The idea was considered without enthusiasm, but it was decided that the threat to our agents already in place there would be greater than the psychological benefit in the destabilization.

The hijacked plane. Early in 1953 four Czechs high-jacked a domestic flight from Brno, the Czech Pittsburgh, to Prague and forced the pilot to fly to the West. As the pilot crossed the West German border, he radioed blindly that he was under duress and wanted to be cleared to land in London. An alert Air Force tower man at the US base in Wiesbaden, just west of Frankfurt, radioed back that London was fogged in and to land at Wiesbaden. Just after midnight the phone rang on my night table. It was Colonel P., the Air Force intelligence head at Wiesbaden, calling me in fairly transparent verbal code to ask me to please get my "Cee-Zees" meaning Czech speakers out to the field promptly, that "we got us a fistful of folks" and need help at once. A few more guarded comments and I got the drift of what had happened.

I phoned and woke my executive officer, Bill Farrell, who at the time was an active duty lieutenant colonel, a status that facilitated his access to the airfield. I told Farrell that I had an idea of what was happening, that a plane must have landed off its normal schedule and that we have been asked for a full spread of our resources.

Regardless of time of night, would he mobilize the right people, get out to the laboratory, round up needed equipment and form a convoy to get out there. Take only needed people and let no one know what's doing outside TAD. He did. He rounded up John Zinski and John Zarek plus two photographers and their gear and a chemist for flaps and seals work.

They got to Wiesbaden before dawn, set up three adjoining rooms, one to hold the passengers and crew before interrogation, the second the interrogation room and the third the holding area. Zinski addressed the Czechs, welcomed them to the Free World, noted the unusual circumstances of their arrival and asked cooperation one at a time so that they could be returned to normal life as soon as possible. Most were steel executives returning to Prague after an annual planning conference for the industry in Brno. It took two full days to do the interrogations and photograph all documents the passengers carried in their wallets and brief cases. Meanwhile the chemist opened the safe on the plane, opened every registered mail letter for the photographers to film the contents and restored the letters to their envelops so that it would be hard to be sure they had indeed been opened. The safe was similarly resealed.

On the second day the news had begun to spread and State Department and Army counter-intelligence people began to demand to have access. Colonel P. called me frantically to ask how soon we would be finished and how much longer he had to hold off the other agencies. The TAD team finished the evening of the second day. All the passengers except the four hijackers wanted to return to Czechoslovakia. As they said, defecting would be pointless exposure for themselves and their families; we could be sure they would welcome our arrival to liberate the country but meanwhile it would serve little purpose to add them to the displaced persons camps in West Germany. The hijackers remained behind in Germany.

The plane was released that evening. How Air Force squared matters with other departments of the US Government or anyone else is not clear to me. However, I still see the glowing commendation Col. P. wrote to General Truscott about TAD's "outstanding and professional work." Gordon Stewart forwarded it to him with an endorsement. The endorsement said: "This is the kind of thing Karlow does well." My special pride was in the fact that the TAD people were so good and so ready, that the job was done on no notice at all without my being involved except for that initial phone call. I hope I was equally effusive in my letter of commendation to Bill Farrell.

Four-color background print. New East German documents were issued, featuring a multi-colored background print called Zammeldruck, collecting printing. The Zammel successively printed out colored patterns so that the dyes would gently blend into one another in a rainbow effect designed to be hard to reproduce. Jeff Marzen, our operations chief, "Big Paul" Szego, the head of printing and "Little Paul" Toth, his assistant, took on the job. They called me over to the shop a few weeks later to show me their progress. They had taken apart an aging American Addressograph Multigraph offset printing machine, built some straight gear-toothed tracks the length of a long work bench. They then ran the printing cylinder down the tracks so that the printing plate would hit the four variously colored inking pads in sequence, each time taking on an additional color, then printing the gathered inkings on paper. The result was a remarkable match, detectable but only on direct and close-up side by side comparison on the spot with a genuine document.

Not everything was trouble free. I hit one nasty snag where I had not adequately followed the bureaucratic principle of "CYA." It concerned my G-4 function, services and procurement. We bought heavy printing and photographic processing equipment on the German market. Our supply man hired Horst W., a German contractor, a bright and eager tall, blond, Teutonic type, with initiative and drive. Horst's father had been in the photography equipment business and Horst knew where to order and buy equipment and supplies of the type we needed. For example, he found out which manufacturer prepared certain watermarked paper similar to what was used on East German documents. As a German, he could snoop around for something like this in a way that might not have been possible for an American. Also, he could obtain standard German professional discounts, usually between 30% and 40% of list price. US Army procurement policy was to take no more than 15% discount from German suppliers, to help stimulate German economic recovery. We worked out a deal with Horst, that he would have both a salary and a share of premium discounts he could obtain from what he could negotiate with the German suppliers.

He earned his keep amply just in his ability to locate the proper supply sources for some pretty esoteric supplies and equipment, such as is needed for document forging. I documented this in a memo to German Mission Headquarters, because I knew there was a latent problem in having an employee also used as a contractor. I hoped the specialized nature of our procurement would let us waive this. There was no problem at first, until other parts of the German Mission found out about the discounted prices we could get and asked us to procure certain items like cameras for them. At this point, some of the frictions I had created with Technical Services in Washington came to the fore. An Inspector General survey of TAD was ordered and it discovered the procurement situation and made an issue of it. The IG report commended TAD on its excellent work, but recommended I be fired because of the procurement malpractice. At this point Gen. Truscott stepped in and endorsed a rebuttal to the IG Report with a strongly worded paragraph commending my good work and the products of my imagination and leadership and stating that he would especially want me in any future command of his. The matter blew over, since my three-year term was up and I was ready for reassignment.

In June 1953 TAD gave a farewell party for me and for Libby, by then my wife. It was a sentimental occasion. TAD numbered 72 people at its peak. Somehow, a chemistry had developed between us all, which led to high morale and high productivity and a real camaraderie. One of our artists designed a small brass medal that I had struck at my expense and handed out to each TAD person, in gold for the original two dozen members, in silver for the more recent arrivals. It showed a slim messenger holding a half opened scroll in on hand, the scroll covered with writing, and a rolled up scroll in the other hand. The motto around the edges said; *NOVE SEAT - NOVE DUNT* as though in Latin. Read quickly and phonetically, it said "Now we see it, now we don't," our TAD motto. It was corny but went over well. I was happy to learn that over the next years Jeff Marzen, Paul Szego, Paul Toth and some others were called to Washington to take over most of the key responsibilities in the Technical Services Division.

•••

We had several months of home leave in mid-summer of 1953. These five years, 1950-1955, were among the happiest of my life. In my job, I was exhilarated at how well TAD had worked out, from a barebones concept that I thought about in 1949 to a useful and respected service function in 1953. Personally, getting married in 1952 was a particularly good idea, even if Lib really had the idea before I did. I was happily getting used to being married and to calling her "my wife" and enjoying her company. As to living arrangement, we were on an extended honeymoon in the "B.C." (before children) years 1952-1955 and we both enjoyed the attractions and contradictions of living abroad in a time when dramatic changes were taking place in countries rebuilding after the war.

•••

Professionally, I had a tempting offer from the Ford Motor Co. in 1953, when the "Whiz Kids," the brilliant group of managers headed by Robert McNamara, were rebuilding the company. The offer was highly informal and was made by one of the executives in charge of Ford's 50th Anniversary celebration in 1953. Would I come out to Detroit, get family and myself settled and "come to work?" I flew out to Detroit and was given a very-important-person treatment of a nature I had not experienced before. It happened in early summer of 1953 while I was on my annual in-person report trip to Washington. A black Ford sedan with driver met me at the airport. The driver was a cheerful fatherly talkative type, a black man probably in his early 60s with gray hair. He told me how he had been recruited by "Mr. Ford himself" some 30 years before. He said he was manning a steam shovel for the local utility company when a car stopped near his work area. The driver came over and said he though the motor was not running right. It was Mr. Ford and he sought out the project foreman about this, to no avail. So, Mr. Ford went to the nearest telephone, called the utility company's president and arranged to buy the machine on the spot. He sent a flatbed truck to pick it up, hired the driver and took them both to Dearborn. Apparently Mr. Ford was right, the engine was indeed defective and the driver had been working for Ford ever since.

Various company executives showed me around, from the River Rouge steel plant to the museum complex being developed at Dearborn Village. I was shown through "Fairlane," the Fords' house that contained an auto service facility in the basement and several hobby rooms, which were storage rooms, one for string and fasteners, another for clocks and clock parts. Mr. Ford was a true packrat, keeping all sorts of things for possible future use. In the offices I spent most time with Ford International people, then just beginning to think about the nature of the relationship the Ford Co. should have with its overseas subsidiaries.

Maybe I was unused to the informality; maybe I didn't sell myself. Still, the private sector seemed tame to me at the time, as compared to the challenges presented by the Cold War. When I left to go back to Washington, there was still only a general invitation to come and join the company. No solid job offer that I could look over. No specifics. I begged off. Oh, yes, the drive back to the airport was a repeat performance of my arrival. This time it was in a gray Ford, again with an older black driver who had a story to tell about how he "got in with Ford." It seems he was working for a contractor at Mr. Ford's house and was doing some extra work for Mr. Ford when he was seriously injured in an on-the-job accident. Mr. Ford visited him at the hospital and promised him a job for life. That had been some 20 years ago...

•••

What about my artificial leg? Could I spend more time abroad? The new "suction" fit turned out to be serviceable and satisfactory. The leg was at times a hindrance to me, actually more a nuisance than a "handicap" as I would define the term. In fact, much of the time I literally forgot that I had an artificial leg. I was comfortable; I walked well. I only rarely had sores or abrasions on my stump. And most of my colleagues were not even aware that I was missing leg. Most seemed to think that I had a stiff knee or maybe a hip problem. Heat and especially humidity did bother me, in that perspiration could cause the leg to slip and be out of fit. I tried to make it a point to remove the leg and refit it once a day, usually upon coming home in the afternoon, to be sure it was dry and put on correctly.

I went back to Philadelphia for a thorough check-up by Bill Peters that same summer of 1953. He redesigned the socket of my leg, the part that holds it on to my body, to what was termed a "total contact" fit. This was a new way of fitting whereby the socket is shaped exactly to the muscle structure of the entire leg stump, not just the top rim. This was one key to Peters' approach: Not just to fit the shape of the muscles when they are fully tensed, but to project how those muscles would develop with proper exercise and to allow for this expansion. As before, the new leg was held in place entirely by vacuum pressure. To put the leg on, I would still pull myself into the socket with an open-ended cotton stockinet, which pulls out through the valve opening at the base of the socket. Then I would make sure there was no air left in the socket, by flexing muscles and that the position or alignment was right, which you learn with practice, and seal off the opening with a screw-in valve. I still follow this procedure today. A number of prosthetists were not up to the extra work and attention that this total contact design required and fell back on various types of "soft" or padded sockets to compensate for inadequate fit. The arrival of computer-aided design may help this development in the future. Exact fit is essential.

Another key innovation that Peters pioneered: He designed a mechanical knee control, a device that wrapped around the knee bolt and in effect added a mechanical brake to provide resistance to an otherwise free-swinging knee. Its purpose was to give the wearer a constant level of resistance throughout the entire stride. This in turn forced the wearer to use his muscles both in the stump and in the waist. Hard to get used to at first, like taking up a new sport but, once the muscles adjusted, it prevented atrophy as well as helping materially to stabilize the fit and make one a better walker.

So equipped, I was off for another three years overseas, back to Germany.

•••

My next assignment was to Munich, to join the small team of Americans working with the newly developing West German intelligence service. This was the organization headed by German ex-General Reinhard Gehlen, the former head of military intelligence for the German Army Command on the Eastern Front (*Fremde Heere Ost*). In 1944, as German troops were driven back and out of Russia, Gehlen and his people foresaw the imminent military collapse of Germany and anticipated hostility by the USSR to the west after the end of the war. Gehlen maneuvered to have copies of their intelligence files stashed in a mountain chalet in Bavaria. When the time came, Gehlen expected to use them as bargaining chips to make a deal for himself and his group, through making contact with the American military authorities and offering the files to them. The files were remarkable: Over six years' comprehensive records on Soviet "order of battle," meaning lists and locations of Soviet military units down to regiments, complete with names of officers, equipment, strengths and weaknesses, command subordination, etc.

The maneuver succeeded. Gehlen and a nucleus of his officers were put under the auspices of the CIA, to provide detailed military intelligence on the Soviet armed forces in eastern Europe in the critical Cold War years and if successful, to play a part in a future German government. A forceful and highly diplomatic American, James M. Critchfield, was put in charge of this project. Critchfield was from North Dakota and became one of the youngest full colonels in the Army. He agreed to accept the position as a civilian with the mandate to give the Gehlen group enough autonomy so that it could develop its own momentum, yet maintain for the CIA an adequate flow of information and degree of control over its activities.

As first step, a core group of Gehlen's people was brought to the US and set up in military barracks near Washington, DC. Gehlen's information was strikingly important to the Defense Department in view of the real possibility of armed conflict breaking out in Europe with the Soviet Union. Gehlen's people were authorized to mount new low-level operations based in West Germany. Shortly, he and his staff were moved back to Germany, where they developed a sizable base for operations located in the estate of former Nazi bigwig Martin Bormann in Pullach just south of Munich. There were several larger buildings on the premises, also a rabbit warren of tunnels and air raid shelters underground, including secret meeting rooms and storage areas. As CIA defined the mission, the avowed objective was to provide tactical information on Soviet military activity, also on developments in East Germany in the political, military and intelligence fields. The broader objective was to judge the Gehlen organization by its output and if successful to support Gehlen in his efforts to have his group become the nucleus of the future German national intelligence service. In the end, this succeeded, too.

My assignment was to evaluate the intelligence production of the Gehlen organization. I developed good relations with several key Germans and found that most of them were former German General Staff officers who had been active on the Eastern Front. The German who headed this intelligence responsibility was Heinz Danko Herre, a tall, distinguished General Staff colonel who was also a writer and historian in his own right. I programmed some briefings for him and his staff on the basic intelligence research and analysis procedures to OSS R&A days. Then I tried something new, something I said we did regularly in Washington, I postulated that every intelligence report should be a reply to a question. I proposed that they review each incoming report, listing the question or questions that each answered. They should tally the number of reports that were received in answer to each question into a regular monthly report to us. It took several months until I could develop this into a routine, but it became useful very quickly. One subject showed up with inordinate frequency: Hoof and mouth disease in cattle in East Germany. I asked Herre what difference it would make to the strategic situation in East Germany if the Soviets killed off every second cow in the country. He investigated and reported back that his people had received such detailed questionnaires from the US Department of Agriculture and then received such glowing commendations for their work, that it had been enough to distort the collection priorities for the entire organization. He was grateful to me for suggesting a system that could detect such collection distortions.

Meanwhile, we were better able to calculate overall intelligence production by the "Org.," as we nicknamed it, allocated between East Germany (most of it), Poland (little), Czechoslovakia (some) and USSR (a trickle). Most of the information was on Soviet military movements (the most valuable production), some on German economic developments (sometimes a first, often more useful as confirmation of intelligence from other sources). There were occasional unique reports indicating coverage potential whose important to us the Germans could or did not realize; which we might follow up through them or independently and there were reports we were sure they withheld from us, such as on German political personalities.

In the course of our work, Herre and I became good personal friends. He called me into his office one day and began with pleasantries and small talk, at which he was not at his best. Finally he revealed the purpose of the meeting. In his General Staff background, he explained, when one had shared a rappel mountain scaling of over 3,000 meters altitude, or was classmate in the General Staff School or War College, or shared a significant adventure, one went on the informal *"du"* terms. He had called me in to ask me if I would agree to go on *"du"* terms with him, as we had already shared a great adventure. It was a pleasant surprise if somewhat charmingly anachronistic and I agreed. He nearly leaped over his desk at me to kiss me on both cheeks. Then he made it a point in talking in German with me in the presence of his fellow officers to use the German conversation to show that he and I were on *"du"* terms.

After eight months I reported my findings to Critchfield who was pleased. He leaned back and with a broad smile, complimented me on my work. He told me that I had accomplished in eight months what my predecessor had not been able to accomplish in four years.

• • •

Meanwhile, in these two years 1953 to 1955, Libby took on a sensitive job with the SR Division's counter-intelligence people at the Munich operations base. She was working for Harry Rositzke preparing detailed analyses of interrogations of Soviet defectors and walk-ins. Her data were increasingly used as basis for further interrogations, with remarkable results. It seemed that in the Soviet spy training school in Kiev the director had a brass cigarette box on his coffee table. The box was unusual for its design, which consisted of a red enamel crocodile straddling the lid of the box. As I recall the story, inclusion of questions about that box so unnerved one potential defector that he unwittingly admitted he had been trained at that school and was indeed a plant, not a defector.

We decided to start a family while still in Germany, partly because of the ready availability of household help. Lib, never a high fashion dresser, looked her best in sports clothes. However, with her newly arrived pregnancy, my sister transformed her into a veritable fashion plate with the modern American stylish maternity dresses she sent over.

German women then were still traditionally diffident about appearing publicly when pregnant, or at least in the last months of pregnancy, what the Germans called "high pregnancy" (*Hochschwange*). There were several parties we attended with Germans where Lib and her clothes were the topic of the evening. Once I recall we were with members of the Munich movie colony and there was Lib in the corner surrounded by starlets eagerly studying the cut of the maternity wear. Duly according to plan, son Jim was born at the 2nd General Hospital, the old Luftwaffe installation in Munich that the US Army had taken over on Saturday night, May 29, 1955. We returned to the US in August for home leave and reassignment.

• • •

Back to work at headquarters before year's end and the question of the next assignment arose. One senior position in EE (Eastern Europe) Division had been unfilled for some months. It was chief of psychological warfare for Eastern Europe. I was encouraged to take the assignment to gain valuable first-hand experience in this field, as this broadening of my career experience would be a good thing. I agreed, if the OPC heads agreed.

At this point, with the success of the joint OPC-OSO venture in TAD still fresh in their minds, I was greeted as one of the group by OPC and a series of intensive briefings and meetings in covert action activities were arranged for me by Desmond FitzGerald, then chief of the activity and Tracy Barnes, his chief of operations.

We went over the whole gamut of psychological warfare to covert action or "dirty tricks" approaches: subtle attacks on individuals, leaflets and rumor spreading, infiltration of existing groups and support to dissident elements; creating new or "notional" groups (would we use the word "virtual" today?), exploiting local fears and superstitions; underground newspapers and radio stations; identifying and supporting the growth of future leaders; relations to political, artistic and technical groups and foundations. There were themes, too, to compete toe to toe with Communists and Soviet "front" groups, groups that pretended to be democratic but were controlled by Soviet officials nearby or by remote control. We, too, tried to operate groups that were purportedly national or non-partisan and tried for ways to take a communist but nationalist line, not anti-Communist but just anti-Soviet imperialism.

I have at various times quoted with perhaps excessive levity what I heard once as the "rules" for psychological warfare:

Rule 1 - Stay "in" with the "outs;"
Rule 2 - Exploit the inevitable, and
Rule 3 - Don't get between the dog and the tree.

Other "rules" might be: that you do not need to be consistent as long as you are coordinated, or that the enemy of your enemy may be your friend, or that paraphrasing Churchill's comment that England and the U.S. were "separated by a common language," use English to confuse rather than communicate.

•••

I had not realized how different the objectives and methods of operating were between intelligence collection and covert action. The intelligence approach starts with determining and defining the targets, what actually needs to be known. Then one considers where the information might be, and the most practical approaches to get at or near it. Then comes the careful search for the most recent and reliable sources, and how to find, then recruit, and then win control over agents who might provide access. Then comes the painstaking effort to review or evaluate the plausibility of the information and the reliability of the source or sources, and finally the preparation of the estimates or appraisals on the significance of the information as the basis for decisions or action.

Covert action in contrast is almost mirror image in its approach. The objective is to create an effect on the basis of which a target, whether an individual, or an organization, will take action it otherwise would not take. You search for vulnerabilities, ways to make themes out of them, and then choose places or events at which information or misinformation can be floated or planted. You use members of a rival organization, or individuals with an ax to grind, but their recruitment is far more casual and the control over them frequently near non-existent. For a political dissident group, money or communications or weapons are the currency, or the leverage, as the case may be, and their supply or withholding of supplies is a form of control. The ideal is to see leaders with whom you are in touch emerge in the group, and have the group or movement you are backing take on a momentum of its own. With this should come a degree of local identification, or reputation, or recognition. Above all, the prime consideration is to maintain the possibility for maximum plausible denial of direct U.S. official involvement. The operating people involved must be imaginative in their approaches, and have an understanding of the milieu, the thought processes and attitudes of the group and of the environment of the target or area involved.

There were also "rules" that came with the territory- that you do not need to be consistent as long as you are coordinated, or that the enemy of your enemy may be your friend, or that, paraphrasing Churchill's comment that England and the U.S. were "separated by a common language," use English to confuse rather than communicate.

These contrasts help explain some of the misunderstandings and points of friction that arise between intelligence collection and covert action officers. Covert action people regard the intelligence types as stodgy, over-cautious and unimaginative. In return, intelligence people regard covert action operators as unrealistic Don Quixotes and a risk to national security. Intelligence operations must be painstakingly documented, with careful records kept. In covert action operations paper trails are often anathema, to be avoided. While there is a broad band of mutual understanding, the basic difference is intelligence people believe agents are first and foremost the means for collecting intelligence; covert action people see their work as an essential additional dimension to foreign policy and, in effect, to putting intelligence to positive use.

CHAPTER 11

THE HUNGARIAN DEFEAT...

I started on the job, Chief, Psychological Warfare, Eastern Europe, in January 1956, part-time at first, to have time for the background. I quickly found that a statement of objectives that I had tried to define for myself, to move slowly and carefully through this new area, never had a chance to develop. Events literally exploded on the scene. In brief, my hopes to combine the best of my experience in intelligence with the special needs of covert action came up headlong against official U.S. foreign policy, and left me stunned and disillusioned.

Hungary was the subject of most of the papers and messages crossing my desk.

My knowledge of Hungary was sketchy at best. The people were well described as enthusiasts and perfectionists. Descended from Mongolian invaders, they were defensive towards any people that would share their land. Hungary's Iron Guard fascists were perhaps Hitler's most dedicated non-German followers during World War II. The country now seemed to be ruled by a group of super-dedicated Communists, hardly an atmosphere where opposition to communism could be expected to develop. And yet here was a growing stream of messages from the small open opposition Hungarian Socialist Party about building a nationalist communist state, by more than inference without the USSR or Soviet troops present.

A grisly series of events came to light. In 1949 a widespread purge of the Communist Party took place. One time Communist foreign minister Lazslo Rajk was overthrown, tried by the Communists as a Tito-ist, and sentenced to death. Reportedly, the sentence was carried out in the courtyard of the Interior Ministry. After a summary court-martial type procedure, his head was cut off by piano wire, apparently in the presence of his wife. Another major Party purge in February 1953 rocked the country, and a moderate, Imre Nagy, was named Prime Minister. Two years later, in 1955, Nagy was denounced as a right wing deviationist and expelled from the Party. Unrest inside and outside the Party continued, and in 1956, Rajk's name was cleared. He was ordered to be "rehabilitated". In a ceremony on March 29, with his widow and family present, he was declared restored to political honor and absolved of Titoism and treason.

Meanwhile, the head of the Social Democratic Party was released by the Soviets from five years in prison in Siberia. He and his closest followers were attempting to open contact with Western political parties. The banned Smallholders Party revived. Student unrest was on the rise, and there was growing criticism of the government in organized labor ranks. This, in very terse form, was what was in the reports coming in, largely from active Hungarian exile groups in Vienna, London and New York. The U.S. propaganda voice, Radio Free Europe, was blasting out words of hope, based on émigré reports, to people "seeking freedom," obviously nearly getting out of hand as far as Soviet control was concerned. From the psychological warfare standpoint, we were waging a battle of wills to weaken the hold of the USSR over the Soviet bloc nations of Eastern Europe. Hungary was coming sharply into the spotlight as the main battlefield. The road to the battlefield seemed to run directly across my desk.

I announced as my first priority project the preparation of a situation report on Hungary. I met with émigrés, with State Department, with the U.S. Information Agency and its Voice of America people, and representatives of Radio Free Europe and Radio Liberation (another U.S. sponsored activity with a mid-European outlook). From an intelligence standpoint, there was virtually no independent agent source inside Hungary, only some occasional travelers to the country. I found the State Department was little interested in Hungary. All diplomatic eyes seemed to be focused on the Arab-Israeli conflict in the Middle East, where Egyptian president Nasser threatened to nationalize the Suez Canal. I submitted my report to Des FitzGerald and also to Dick Helms, who appreciated being kept informed.

A special inter-agency meeting was arranged with a special Task Force in State Department. Outerbridge Horsey, a prominent Foreign Service officer, headed the task force. To say we got a cool reception is to put it mildly. We got a lecture on reality as seen at top foreign policy levels: Didn't we know that the *real* crisis is in the Middle East? Hungary is a sideshow. Anyway, nothing is going to happen there, the Communists' control is too tight. Also, there is no breaking away from Communism; once a Communist, always a Communist. I couldn't believe my ears. Finally, we must realize that we are up against a Sino-Soviet Bloc, and we in CIA should not make light of this. The date for the meeting was unfortunate, and practically foredoomed anything constructive: It was on July 28, two days after Nasser nationalized the Suez Canal.

Despite this, reports became more intense and threats of action more imminent. One Hungarian group asked us how they could establish their bona fides with us, to show they were real. They suggested actions like toppling the statue of Stalin, a general strike, or an attack on the USSR Embassy or propaganda office, or, of all ideas, closing down the Secret Police. I passed these reports on to the State Department and asked for another meeting with their Task Force. It was scheduled for October 25.

By October 23, widespread rioting broke out in Budapest. Crowds carrying the red-white-green Hungarian national flag attacked and tore down the statue of Stalin. By October 25, Imre Nagy, the moderate, was readmitted to the Communist Party and named Premier, and open revolution took over in Budapest. At the October 25 meeting, we were told in direct terms that we were to do nothing to incite revolution in Hungary or to admit that the U.S. had ever tried to promote revolution in Hungary. The USSR has the atom bomb and might not hesitate to use it to start World War III. The saying was that the wounded bear was the dangerous bear.

Two days later Soviet troops began to pull out of Budapest. Crowds of students and workers and soldiers among other things broke into the Secret Police headquarters to release all prisoners and seize the Secret Police officials instead. A true spontaneous popular revolution was in full bloom.

On October 29, Israel invaded Egypt and cut the Suez Canal.

On October 30, Soviet troops withdrew from Budapest and Premier Nagy, in a radio speech, promised free elections. He sent Mrs. Anna Kethly, prominent educator and parliamentarian, to address the United Nations in New York on Hungary's behalf. The State Department issued instructions that no one was to contact Mrs. Kethly. I personally examined Mrs. Kethly's "Diplomatic Passport No. 1" from what I recall was called the "Hungarian Popular Socialist Republic," and returned it to her along with other envelopes. I am vague on exact times and details, partly because there is no paper trail, and partly deliberately.

Clandestine radio stations sprang up all over Hungary carrying news of revolution and resistance. Martin Himler, our principal Hungarian-speaking expert, was on vacation in Greece. Our people in Athens contacted him, and he got together with my good friend and colleague of Germany days, Richard P. Scott, who was Chief of Communications in Athens, and was in daily communications with me. Between them they mounted a clandestine station notionally in the suburbs of Budapest. With FitzGerald's full support, we tried to provide guidance; our line was to be national Hungarian Communists outraged by this blatant Soviet imperialism, and let's drive the Soviet occupiers out and get Hungary going again for the good of the Hungarian people. "*Ruszki haza!*" (Russians go home!). I urged that we be fervent but cautious, for the revolution to take place a step at a time and wait for world opinion to espouse our cause; don't get carried away and risk losing everything. We called the station "RADIO RAJK," after the murdered then rehabilitated Communist Party official. Above all, we warned that the Soviets were sending in reinforcements (we had some intelligence reports about Soviet troop reinforcements crossing the Hungarian border) and predicted that they would not give up if they felt a hostile regime might take over Hungary from them.

"We Hungarian Communists will make sure what persons and circumstances were responsible for calling in Russian troops. The guilty will meet the fate they deserve, the gallows..."

The trouble was that its signal was so authentic in sound, and its messages so topical, that to our horror it was quoted by name in the daily U.S. Information Service's daily Foreign Broadcast Intercept Summary! This, of course, was a "no-no" but, before we could do much about it, events reached their unavoidable climax. The Soviets invited resistance leaders to confer about Soviet troop withdrawals; the resistance leader, Pal Maleter, and his staff went to the meeting and were arrested and not heard from again. Maleter's deputy, Bela Kiraly, took over, but in a few days strongly reinforced Soviet troops plowed their way back into Budapest. We ordered Himler to stage a break-in and go off the air dramatically, which he did, complete with a sweatily whispered, "World help us! Long live Hungary."

We helped Kiraly get out of Hungary and to Switzerland. We provided civilian clothes and the arrangements to fly to New York. I met him there at plane-side; in those days special passes were available to let me get right into the plane's debarking point, pick up the luggage as it was off-loaded from the plane, have a special route through Immigration & Naturalization, and right into a waiting limousine. Kiraly and I went straight to Pennsylvania Station to the train platform; I had a parlor car cabin reserved on the 4:00 PM Congressional express to Washington.

The train moved out silently through the dark tunnel under the Hudson River and out onto the featureless Jersey meadows. Tall, brown hair, athletic figure, his English was hesitant, and we settled on German. I broke the ice with a straight question.

"General," I began.

He cut in sharply. "*Nicht* general...the generals all fled, they were all Russian appointees. I'm a lieutenant colonel."

"All right, colonel. Tell me…what should we have done to help you?"

"No, not you," he replied. "This was our doing." Then he sat back thoughtfully, cradling his chin in his hands.

"Yes, there was something you could have done," he said.

It would have been in helping him contact the rest of Hungary's army around the country. It seemed the Soviets controlled the signal corps and when revolt broke out they simply shut it down. Kiraly described how he and his colleagues were trying to get the other Army units to join the revolution. All they had was the public long-distance phone system, which they used to call their friends and classmates to identify themselves and ask for help.

"If you could have had *acht Gruppen Paras*, eight parachute teams, two-man teams with two-way communications that could have dropped onto each of the military headquarters around the country, it would have shown that we were in a genuine revolution," Kiraly said with some animation. "Then we could have had a chance to drive out the Russians…"

He hesitated, and added that it would have been possible to win at least a partition of Hungary. As it was, only elements of two divisions were active in the fighting in Budapest, and the rest of the country was relatively quiet except for some sporadic outbursts—stimulated by radio reports.

"Would that have been possible?"

The question struck me like a blow on the head. My mind flashed back to the State Department Task Force presentations. An iceberg in Hell. That's how much chance that idea would have had at best. And yet, I will believe to the end of my days that Hungary at that time was the real Achilles Heel to the Soviets, not the Middle East. A rollback in Hungary would have been a bitter pill for the Soviets, and a real psychological loss. I cannot believe that it would have led the Soviets to open atomic warfare to maintain their position in Hungary.

The Israelis withdrew eastward across the Sinai Desert; direct U.S. pressure, by President Eisenhower in person, caused the British and French to evacuate their troops overnight from the Suez area and turn it back to Nasser.

How hollow our protestations about liberation of Eastern Europe sounded! Our bluff had been royally called. I was disgusted, and emotionally shaken. I took two weeks off, to cool off and decompress. The Hungarian revolt debacle literally made me ill for a few days, and I felt like quitting, resigning.

Lib and I discussed this seriously, and she was all for it. We did not need another summer of that kind of frustration. We discussed our career planning; where did we want to be, and doing what? I did not believe that I needed to be in government, or in intelligence, for the rest of my life. I thought that I could make use of what I had learned and apply it in the private sector. But how to make the transition, and when? What would be the next step? Yet I felt that quitting now would be like running away. Also, where would I go? The opportunity to go with Ford had come just a few years too soon and was no longer open. I didn't feel like going off to graduate school. Too much still seemed to be going on in Washington.

Lib herself realized by this time that she could not comfortably hold a full-time job in CIA in the U.S. with me working there. It still was not a preferred course of action for wives to be staff members on their own. More important, she did not want full-time work, what with son Jim on the scene and our firm expectation to provide him with a kid sister in the near future. Lib left CIA in 1956, shortly after our return from Europe, and became active in the League of Women Voters. In a few years she was one of the heads of the Washington, D.C. League and was named a member of the League's national board of directors. She took a particular interest in the Overseas Education Fund, a branch of the League of which many League officers were skeptical, as the League's focus was on domestic issues. Lib was elected president of the OEF, and served for several years in that position. The OEF thrived under her leadership, particularly in projects in several developing countries in improving the earning power of women through developing their own cottage industries or money-earning activities.

CHAPTER 12

STATE DEPARTMENT: A PARODY OF POLICIES...

Ideally, I wanted to see if I could find a position in the Agency whose function would be working with business, so that I could make a gradual transition out of CIA. The Technical Services end of the business seemed to offer the most promising channel for this, but some of my colleagues from TAD days in Germany were just beginning to take over key positions and I felt it more politic not to push this path for myself at this time.

An alternative opened up for me. Within the Covert Action structure there was an Economic Action Group that had been operating relatively ineffectively and needed new leadership and a new mandate. I looked into it. The basic question it faced was how the influence of private companies, or of individuals in the private sector, could be brought to bear in situations where their activity would help compete with or undermine the growing number of state socialist advocates spreading in the Third World. At that time, United Nations agencies were undertaking programs that actually helped spread socialism because there were few alternatives presented from "our" side. The challenge lay in making Americans with appropriate interests and skills aware of political implications in countries in which they were interested and where they might be encouraged to involve themselves appropriately. It also meant looking for business opportunities for foreign private investors. It also meant hearing of executive positions in international agencies and projects and finding someone to nominate for the position that would offer chances for exercising influence. For example: There was a chance to nominate an American for a prominent international banking position, were a candidate available. An open recruitment effort officially sponsored by the U.S. Government might blackball any American nominee and keep him from being elected, in view of the anti-imperialist fears voiced by so many of the Third World spokesmen. Similar considerations might apply in the case of a state-owned distribution outlet for soft drinks in Africa that was looking for a European or American partner. Or a major company in the extraction field (oil or minerals) that might be interested in offering training courses to promising young leaders in some of the developing countries. How could suggestions be made without appearing to come from or involve the U.S. Government?

I agreed to come on board as deputy chief, Economic Action Group, for up to three months, then take over from Robert Moran, the present chief. He was a relatively youthful-appearing man, brown haired, slender and of above average height. He was bright, but very rigid in his views. His easy manner with people belied a degree of inner tension, a fanatic sense of mission, and concern about any criticism. His English wife cooked a very English dinner, right down to the Yorkshire pudding, and she disdained "American" cooking as not good for your health. He carried a bible in his attaché case. I thought of him at times as being like the hero in "Music Man," an intense salesman but without real knowledge of or enthusiasm for the subject at hand.

Robert welcomed me, thought I could bring in some support for the function from the intelligence side of the business about which he openly admitted that he knew little. More than this, I began to sense that he did not regard the intelligence function as particularly necessary as compared to the covert action functions.

Some of the ongoing Economic Action projects puzzled me. I could not always fathom their basic purpose. One project involved a prominent lecturer on management principles who was on a retainer to spread his private sector curriculum to some of the larger developing countries. Particular target countries were in Latin America, where communist and Cuban influence was a matter of concern. The idea was defensible but I felt that the lecturer should be able to break into those markets on his own. I asked in vain about whether we were gaining any contacts in the target countries, with people who might be future leaders or at least sources of information. Neither of these considerations was part of the project.

The project to recruit a prominent retired banker to be a candidate for the position of operating head of a regional bank was potentially interesting. The idea, however, was not to obtain information on who is seeking what and who wields power where, but just to exert influence in an anti-Communist direction.

The project taking most time at the moment had to do with setting up a bulk commodity trader to open a wholesale or retail level business in ex-French Guinea in West Africa. Again the idea was to show the private sector way of doing business. The principal agent, *AMADOR*, was to try to develop a market for Guinean bananas in exchange for consumer goods. The problem, however, was that Guinean bananas are covered by a green peel with black spots. Their taste is quite unique.

To put it mildly, I soon felt like a fish out of water. Robert and I always had cordial relations, because he was doing a dedicated job that he truly felt should be done and I respected him for it. I quickly realized, though, that I would have to sit back until our three-month overlap ended before expressing myself. Well, the overlap dragged on and did not end, as Robert could not find another job. But I could, and I did, transfer out without further delay back into the technical equipment field.

•••

There was again a need for sorting out what technical equipment was required for "*HUMINT*," a new term referring to human intelligence. In 1947, the need was to see what had been developed in World War II that could be adapted to improve secret intelligence operations. In 1958, science and technology combined to bring out space satellites, the U-2 plane, and a growing range of sensing devices and traffic monitoring capabilities that put a whole new dimension onto the overall range of intelligence collection. In fact, the technocrats even began to question the need for secret intelligence or *HUMINT* operations in view of the inevitable limits on what espionage agents can really produce. That is, as compared to the growing wonders of *COMINT* (meaning communications intelligence, intercepts of all kind plus highly advanced code-breaking), or *SIGINT* (traffic measurement, and gleaning information from tracking stations on the ground, in space satellites, under the oceans, etc.). Similarly, the arrival of computers made collation and analysis of bulk information possible as never before. Again the question arose about whether agent operations were being slighted in the drive for advanced technology. I proposed establishing a new Technical Requirements Board, and was assigned the job of surveying the situation and proposing a program or mechanism to meet the operational needs of the operations element better.

I was introduced to much of the new technology. It was amazing to see the detail in the photography taken from the U-2, and the types of results expected from prospective families of space satellites. I set up a network of Technical Requirements representatives, senior operations people from each operating division to attend our periodic meetings and who would reflect the needs and particular problems of their respective divisions.

I had heard and read about problems in businesses that required them to bring more realism into the R&D function. I set as my objective to develop more hardware that was more immediately responsive to customer needs. Favorable response from the operating divisions was surprising and quick. I consulted closely with Cornelius Roosevelt who headed the Technical Services Division. He was a tweedy scientist type, with a wealth of charm and international experience who had been for many years an overseas representative of the American Bank Note Company when it was making currency for smaller countries abroad.

Again, as in 1947, there was no clarity between true research work and development engineering. Technical people did not regard the needs of agent operations as challenging as those of advanced collection and sensing devices. At the same time, there was a lot of groping and outright waste through lack of communications between engineers and customers.

It took prodding to get attention, and I did not always feel popular or loved in my approach. One gadget, for example, I called the BUICK CONVERTIBLE. It was a small metal box, the size of a king-size pack of cigarettes, requested by the Air Force, to tell a downed pilot where he was. Intrigued by this, I looked into it. It was designed for the U-2 pilot overflying the USSR. Should he be shot down, he would have this box around his neck. Once on the ground, a peephole in the box would show him a map of the area and the routes to urban centers and possible avenues of escape. Apparently there was an ingenious array of maps inside that could be moved around by knobs, and magnifiers to enlarge the scale of the map and show details. What about at night? I asked the question somewhat sarcastically. Oh, I was told, there is a model that has an in-built light source, like a small slide viewer. Well, suppose the map tells the pilot he is near Sverdlovsk. What can he do about it, map or none? Aside from being useless to the point of being silly, each of the dozen or so prototypes cost about as much as a Buick Convertible, then around $4,500.

At the same time, some of the items discussed by the Technical Requirements Board were well used in the future. Also, it was obvious that other countries were being assisted by technical innovation such as in the case of the American Embassy in Moscow. The Embassy was steadily being bombarded by a flow of microwave radiation that our people could detect without knowing its source or its purpose. It turned out that this was indeed a highly sophisticated electronic surveillance operation. The flow of microwaves served to sensitize special passive microphones implanted in the walls of the U.S. offices in the American Embassy itself. "Passive" means without their own power source; the units look like silver dollar size microphones with a tadpole-like tail as antenna. The microwave stream from outside the

Embassy was modulated by the audio frequencies picked up by the microphone and transmitted by the tail-like antenna. Receivers on the other side of the Embassy could pick up these modulations and from them reconstruct the original voices that the microphone overheard. In other words, a passive microphone could be installed without requiring any batteries or power source, and so could last unattended indefinitely. One was actually found in the Great Seal above the desk of the Ambassador. This system was given the name *EASYCHAIR* although the British had referred to the system as *RAFTER*.

Joe Burk, representing the Counter Intelligence Staff, briefed the Technical Requirements Board on this, and the idea of a passive audio penetration system promptly was voted one of the Board's top priority projects. Neither Burk nor his boss James J. Angleton, Chief of Counter-Intelligence, nor anyone else in CIA knew until two years later, that is, in 1961, that the British had figured out how to duplicate and even improve on the system. The British had informed the FBI of this, but no information reached the CIA.

Among other operations on which I was briefed in 1959 was the build-up to a veritable invasion of Cuba. I recall one of our "in" jokes in the intelligence operations crowd was about the greatest oxymoron one could imagine was that of a covert regimental combat team, meaning a secret or plausibly deniable band of 1200 soldiers. And yet here it was, shaping up before our eyes. How could such a regimental combat team, some 1200 men, be kept "covert," meaning plausibly deniable in case of premature discovery or breach of security? I became involved because one of the strictures placed on the operation was that no equipment issued to the participants in this venture could be purely of U.S. origin, meaning that every item should have been purchasable on the gun-running and armaments markets of the world. I was asked to help in establishing availability of numerous types of weapons large or small on munitions markets in Europe, Latin America, and the Far East. The effect of this stricture was that, when the group did land in Cuba, there were no newer-type heat-seeking anti-tank missiles along that might have given the participants a chance against Cuban tanks. In the course of doing this study, I was surprised at how many people in CIA knew about the Cuban plans. Inevitably a number of newsmen must have known about the plans, too, but in those days they were still deferential to national security restraints in a way not seen since. More troubling to me was that the enthusiasm for the project among the covert action people was in sharp contrast to the way in which the intelligence people studiously ignored the venture, giving it no help but yet not able to get the venture killed off.

One day over lunch I asked Jerry Domann, one of the operations heads of the venture, what the plans were, should the operation succeed, to replace Castro? No problem, I was told. "We've got Ramón, and José, and Martín, and Mario..." I was appalled that there was no single candidate designated to take over, and no apparent structure behind him. I was assured this wasn't a problem as there would be people who would rise up on their own accord to depose Castro. My immediate superior and mentor, the tall and aristocratic Dan DeBardeleben, a West Point graduate who left the Army early and was a senior advisor to Helms, was equally hung up on this point. I asked him directly whether he thought it possible that this whole venture could fail?

He stated without hesitation he was convinced that the whole program was highly vulnerable and would probably fail. The Bay of Pigs landings occurred the next month to the day.

In brief, the Special Operations part of the Agency was "gung ho" on proceeding with the Cuban invasion. The Foreign Intelligence part sat on its hands, aware that nothing they could say or do would discourage the advocates and participants to review the operation. The basic assumption was that Cuban people would rise up on their own to revolt against Castro as soon as the landings took place. There was no hard intelligence to support this, in fact, I recall only reporting to the contrary.

News reports from and about the Bay of Pigs quickly turned negative. The whole brigade was captured after a few days of one-sided fighting. Still fresh from his inauguration, President Kennedy promptly and courageously accepted responsibility for the poor decision on Cuba. One of the remedial steps he took was to order better communications between the various agencies involved in foreign policy. To this end he ordered establishment of an Operations Center in the Secretary of State's office where "everything concerning foreign policy" would be known in advance. Every agency of government was ordered to make available a well-informed officer who would be attached full-time to State Department and keep the Secretary informed of actions taken or planned by the respective agency. It was an idealistic proposal, but it might do the trick. Richard Helms, by that time Deputy Director Plans (Operations), nominated me to be the Agency's representative, and Richard Bissell, the head of the covert action elements, concurred.

•••

The Seventh Floor of the State Department, where the Secretary's office is located, looks sedate and composed. Just now there was staccato hammering heard all over the floor as partitions were being installed and doors mounted to make an area ready for the new Operations Center. A central conference room was near ready, carpeted and with a long central conference table with some fourteen leather-upholstered chairs with arms and an extra row of the same type of chair around the table along the walls. Despite holes in the walls for projectors and screens to help in presentations, not yet ready, the room was to be the scene of the Center's organizing meeting.

"We are sailing in uncharted waters, but it's up to all of us to find the best ways to make this work." With these words, Theodore C. Achilles greeted the initial group of a dozen Foreign Service Officers and four representatives of other agencies—Defense, CIA, USIA and AID. Other observers were seated in the chairs along the walls.

Achilles was Counselor to the Department, a position befitting his senior rank in the Foreign Service. Gray haired, medium build and slightly stooped, his infectious smile and inevitable unlit pipe made him appear as the consummate diplomat. Responsibility for organizing the Operations Center was assigned to him, reporting to the Secretary, Dean Rusk, and his immediate assistant, Lucius K. "Luke" Battle, whose official title was Chief of the Secretariat. I felt special attention was placed on my status because, after all, CIA had been the cause for the Bay of Pigs fiasco and State/CIA relations were most in need of definition. It was Battle who arranged the details of my work in State, as he wanted me as much as possible to be integrated into the Foreign Service for the extent of my assignment with the Operations Center. I was indeed made to feel at home there; I had not had many direct dealings with State Department, certainly not in the U.S. I enjoyed getting to know and working with a truly outstanding group of Foreign Service Officers.

The suite of offices that had been made available on the Seventh Floor, close to the Secretary's offices, emphasized the importance that Secretary Rusk and his top assistants seemed to place in the new Center, at least at first. I never found out whose offices were cleared out to make room. A name board appeared across the top of the front door proclaiming OPERATIONS CENTER, and a receptionist was stationed inside the door to restrict admission. Still, the hallway was open to the public, and both the Defense representative, Colonel (later General) Mike Rogers, and I protested this. On one occasion, I was actually stopped by two men outside the Operations Center, one with a camera, who openly identified themselves as representing TASS, the Soviet news agency. They wondered if I would agree to a short interview? I begged off, but used this as a vivid example of a security problem. Duly and reluctantly the whole corridor was blocked off. As one Foreign Service officer remarked, "We don't want to become like the CIA." Well, in short order, the entire Building instituted entrance restrictions, to the concern of a number of Foreign Service officers who were overruled in their belief that public buildings should be open to the public.

The Operations Center rooms were quickly equipped with teletypes and appropriate desks and reading boards, somewhat like a movie version of a newspaper's news-room. I was able to develop new dissemination schedules for the CIA's current intelligence briefing papers, and arrange for meetings between area experts in CIA and State, to the mutual benefit of both. Through informal meetings, in offices or over lunch, I believe I did a good deal of educational work on how best to use CIA; I certainly learned a lot about the perspective of the Foreign Service, and passed this along to my colleagues back in the Agency. But there were adjustment problems on all sides.

Col. Rogers arranged a major step forward when he gained approval to tie State Department into the global Defense communications network. Foy Kohler, Assistant Secretary for Europe, made the first call on it by contacting Allan Lightner, his representative in Berlin. Up to this point the only official communication with Lightner had been conducted by diplomatic pouch or coded cable messages. Here now was the opportunity to talk openly over secure telephone lines. They talked like kids with a new toy for perhaps forty minutes, which meant tying up the vital global communications link beyond the terse emergency-type messages it normally carried. Kohler was delighted and, as this was his first visit to the Operations Center, asked to be shown around. John Stutesman, Achilles' executive officer, led the way. They got only to the next room, where a junior officer was present and busy rewinding a tape recorder that contained the recording of Kohler's entire conversation. He hit the ceiling, objecting that his phone had been bugged and vowed to take it up with Secretary Rusk. He did, but Rusk backed the Operations Center in that a verbal conversation is every bit as official as an exchange of messages. There were frequent instances where Rusk had to, and did, back the Center.

The task forces conducted much of the major policy-related business. These were groups representing each of the many agencies involved in a policy problem. An immediate problem was that there could hardly be a government-wide foreign policy discussion without involving some two-dozen government offices or agencies. For example, aside from several offices in State and Defense, there were CIA, FBI, USIA, and AID. Then there was Dept. of Interior for minerals or pollution, Agriculture for crops and import/export problems, Commerce on trade, Treasury for foreign currencies and credits, the Federal Aviation Agency for air safety, the Federal Communications Commission on radio frequencies and traffic problems, and several others.

Sometimes the task forces worked, and sometimes they didn't work right. For example, an early initiative I attended had to do with Portuguese colonies in Africa. The immediate issue was that U.S. military planes could not yet successfully fly non-stop across the Atlantic to get to the American bases in Europe. We needed continued access to the Portuguese islands of the Azores, where we had a refueling base. This might be endangered if we push the Portuguese too hard to liberate their African colonies like Angola and Mozambique. Who would chair the task force? Mennen Williams, President Kennedy's new appointee as Assistant Secretary for Africa, volunteered for the job. Foy Kohler, Assistant Secretary for Europe, argued that Portuguese colonies belong to Portugal and so come under Europe. The decision as to who chaired the task force virtually decided that which the task force would ultimately recommend.

The Berlin Task Force was galvanized into action on August 13, 1961. It was a Sunday, and I was at the Ops Center when the first reports came in about the East Germans building a wall straight through the heart of the city, along the demarcation line. Such a thing seemed incredible, and the Task Force members were in turmoil. The military representatives asked whether they should order tanks or bulldozers to push down the incipient structure? Martin Hillenbrandt, the senior Germany specialist in the State Department and head of the Task Force, demurred. Wouldn't they just build it one block further back? Would there be any point in recommending to the Allies, France and Britain, that we play this game? The realization grew that this wall was not to keep the West out, but to keep East German citizens in. At this point I volunteered to give a briefing on how Soviet controls over the civilian population worked, illustrating my comments with videographs. The idea of controlling a civilian population not just to prevent flight but to keep controls over everyday life seemed to be new to most of the task force members. One whole hour of a subsequent Task Force meeting was given over to this. I was commended for my presentation, although many thought it seemed "too spooky-too CIA" as an evaluation of the problem.

In due time the Berlin Wall hardened, and the East Germans took measures to impede Western access into West Berlin. The airlift resulted, and the Task Force gave consideration to ways to facilitate access despite Soviet and East German opposition. One suggestion was to offer to build a four-lane elevated super-highway from Helmstedt, just east of Frankfurt, to West Berlin. This would preserve East German sovereignty and allow free flow of traffic. I had a hard time believing that something so unreal would even be considered, but it was. I interjected a question: What if some careless driver flicks a cigarette butt out the window, and it starts a fire on the ground…who is accountable for the damage it would cause? Good point: Ironically, someone was delegated to investigate possible plastic shields that could be installed on both sides of the proposed freeway to prevent this kind of accident.

Back in Langley I called on my technical connections to see if I could glean any information that I could contribute to the Berlin Task Force. I had clearance for the U-2 type data and for certain advanced levels of communications information. It was sufficient for me to realize that data were available beyond what I was cleared to read and, while I was given some glimpses, there was nothing for which I should be the channel to any customer agency. I should not touch or be aware of any information until it hit Current Intelligence channels, by which time CIA's Office of Current Intelligence disseminated it to its limited list of customers in the daily top secret intelligence briefing routines. My job was to propose optimal channels where none existed, not to be the messenger myself.

As procedures were established, I realized that my job was nearly finished. I believed the liaison to the Operations Center should not be from the Operations side of CIA (which I represented) but from the Intelligence and national estimates side. I began to formalize arrangements in this direction, and make recommendations on this in reports to Dick Helms back in CIA, and to Luke Battle and Ted Achilles at State.

Then there was a security flap as a State Department document of some sensitivity was leaked to the press. Checking the names of those who had access to that document, the only non-Foreign Service names on the list were Col. Rogers and mine. Rogers by this time had openly requested relief; he went back to Air Force where he in short order reached the rank of Lieutenant General. I realized my vulnerability should there be future incidents like this, and increased my feelers for another job back in CIA. An interesting thing happened just at this time: One of the Security people at State called to inform me that they wanted to remove my name from the top secret cable traffic. I agreed, noting that I felt I was at the end of my tour of duty in State depending on the wishes of my bosses back at the Agency. This was around late March or early April of 1962. I did not learn until a year later that an approach by CIA led to this - but this gets ahead of events.

•••

Battle assured me the Department wanted to keep me (or a corresponding replacement) as they felt my stay had been constructive. There had been several times when the work of an individual Foreign Service officer was facilitated by having a "captive" CIA man at hand to make connections on one matter or another. He cited two cases, and I was surprised that either had come to his attention. One concerned the Dominican Republic after the dictator, Trujillo, was assassinated; the other Kenya after an outbreak of tribal violence. In both cases I asked our operating division to prepare a situation report of popular sentiment in the area and to have the desk chief come or send someone over to give a verbal briefing. In both cases I was proud of the caliber of CIA man who briefed us. Still, I told Battle, for the longer term I would rather be a participant in an operation than a general liaison man.

For my part, I began to realize that I was facing a re-entry problem in CIA after 15 months outside the agency. It was like my return in 1955 after six years in Germany. This time I thought I had something in my favor. Before the assignment to State Department, I had applied for one of the two fellowships to the National War College that is open every year to representatives of CIA. I had applied the previous year and was runner-up; this time I felt that I had a good chance to be designated to one of the two openings. Nomination to attend a senior War College is a prestigious step in a Government career. Most of the military attendees were earmarked for promotion to flag rank. It would be highly valuable for a future government career to have worked with this caliber of military officers and to be considered one of them.

I went in to discuss this with Dick Helms, by then Deputy Director of Plans, meaning the head of operations and therefore the person to whom I reported.

This time, to my surprise, I found Helms hesitant and, more than that, he seemed determined to talk me out of applying. After all, he said, you have just been mixing with people from other agencies for a year, and to take another year now to do more of the same would keep me removed from the Agency and the scene of the action too long. He agreed that I should be replaced at the Operations Center, and asked me to come back and serve him directly as special assistant to look into some operations that seemed no longer to be the type of thing we should still be doing. He asked me to work out details with Dan DeBardeleben who would be my immediate backstop, and then to come back to see him in a week for further instructions.

I checked at once with DeBardeleben, with whom I had worked well over the past four years. He hinted at the imminence of major changes, and said that Helms' proposal made a good deal of sense. Helms needed the services of some people he could trust, and that this was not only a positive move for me but also a command performance. This was encouraging, but I still began to have a feeling of frustration. I felt "out of the loop."

The following week I made an appointment to talk over my future assignments with Helms. It took a few days to fix a date on his schedule, but his long-time and faithful secretary, Liz Dunlevy, pinned a time when we would have an uninterrupted half-hour. I had a strange foreboding about this meeting. I knew it would bring on a major change in my career, but I had no idea what or in which direction. I had begun to feel in limbo professionally, but I had no idea why, or what to do about it.

CHAPTER 13

OUT IN THE COLD...

It was the Saturday after Thanksgiving, November 27, 1962. The Matthews, our neighbors, had just come by to pick up our children, Jim and Alexandra, for a day's outing with their children. Jeanne had been one of my wife's classmates at Smith College and had majored in modern art. She enjoyed modern paintings, and incidentally owned some stunning ones. Her husband Jack, an ex-Navy officer, was in the Agency's Personnel Department under the Deputy Director for Administration. It was to be a Navy Day type open house in Annapolis. My son Jim, in particular, was looking forward to visiting a real submarine, and Alexandra looked forward to the adventure in general.

Lib and I looked forward to a quiet late breakfast. She was dressed in blue jeans in which she looked particularly trim, and a heavy Norwegian hand-knit sweater that had been a Christmas gift last year from her parents. I knew it would not be a quiet but intense breakfast when she pulled out her yellow clipboard, the sure sign of the logical female mind at work, doing some mental organizing. She showed me the clipboard. On the top page of the pad of yellow lined paper, she had drawn a line down the middle, and titled the two columns: "GOOD" and "NOT GOOD." There was no text yet in either column. She very soberly went down a mental checklist that she had obviously been rehearsing and refining to herself.

"Let me tell you my present reactions," she began.

"You say that you are on ice in your job, and obviously you are, whether on ice or on hold. You seem to be assuming that this 'on ice' condition is a prelude to some new assignment, and I want to hypothesize that it may not be for good, I mean for a good assignment."

She reached for the clipboard and began adding notes as we talked. Her first note made reference to the tapping of our telephone. We knew the phone had been tapped for some time, but dismissed it since I had been subject to many security checks in my lifetime, as had she. However, it had never before reached the extent of total phone monitoring. Lib assigned this entry in the NOT GOOD column.

Next, she considered the broker's call from the week before. Tony Lytton, our reliable but not overly energetic trust officer at Chase Manhattan Bank in New York, had phoned and in an amiable tone asked what sort of trouble I was in this time. It seemed that a pair of FBI agents had visited him to inquire whether Lib and I were living beyond our means. Any security check before had been done by a phone call.

"What did you tell them, Tony?" I asked.

"Aw, let's put it this way." It was Tony's favorite saying, and he chuckled at his own wit. "I told them that as far as the bank is concerned, with those trust funds building up for you back there in Plainfield, you and Libby could spend the rest of your days sailing the Caribbean on a schooner with a full-time crew of two."

"Boy, Tony. You must know something about our accounts that I don't know. Let me know when your great advice gets us to that stage, and we'll invite you along..." Lib grinned, but she had little time for Tony.

"Dear, dear Tony! You didn't tell me about that."

She made a note on her clipboard – "Security check—financial".

"That may explain something," she elaborated, "You know that Marie lady, the nice teller at the Community Bank here. She mentioned to me that some FBI people had been in to see the branch manager to ask about you. I didn't take it seriously as I couldn't imagine the FBI would be so obvious or so loose-mouthed if they were doing a check."

"Did she say what questions they asked?"

"Same as with Tony. Why did you periodically have four-figure bank account balances."

"What did Marie say?"

"It was the branch manager, not Marie, but apparently it was the same theme. They wanted to know if we were living beyond our means?"

"You say they asked about my bank balances. What about yours, which are a lot fatter than mine."

"No," Lib replied. "It's only about you." As Lib saw it, the inquiries were not so much about bank balances in the sense of a credit reference. The questions seemed more to be about whether there were periodic changes in total amounts, or whether there had been a recent change, a recent inflow of new funds. But again, why would the FBI openly send people to the bank, or to the trust officer in New York, both things that could be done by phone. It did not seem that this made sense, if indeed I was being checked for a new job. Lib put both down as "NOT GOOD" entries.

Next came the phony-sounding interview I had with two FBI agents about that engraver from Germany named Ziffer. At the time, the agents felt me out on the plausibility that Ziffer would re-defect to the Germans. Of course, there had never been a genuine issue; the agents just wanted to see my response. Lib entered "German-*phony interview*" into the "NOT GOOD" column.

Actually, I had become aware that there was a comprehensive security-clearance procedure under way while I was finishing up at State Department, back in June or July. I had received calls from several people, saying that FBI agents were asking questions about me. I also had a call from someone at the alumni office of Swarthmore College, also from Dick Smith, my stock broker and college classmate in Philadelphia.

Then there was the evening that two FBI men came to our house and asked to use it as a listening post...for some "remote investigation" they were conducting. Lib had another entry, *phony listening post*, in the "NOT GOOD" column.

"Well. Just a minute, now," I said reaching for the clipboard. The score showed NOT GOOD - 6, GOOD - 0.

We began to conjecture what could have gone wrong and where, but nothing seemed to make sense. Not having been a State Department employee, I had been in a very exposed position in the Operations Center, but I could not think of any incident that would warrant a hostile security check. I still expected the other shoe to drop, and the result to be a job offer. Lib suggested seriously that I resign or change careers. I felt that if something were wrong, I had to stick it out to see what it was. Otherwise, it would seem that I was running away.

• • •

Right after New Year's 1963, I met Barney Bland for lunch. He and Carolyn were the ones who had arranged my marriage in Paris; he was now involved with the housing and caretaking of defectors for the administrative part of CIA's Operations structure. Almost casually, he mentioned his surprise at hearing that I had withdrawn my name from candidacy for the Technical Services job. I did a quick double take at this and told him I had done no such thing. Apparently the job had just been given to someone new to Technical Services work, and Sid Gottlieb would be his new deputy there. This news shook me. I tried not to show my feelings. Then Bland mentioned what a busy Christmas season it had been for him, what with a high-powered defector and his family arriving and requiring housing and attention. Had I heard about him? When I drew a blank, he left me with a hint that he had some other news for me but had not yet received the full story. He gave no picture of what this would be. I was hardly listening. I wasn't interested. What did his "defectors" have to do with me?

More plainly than ever, I was professionally on ice. The concept was still with me, oppressive and demoralizing. I thought to myself that a better description might be "on fire." I felt angry, without knowing with whom to feel angry. Lib had no such hesitation. She felt that Helms had got me into this situation. That made sense.

It was the weekend. Nonetheless I phoned Helms at his home. He was away, but called me Sunday evening when he returned. I told him without wasted words that I was on my way over to see him, that it was very important. Ten minutes later I was at his home on Fessenden Street. I was furious, but felt under control.

I point-blank asked what was wrong. If he wanted me to resign, I would. But obviously something was badly off the tracks somewhere, and I expected him to do something about it. He begged me to be patient just another week or two, saying that "it would be worth it" for me. It was a promise. For the moment, I had no choice but to accept it.

• • •

The following week I drafted several versions of a letter of resignation. I stated that since I had been side tracked for reasons unknown and unexplained, I assumed my career was over. I asked for permission to make my resignation public. It all sounded so lame somehow.

I went to work every day, mostly in my sparsely furnished office. I spent much of the time studying personal investments, the stock market, trends and individual issues. It was a good time to do this, what with an expanding U.S. economy and a long-term bull market sending stock prices ever higher. My efforts paid off well in terms of the net worth of both Lib's and my investment accounts, but it was hardly what the CIA was paying me or anyone else to do.

CHAPTER 14

THE FBI...

The telephone's ringing jarred me out from a heavy sleep that had been filled with vague dreams, mostly scenes of my somehow losing something. How long had it been ringing? I glanced over at the other bed to see if Libby was making any effort to answer it. No, the tousled brown hair just showing over the pulled-up sheets gave me the impression that a studied game of possum was going on.

I reached for the phone noticing the electric clock on my night table showed Monday, 6:17 A.M. My Laugh-a-day cartoon calendar was open to February 11, 1963. The chilliness of my "hello" would have congealed anyone who was calling a wrong number, but this call was intentional.

The caller was Howard Osborne of the Security Office. Sounding somewhat out of breath, he said that he was glad to catch me before I left for the office. (What, at 6-something a.m.?) A top priority assignment had just come up, he said, one that I was well equipped to handle, and Mr. Helms had approved my taking it on, even on this very short notice. It concerned a serious security matter on which my help was badly needed, working with the FBI.

I recalled that Osborne had arranged that phony meeting some weeks ago when two FBI agents came to ask questions about Ziffer, the Polish/German engraver whom I had known from Munich days. I asked if this was related to the Ziffer case? Osborne assured me it was a different matter, and I should check it out with Helms' office if I had any question. At any rate, I was expected at the FBI building at 12th and Pennsylvania, the old post office building, at ten this morning. Just drive in, there would be a guest parking space held for me. I was to ask for Special Agent Taylor. He repeated, "12th and Pennsylvania..."

I got up and dressed, and Lib and I fixed some breakfast. I said to Lib that this call made no sense at all, but at least there was some activity, some movement. The dénouement might well be at hand; perhaps we will now get at the bottom of my being on ice...or on fire...or, she added, "on nothing".

Around eight-thirty I put in a call to Helms' office to confirm Osborne's words. Liz Dunlevy, Helms' secretary, was already in the office and took the call. She said that Helms was away, but turned me over to his deputy, Tom Karamessines. Tom came on the phone immediately. (Was he perhaps expecting my call so soon?) He assured me that he knew of the assignment and of its importance, in fact of its top priority, and that he was sure that I would handle it competently. He told me to report back when the matter was completed. I hung up with foreboding.

I got the Packard out of the garage and headed downtown. I took the same route I followed most days commuting to the H Street office. Yet today it seemed different. The motor seemed peppier; the ticking in the odometer stopped, the tires sipped softly in the slush on the streets. Down to Canal Road and the Whitehurst Freeway, then down Constitution Avenue past the White House, right on Twelfth Street and into the parking lot for the FBI offices in the old post office building on the corner of Pennsylvania Avenue. As instructed, I parked in one of the visitors' reserved spaces, went in and asked for Special Agent Taylor. A visitor's pass in my name was ready for me.

• • •

The old post office building looked like the relic it was, ponderous, stained, unkempt. It stood at an angle to the direction of Pennsylvania Avenue, as if it had been there first. In the blustery February weather, the big old building was stuffy inside. There were four receptionists behind the counter; each dressed in a drab gray smock. One of them gave me an unsmiling "can I help you" look and checked off my name on the list on her clipboard. She handed me a visitor's pass without a change of expression or more than a cursory glance. Clip this on the lapel of your jacket, she said, and "proceed" to the fourth floor. She waved me towards a bank of elderly art deco style elevators, complete with gilded ironwork bedecking the sliding doors.

On the fourth floor, a man with a forced smile held out his hand in welcome. Gray suit, brown shoes, white shirt, waxed-down hair.

"Mr. Karlow, I'm Maurice Taylor. Nice to meet you," he said cordially, asking me to "please" come with him. A soft, New England accent, I thought, if those terms were not a contradiction. Maurice? Unusual name, I pondered where I had recently seen it? Yes. He had been one of the FBI men who came by my house asking us to let them use our garage area as a listening post. I wondered vaguely if that would be brought up. He led me along a balcony that looked down on a huge internal atrium four stories down. I tried to picture it in the past; was it filled with packages, or postal clerks, or lost mail? For that matter, what were all those people at those little desks with all those file cabinets down there doing just now?

Taylor went on further, then turned to the right around the corner, down a corridor, and into a drab but brightly lit inside meeting room. On one side was a government-issue medium-echelon conference table and four standard wood armchairs with their leather seats. Around the room were a small telephone table, two additional government-issue leather-seat straight chairs and a metal file cabinet. Looking down on the scene was a strong jawed, 5 x 3-foot picture of The Director, Mr. J. Edgar Hoover.

"This is Pete Brent," Taylor said, introducing the other man in the room. Another wan, forced smile, gray suit, white shirt, dark brown shoes. Yes, I had met this man before, too. Where? I commented that he and I shared the name Peter. No, "Pete" was only a nickname for him, he explained. His name was Aubrey. Aubrey? Also familiar somehow, but where?

After some pleasantries about the weather, Taylor led off.

"Are you familiar with the nature of what we are here for?" He asked.

My instructions were, I said, only that I was to be of whatever help I can be to the Bureau in a priority national security case.

"That's it. We would like to go over some questions with you and hope you will be cooperative."

"That's why I'm here. Where do we start?"

Silence. My eyes wandered idly around the room. Well lighted for an inside room, the small conference table was big enough for four to sit facing each other, two on each side; some file cabinets on the other side, and a small table with telephone placed so that it blocked another door leading out. No other pictures or decoration except, of course, the double-size photo of Director Hoover. A neat stack of a half-dozen thinly filled manila folders and a leather top opening briefcase with handles and two leather snaplock straps, the government issue type, rested on the floor next to the table leg.

Finally Brent spoke up. "Before we start," his voice was somewhat rasping and officious, but perhaps he was nervous, I thought. "We want you to know that whatever you say will be a matter of record and can be held against you in a court of law. You have the right to keep silent, and you have the right to counsel, to have a lawyer or an attorney with you."

There was silence again.

Whoa!

Just for a moment I thought of the saying attributed to Winston Churchill, that your mind is never clearer than when you feel the noose tighten around your neck.

"Just a minute," I said. This was a strange twist, unexpected at the least. "Would you repeat that?"

Brent went over it again. "What I said is that you have the right not to answer, to remain silent; to be represented by counsel, to have a lawyer..."

I was given the so-called "Rights"...those that have come to be known as the Miranda Rights.

The Rights? Applied to me?

Things were indeed off the track! Clearly I was the target for whatever it was. My stomach tightened. I felt that I was facing a closed door and the door was opening, but I had no idea what was behind it.

"Let me get this straight," I said slowly. I reminded them that my instructions were to help in a major national security case. This then is about me, not about any national case?

No reaction.

"Look, I didn't come here to remain silent, but now, since this is about me, what is the story? Anyway, why should I have a lawyer? And what kind of lawyer should I have?"

There was silence again in the room.

I asked flat-out whether I was in some way accused of something.

"You are not 'accused' of anything," Brent stated quickly. "There *is* a national security problem, and a serious one." He cleared his throat, as though the rasp in his voice was from a sore throat. "We just wish you to know that..."

I stood up. OK, I was under suspicion, but of what? I told them that I've had a feeling for some time that something very wrong has somehow cropped up and was hanging over me.

Taylor spoke up, softly. "As we said, this concerns a high priority case of national concern, and we hope you will cooperate."

I told them that I was delighted to cooperate. What is it that I'm accused of doing?

Brent spoke up, his voice sounding a growing irritation.

"We have told you, you're not 'accused' of anything."

Just sparring, but on their terms.

"We have some questions to go over with you, and these are our procedures if you would be cooperative." He motioned towards the chair on the left side of the conference table; he and Taylor sat down on the other side.

TARGETED BY THE CIA

I looked around the room, and could not help taking in the details of the classic interrogation room. The whole scene could be photographed if there were a concealed camera on the right-hand wall. I tried to see where one might be. Was there one? Funny feeling, I thought to myself, to realize that I was inside one of these interrogation set-ups that you usually read about only in detective novels. So this was the FBI, living up to the popular radio program, "The FBI in Peace and War." A classic interrogation was shaping up here; Brent was playing the "heavy," to intimidate me. Taylor, the "nice guy," served to befriend me. Well, if they want a show, let's put one on. But why, what?

"You see, we have these standard procedures," Taylor added breezily. "We would like to go over a number of things with you in the form of questions about which we hope you can shed some light and which we will take up..."

My eyes were on the picture on the wall to the left, above the end of the table. There was J. Edgar Hoover's standard austere expression framed and staring out sullenly into the room. I wondered if they had microphones set into the photo...maybe a camera? Hardly, certainly no obvious sign of one. And the microphones would more probably be under the table rim, or in a drawer of the table. Or, more simply, in the briefcase.

"...assure you this is of priority importance to the Bureau." Taylor's voice trailed off.

"So it is about me," I said, focusing back on the two men. They were game playing, which I called misplaced if they really were serious.

Again the two special agents exchanged glances.

"As we said, it concerns a serious security matter on which we will appreciate your cooperation." Brent's voice had an even sharper edge now.

I looked at Brent, suddenly remembering when we had met. The Ziffer interview! "Is this connected with your questioning me about that Polish forger?" I asked.

No, it wasn't. He didn't want to discuss the Polish case now, beyond saying that it was apparently "under control." It may be for him, I pointed out, but I had some strong reactions on that interview from my superiors, and since the subject had come up, whatever did happen in that case?

Suffice it for now, nothing, Brent said, in a steely tone. But I persisted, pointing out that the Ziffer case hardly made me feel that anything else they worked on would be any closer to the mark. This is not, Brent said tartly, the place to discuss this further.

Taylor broke in. "Mr. Karlow, we have a serious matter to go into here. Are you ready to cooperate, and do you understand your right to remain silent or have a lawyer?"

"I do want to call a lawyer," I said, "but I have no idea what kind of lawyer to call."

I felt it was time to check back with the Agency and call Larry Houston, the CIA's general counsel. And furthermore, I would be glad to have them hear the conversation.

I moved towards the dial phone on the side table blocking the door across the room, and looked over at Taylor and Brent. "Mind if I make a call right here and now?"

They looked at each other. "No, fine, help yourself. Dial nine to get outside."

I dialed the Agency, and the extension of Larry Houston, the General Counsel. Mary Jean McDermott, Houston's long-time secretary, answered.

"Mary Jean, it's Peter Karlow. I'm here at the FBI and need to check something out with the boss. Could you put me through to Mr. Houston? As I say, I'm over here at the FBI, and I have an immediate matter to take up with him, please."

"Pete," Houston's slight old-Virginia drawl still showed through as he came on the line. "What can I do for you?"

"Lawrence," I called him, more formally than usual. Houston and I had worked on mutual Agency problems since World War II days. "I'm here at the FBI. Osborne in the Security Office seems to have arranged with Dick Helms that I help out here on a priority security project. Do you know the background of this?"

"Well, let's see. You're at the FBI now. Tell me what has happened."

"As much as I can, Larry. You know Howard Osborne in Security. He called me at home this morning at the crack of dawn, to tell me that Helms wants me to report here to the FBI for a special assignment to what he called a priority national security project. I must assume you know something about this; Osborne said Helms had approved it."

"Well," Houston seemed to hesitate. "Has something special come up about which I should know?"

"Yes, Larry. When I got here, I found out that it's no security project but something about me and that I seem to need a lawyer. Before we have even gotten started, the people here have read me my Rights. I am in the dark as to what this is, and what I should do. They say a lawyer could represent me. If so, whom do I get? What kind of lawyer should I have? And for that matter, what about security clearances for a lawyer from the outside? I can't just call someone in off the street. It seems to me it's part of your job to protect employees and if so, do you assign someone to me on this?"

Houston's response was measured, even beyond his usual thoughtful and meticulous way. I was surprised that he was so obviously hesitating, and trying to indicate that he had only a general idea about what this was all about. "Until you find out more about what the problem is, I'm not sure I can do much for you."

What about the job I did for him with Chuck Ferguson of his staff, back on the Economic Action business last summer, the AMADOR project that involved the agent whom I used to call the banana salesman. Chuck and I had good rapport on that job, was there any chance he could help me in whatever this business here implies?

"No, not readily." Houston said that this was for him a bad time to spring anybody. "I don't have anyone available just now."

No.

I was on my own, more so than I could have expected. There was a moment's silence.

Houston went on cautiously to ask if I thought I could proceed at my own speed on this. I could simply stop or step aside whenever I felt anything troublesome would come up.

I hesitated. I frankly had mixed feelings on this. In a way I wanted to get at whatever it was that was hanging over me. In another way, I appreciated the seriousness of needing counsel... but, what about a lawyer? If I didn't get support from Houston, to whom should I look? What kind of a lawyer would I need? What about security clearance problems?

Chapter 15

On my own...

"And for that matter," I added. "Who would pay for it?"

There was another awkward silence. Then Houston came on with a slowly enunciated sentence, to the effect that I should try to work with the people there, and simply reserve on any matter that might bother me.

I reminded him that I was calling directly from the FBI office, with the two Agents present and listening. Whatever it is, as I told them and Houston, I can't think of anything I have to be concerned about, or on my conscience. But why the "national priority" foolishness?

Houston said evenly. "Keep me informed on what happens."

Sure. I hung up.

Taylor and Brent were looking at me expectantly.

"Do you know Mr. Houston?" I asked.

Taylor answered: "Not personally, no. He's legal counsel at the Agency, isn't he?"

"Yes." I went back to the table and sat down.

"O.K. I will work with you on the basis of what Houston just suggested. I cannot imagine what it is that would require me to have an outside lawyer cleared and in attendance."

Brent pulled some files out of his briefcase, and some note pads that he shared with Taylor.

"One thing," I added, seeing their preparations. "I promise my full coopera- tion. I am convinced that something, some sort of misunderstanding, has come up somewhere, and I want to do all in my power to get it straightened out."

"Mr. Karlow," Brent put in. "As you have been informed, this is a priority matter on which we hope you will give us your cooperation. If this is agreeable with you, I suggest we proceed."

"It's your ball game," I replied.

•••

They started a new set of role playing, Taylor still in the part of the conciliatory person, Brent the tough man.

Brent began, sonorously.

"What is your name?"

Really, I thought. "Karlow."

"Peter S. Karlow?"

"No, S. Peter."

"Have you ever used any other names?"

"Yes."

They both looked up at this. I noted the poised pens in their hands, ready to take notes.

"When was this," the agent asked in fervent anticipation that he would elicit a response that somehow held the key to the mystery he was attempting to unravel.

"On operations," the obvious answer, " when required."

They both sat back, as though disappointed.

"Well, no, other than that...tell us about other times..."

And so began a routine security interrogation, similar to the many I had been subjected to in my years within intelligence agencies. I thought of the training manual...and how I was now personifying what it referred to as "the subject" and the idea is to put the person being interrogated as much at ease as possible. It became obvious pretty soon that this would not work smoothly. Only longer, interminably longer. It lasted four full working days.

I was expecting the questions on the first day to start about non-controversial matters, my name, residence, schooling, and travel.

The level and pace of questions were not only pedestrian, but on what to me were unbelievably tiny nit-picks. First of all, expectably, there was the family name Klibansky and the legal change of name. To shorten the questioning, I pointed out that in my files there was a record of a legal change of name approved in the court of New York in 1937.

"Kiblansky? I mean Klibansky?" Unconsciously Taylor had touched one of the reasons that would lead one to want to simplify a name, or at least make it more spellable.

With a touch of testiness, I replied: "The legal action mandates the use of the name Karlow. Does this present you with any problem?"

Taylor looked up. "No. Peter S. Now, the 'S' is for Ser-*gei*?"

Was there a difference between "Sergei" on my birth certificate and "Serge" that I use now, if or when I use it, and which my father also used interchangeably? They spent nearly a half-hour on this, and added time on why my first name was spelled differently on my birth certificate than on most other documents?

"Isn't that inconsistent?"

"It's the same name. With a g-e-i in the Germanic form. That is the way it is spelled on my birth certificate. As a matter of fact, I do not use the name, and rarely spell it out."

"It seems you have used both names at different times. In 1941 on a job application you spelled it g-e-i, the normal way. On other occasions you spelled it g-e. Could you explain this?"

Oh, my. They must have had that application form I handed in to the FBI during my senior year from college.

"Look. It's the same name. Like Ann and Anne with an "e," or Jack and Jacques. Does this really make a difference to you?"

"Perhaps. You have not been consistent on your name."

Brent picked up the questions.

"Kiblanski, I mean Klibansky." Brent was a little embarrassed to have repeated Taylor's mis-step. "Would you please tell us why you changed your name?"

I said that this was in 1937, that mispronunciation was common, and expressed my curiosity about how this really could have a bearing on whatever they were after.

"Does this question bother you?" Brent asked softly.

"No, but how is this part of your priority security problem? You have the court record on this; I assume you've seen it."

"Yes. Since we have to go over a number of questions, we'd appreciate it if you'd cooperate with us so we can move along. Now, would you tell us the reason for the change of name?"

"Certainly, but tell me, how does this really have anything to do with what you'd be interested in?"

Brent cut me off. "Mr. Karlow," he said sharply. "Please answer the question, and do not tell us how we should do our work."

A snappy answer died in my throat. This was obviously going to get worse before it got better. The interrogator game was continuing, to have one interrogator, Taylor, be the "friend," the other, Brent, as the "heavy."

"I will say it again, Mr. Brent. We could save time and not play games with this."

A pause followed. Taylor restated the question quietly. "Would you tell us what the reason was for the change of name?"

"Quite simple. I was 15 years old. My sister had started on what she thought might be a career of her own, as a ballet dancer, and wanted an easier name to use professionally. Also, she didn't want to capitalize on her father's name with anyone who might have known him in the music world. Now," I asked Taylor directly. "How is this priority security information? The legal change of name is on the record in my file, and has been from the start. I have stated this officially in personnel forms on at least three occasions that I can recall over the past twenty years."

"But," Brent continued undaunted. "Why did your sister's career affect you?"

"Because through her friends, my mother and I came to be called 'Karlow' too and, when I finished high school, we went through the legal process and all took the name."

"Once again. Your real name is Sergei Peter or Serge Peter?

I'm sure I showed my impatience more than I intended to. I asked whether they really found this line of questioning useful, because I was ready to call a halt.

"No, that's all right," Brent said. He turned over a page of his notes, or was it a briefing sheet?

"Where do you live?"

"No change from the last personal history statement that I filed. Incidentally, I presume you have copies of it, and of the numerous previous PHS's I filled out over the years."

"You live at 5011 Klingle Street?"

I waited a moment. "You say you have seen my PHS's?"

"Yes. You live at..."

"Then let's say no change since the last one I filled out."

"Mr. Karlow," Taylor cut in somewhat brusquely. "Please cooperate on this. We will make more progress if you do."

Brent continued, gently. "How long have you lived at that address?"

"I have not moved. I am still living there."

"I see. What is your phone number there? Is it 229-3666?"

"No change."

"You were born in New York City?"

"There is, I am sure, a birth certificate on file that I trust you have seen."

"And your birthday was March 5, 1921?"

"Look. Let's be reasonable," I said. I felt a flush of anger but wanted to keep my patience.

Predictably, Taylor cut in. "It would be better if you cooperated with us as we go through these questions. Let's go on.

Brent: "You were born at 1190 Madison Avenue in New York. That was a hospital?"

"No. I was born at home. My mother was following some natural childbirth ideas that interested her at the time. She has told me that she was 23 hours in labor with me, and since I was her last child, I guess that put the natural childbirth theory to rest."

I figured a light touch might be timely to help break the ice that I felt was beginning to crust around the edges of the colloquy. Wrong.

"What theory was that?"

A light touch? Not here.

"I don't know." I shrugged resignedly. "If you are interested, please call her. She's living in nearby Georgetown. I'll give you her phone number; it's 965-2252, and I would be glad to call her to tell her you will be contacting her."

Brent continued unruffled. "You went to school at Friends *Semmanary?*"

The name of the school seemed to roll off the tip of his tongue.

"Seminary. Yes…a Quaker school. I believe it still exists."

"Do you remember any people you knew there?"

Silly. "No."

"Then you went to a school called McBurney?"

"Yes…you know, I can't believe this. I suppose questions about college come next?"

"Yes, you attended *Swath*-more College?" Brent asked.

"Yes, Swarthmore." I replied contemplating how often the college's name is misread or mispronounced.

"From when to when?"

"I was in the class of 1941. It's in all of my PHS's."

They asked about courses I took, and my reactions to life at Swarthmore.

"Who were some of the other students, people in your class, whom you knew particularly well?"

I couldn't see any reason for me to cooperate in this. Was it an empty fishing expedition or was someone in or about the college in some way suspect? If so, they could ask me specific names. I felt a tinge of temper flare up, but managed to say quietly, "It's been a while ago. I believe I gave some names as references in past PHS forms."

"Yes, but what names come to mind when you think of your stay in college?"

I didn't see how names of 25 years ago would add anything now, from any reasonable security standpoint. I could imagine, of course, but did not want to go along with that. I suggested that if they had questions about any particular person, name the person.

What about any professors who had particularly impressed you, one way or another? Again, I was not cooperative.

Then slowly the questions began about my association with the communist-front student organization, the American Student Union. I was listed in the class yearbook as a member. I explained that the page in the yearbook covered student groups of all shades of student political expression. It also showed the rival organization, a Town Meeting, that I helped organize. No, I had not been a member of the ASU, just the opposite.

How about names of some ASU members? I really didn't recall any, or at least didn't want to recall any. Other than those listed in the full roster on the yearbook page, that is.

Then came questions about why I wanted to join the FBI while I was still in college. I explained that I had applied while in my senior year at Swarthmore, what with the war on in Europe, I went to downtown Philadelphia, spoke to someone in the FBI office there, and filled out an application. I thought I might elicit interest, since I did have pretty good German and French. I elicited no interest but I did fill out and submit a personal history questionnaire, and they apparently had a copy to compare with similar applications I submitted since.

One point came up, my father's birthplace. Why did I state "Russia" on some forms I submitted over the years and "Germany" on others? I told my interrogators that at whatever time I filled out the various forms; I was giving the best information I had at the time. I said that I had come to believe that his birthplace was in Germany and that my source of information was my mother, and they were welcome to phone her since she lived nearby in the Georgetown section of Washington.

I asked whether they had checked my father's naturalization certificate? This did not help matters as it turned out. As soon as I got home that evening, I checked out my "Vital Papers" file in the old Army surplus safe that I had in my basement at home. There it was, on my birth certificate in March 1921, my father's place of birth duly shown as "Russia." On his certificate of naturalization dated a few weeks later, it shows "Germany" as his birthplace.

I suggested to the FBI men that they bring this up with my mother. I don't believe they made any effort to contact her. It was increasingly clear they felt that, for their task, it was more important to collect possibly conflicting information to use against me rather, than to analyze it and rationalize and pick out any apparent discrepancies.

I tried to explain that it was not too hard to understand if one went back to the temper of the times. I reviewed for them that my father was invited to come to America before World War I and to take a teaching job in the field of voice development for opera singers. He and my Mother arrived in New York from Germany in 1910. I explained how he had become known as the German Baritone, but by the time war broke out, it became less desirable to be the 'German' anything. I told them how my father's friends began to call him the 'Russian baritone.'

"Anyway, leaving politics aside," I said, "the concept of a Russian baritone had a more glamorous sound. I can only assume that my father may have been living his cover, as one would say in the intelligence world, by putting 'Russia' down as his birthplace on my birth certificate even as late as 1921."

I sensed I was facing a mind-set on the part of the two agents that I was not even denting. Why would anyone say he was born in black-haired communist Russia when he was actually born in blue-eyed blond-haired Germany?

Late in the day, we suddenly realized that this line of interrogation had taken all afternoon and that it was time to stop. We agreed to meet again at nine o'clock Tuesday morning.

•••

I only vaguely recall my drive home. I nosed the Packard northwestward, found only moderate traffic as I was slightly ahead of the peak of the Washington evening rush hour. My mind was somewhat in a whirl; perhaps numb would be a better description. To keep alert, I sometimes used to vary my route home. This time I headed toward Connecticut Avenue rather than along the Canal or up Rock Creek Parkway. I saw a parking space long enough for the Packard on 18th Street near a Peoples' Drug store.

I got out and phoned Lib.

"What happened?" she asked.

In very brief, conscious of our home phones being tapped, I told her she was right with her "score card," but I still had no clue as to what, where, or even whether. She would get the kids into bed early and have a drink ready for me.

During the drive my mind was flooded with questions. I couldn't understand what had happened. It was finally coming to a head. Judging from this morning and the Rights business, I was deeply involved. I still clung to the idea that I was in for a new advanced security clearance for some new job. A best-case analysis, but conceivable. But what a strange way, in effect to entrap me, to lure me over for a "special priority job" with the FBI, only to have the FBI agents read me my Rights.

Or, on the other extreme, had I done something, had I left a safe open again, or was some document missing, or had some operation misfired that I in some way might have known about? Possible, but what and why? If so, why not tell me and let me help in the investigation?

Most likely something happened in the State Department, where there was the constant risk of loose document controls, of classified documents being leaked to the press. This was part of the risk I took being assigned there to work in the Operations Center as one of the very few non-Foreign Service officers there. I had expressed concern on several occasions to colleagues in the Agency that I was keenly aware of my very exposed position there, as I had access to some pretty high-level documents in State. This was one of the reasons I had for asking Helms to assign me back to the Agency.

But why this painfully pedestrian review of my personal history statements? Maybe there were some questions because some of my answers to these comprehensive personnel questionnaires, variously known as "PHS" or "Form 47," or background check forms, may not always have been the same. Perhaps in hindsight I should have kept a master copy of my replies, to refer to when facing another personal history questionnaire. Frankly, I never expected to have to fill out so many so often. Each change of job or organization usually required filling in a new set of personal history forms.

I reviewed in my memory how many times I had filled in various versions of these PHS. What, maybe eight times? Counting back: The first was in August 1941, another set when I applied for the Navy commission in April 1942; Another set within six weeks or so when the OSS was formed. October 1945 when the OSS was closed down, and its successor was formed, the Strategic Services Unit, and placed under the War Department. Another when the War Department became the Defense Department in 1946; and in 1947 when I joined the then-new CIA. Then in 1949, when I was removed from CIA rolls, as I was about to go overseas. I had to apply to the Army to be an Army civilian specialist as there was never to be a mention of CIA being physically present in occupied Germany. In 1953, I had to fill out one more PHS when I took my second overseas tour in Munich with the German intelligence. Again, in 1956, when I returned and went officially back into the CIA. Then one or two times for special advanced security clearances, such as for access to cryptographic materials, or information related to the U-2 spy plane, or whatnot. Eleven, twelve in all. And I did recall that I filled out a form for the FBI in early 1941.

I remember being surprised at some simple questions on the forms, surprised when I realized that I was not sure of the answer. Such as, where was my father born? Was it in Russia or Germany? My father was great at telling stories, sometimes bedtime stories. And he had told about Russia, where he had never been, and he had mentioned various cities like "St. Petersburg" or "Nizhni Novgorod," a name my father liked to roll off his tongue when telling stories.

Actually, what difference did my father's birthplace make? He died in 1931, when I was ten. I was immature for my age. I remember being in a haze about his being no longer there, no longer coming back from his frequent trips when each time he brought me a toy or some sort of souvenir. Childhood memories, but how isolated they seem when revived by questions from the FBI? How incongruous can things be?

•••

Tuesday and Wednesday dragged and droned on. There were moments of naiveté in the questions, like in not understanding that a legal change of name need not have a political or criminal overtone,

Wednesday they started on ancestors on my father's side. What was my grandfather's name? I remember wondering myself for a minute what it was—like being questioned on a college exam about a topic on which you had not prepared. I recalled my mother telling me that my father's father died shortly after my father was born, leaving my grandmother to raise the six or seven children. I recalled my mother mentioning the name Misha, presumably "Michael." What was my grandmother's maiden name? Again, it seemed to me that my mother said it was my grandmother's name? Again, I seemed to recall my mother telling me it was Bertha Vohn, sometimes apparently spelled "Von."

Brent erupted at this, saying that the name was "*Vou*," and why did I not have this straight?

The thought hit me that someone had indeed been sent to the city hall in Frankfurt to look up the records, but could not read the old Gothic German script. With slightly exaggerated patience I drew out a piece of paper and wrote out several words in the angular Gothic script including the name "*Von*" which would readily look like "*Vou* " to the uninformed who might not recognize the checkmark like hook superscript which distinguishes the "n" from a "u."

I asked to see the source of their information, meaning did they have a copy of the record that I could see? No they didn't. Didn't they have someone who could read the Gothic script? Apparently not.

What about other relatives? No interest in my mother's sister, who was then living in England. Back to my father. Did my father have brothers and sisters? Yes, but I did not remember how many. I met only two, a sister in Berlin named Anya and known to me as "*Tante* (Aunt) Fanny." Where was she now? I explained how World War I and then World War II had broken all ties across the Atlantic. I referred them to my Mother, who was, after all, the source of my information.

My Uncle Leon in Paris was a banker of some standing. We had had no contact with him since the time of my father's death. That had been a touching moment. His wife, Eugenie, had died the summer before, in 1930. He wrote my mother asking whether she would come over and marry him? Mother later told me that she had considered it briefly, but that she wanted to remain an American. Remember that it was on Leon's behalf that my father had originally been sent to my mother's parents to ask for her hand in marriage.

Questions in the interrogation then shifted to a rather random array of names of people I had worked with or somehow known in my life. Members of the CIA German Mission in the 50s received attention. Why were there so many homosexuals, only they used the term "fairies," among them? There may have been some, I did not think the term "many" applied, but none attracted my attention or approached me. Name after name came out, each time with the question of "was he a fairy?"

What about the people at TAD, the technical laboratory? I recalled none there.

Next, questions shifted to Washington colleagues. I was surprised at the names included. When Richard Helms' name came up as a possible homosexual, I could not help but react.

"Look, with names like Maurice and Aubrey," I said turning my eyes up at the picture of The Director, "maybe I should be asking *you* about homosexuality in the FBI."

Both kept their reactions, if any, to themselves.

When the name Edgar Hamilton came up, I commented that he, in fact, was "an odd duck." They immediately took this to mean homosexual. I said that if they would note the fact that I had brought this information up to them on my own initiative, I'd have a hot item for them. They agreed. I was being impulsive, and felt frustrated. It was pointless to volunteer information about my visit to France with Hamilton so many summers ago. I rationalized that my account would provide a way to test their system of handling raw information.

I told them that I had not had contact with Hamilton for years, not since he arranged that fabulous summer for me in France when I was age twelve, but that my mother was still in Christmas card correspondence with him. He apparently was retired and living with a relative somewhere in Florida. Or was he dead? She had mentioned to me, some years ago, that Hamilton had been in the U.S. on recuperation from an airplane crash and had somehow gone off his trolley and, while in recuperation, ended up having been arrested on a morals charge somewhere in New England. Apparently, he did a stint in jail for it.

Both Taylor and Brent were electrified: they dashed out, presumably to check police archives. I have no idea what, if anything, they found, but they came back smiling. I reminded them to note that I had brought this up to them on my own initiative. I might have known how they would mishandle it! Sometime later, I would learn the agents used my encounter with Hamilton as some sort of seeming proof regarding my own sexuality.

By Thursday, February 14, 1963, 9 a.m., I was getting tired and testy after three days of aimless interrogation, and even the FBI men were showing signs of strain. Taylor was on the greet when I arrived. I cut the canned pleasantries short by moving past him in the corridor and directly into the office. I knew the way by now. Brent was already there, studiously sorting papers and stacking manila files into neat squares.

I figured it was worth one last try, and asked Taylor when he was going to stop the game playing.

"This is the fourth day," I said. "I trust you are finding this rewarding. Just as a tax payer, I must say I'm skeptical about whether you are accomplishing anything." I told them that I still saw no objective in the questions, "except that you are still fishing for something." Trying not to sound sarcastic, I stated that I appreciated that they both must be first-class interrogators, and I said I found their approach interesting to watch. At some point, could I assume we would get to the point where I would be cut in on what they are after?

Taylor picked it up, acknowledged my impatience, and that I had been cooperative. They still had some more areas to cover, but should finish their questions today. Tomorrow was reserved for polygraphing.

"Polygraphing?" I asked. "About what?"

"Please remember you agreed to polygraphing when we first mentioned it."

"Yes, but—" I sat down at the conference table, and tried again to bring up a review of where we were. I stated that I came to the FBI to help on a project; this turned out to have been only an excuse to get me over here. As if any excuse was needed. I was surprised that I was actually the target of an investigation, and I knew enough about procedures concerning polygraphing to know that I had the right to be told in advance the questions that would be covered. Absent this, there would be no polygraphing, or, I stated flatly, no further cooperation by me.

They assured me that they could understand my position. They were confident that I would have adequate explanation tomorrow before the polygraphing.

"Be patient another day," Brent chimed in. "And in the interest of saving time, let's get started again now."

Brent brought a two-foot stack of manila files over from a side table. I noticed that at least a dozen of the file folders had the familiar characteristic of blue tabs. On several, I recognized the subjects from the tabs. They were the actual files from my technical evaluation staff days. I was surprised. Someone had given them actual Agency files; it must have been with Dan DeBardeleben's knowledge and approval. So Dan must know what this all was about, and cooperated with the FBI in its investigation. As director of Support Services, Dan was my present backstop. We had a warm professional relationship that began with the Technical Board venture. But Dan hadn't breathed a word about this to me, and he was not the type to play coy.

"Let's look now at your activities in the Technical Requirements board," Brent began. "When you started on this requirement for improved audio listening devices, what were your objectives?"

"No way," I said to myself. They can fish around about my personal activities, but I was not going to discuss operational matters. I could dig in my heels here with conviction. The lack of cooperation between the Agency and the FBI was well known, particularly in matters of inadequate audio surveillance equipment.

As calmly as I could, I told them that I had no instructions to discuss operational matters or the substance of my work with them, nor the clearance to do so.

Brent and Taylor left the room briefly to discuss further strategy. Obviously they had reserved this time to question me about my professional life and work. They knew it was out of line, so they could not have been so surprised that I turned them down on this. They had no further questions, so we adjourned early, until nine in the morning.

●●●

Friday, February 15, was to be polygraph day. The way it developed caught me completely by surprise. I did not go up to the interview room. Instead, they met me at the entrance lobby and, once I was checked in, asked me to follow them.

It was now clear that Lib's assessment of the situation was correct, that this interrogation, all four days so far, was not a friendly personal security review preparatory to my being offered a new job with a larger responsibility. Something was wrong. But what? There was no need to play games, to lure me over on that national security case excuse to meet with the FBI. Then lamely to spring the warning to me of my "Rights," which simply confirmed that the investigation was about me, and not about some high-level national security problem. Someone must have thought that I might run off and hide if I were tipped off that I was under investigation. Just the opposite. I was impatient to proceed with it, whatever it was, and if the polygraphing were useful and afforded me the chance to identify the problem, face into the problem, and lay it to rest, then let's get on with it.

Also, and I'll admit it, this would be a chance to see top-level polygraphing at first hand, and report to the Agency psychologists about it.

•••

As we were walking briskly towards the polygraph room, my escorts turned left into the main polygraph center, and I deliberately went eight feet farther down the corridor, to the next door which was open, and I went in. It was, as I expected, the door to the observation booth, and the four men inside were surprised and unhappy to see me barge in and wave a greeting to them before my escorts could grab my arms from behind and steer me out and back to the polygraph room. It all happened so quickly that they had no chance to head me off. I apologized innocently for having taken the wrong turn, but I doubt my innocence fooled anyone.

Then, once inside the polygraph room, when Special Agent Neale read out the words that I was the "principal suspect" for being a mole, I was not shocked. I rather felt an instantaneous, indescribable sense of relief.

Principal suspect? Soviet mole? Spy in the upper echelons of the CIA?

How preposterous!

I was overwhelmed by feelings that a burden had finally been lifted from my shoulders. At least I now knew that the investigation was a farce, and not based on anything real, on any act or fact or event or thing that involved me.

For a fleeting moment I thought about the use of the polygraph and what this would have to do with the questioning of the past four days. Could anything be done on a polygraph to put to rest any questions remaining about things like my father's birthplace? Could polygraphing really dispose of these things and get back to normal now that this had all finally surfaced?

I asked again how could this be useful to refute or disprove the vague allegations that faced me? Were there no facts, specific dates or places or things that were supposed to involve me and to which I could react on the machine? They have their questions, they said.

To Neale and the others, I raised again the point about personal motivation. What possible motivation could I have to make me want to consider working for the USSR or becoming a traitor? This was not the point, they explained. The real issue lay in the inconsistencies and discrepancies in my answers, as though I was consciously concealing something. These items were sufficiently clear to warrant polygraphing.

Polygraphing could do that? It wasn't long ago that I had a routine polygraph test given by an obvious novice. He strapped me into the machine, then stated that he wanted to find out the first letter of my Communist Party code name. I couldn't believe it when he started to ask:

"The letter A?" Then he said, "B." When he got to "C" I unbuckled myself from the machine, left and wrote a strong protesting letter about this to the head of the Office of Security. If going down the alphabet worked, we could surely, I wrote, close down the whole Counter-Intelligence department.

I was mentally at the point where I was almost eager to get the proceedings under way. I could not imagine a more perfect acid test of the polygraph's potential.

Yet someone must be after something. How did I get involved? And to see the confidence the FBI people had that this would come out in the polygraph interrogation.

•••

My mind wandered back to an incident in Germany back in the 50s. A Polish lady named Claudia reached West Berlin from her home in Poznan, in southeastern Poland, carrying a newly issued Polish personal identity document of a style we had never seen. This was serious. Was Poland issuing a new identity document and would this invalidate the present document? If so, it could have a crushing effect on our agents in Poland. The American military police unit at the border crossing point took her into custody and called my Technical Aids representative in Berlin to screen the woman. She was willing to be interrogated because she did not recall how she was issued the document or whether anyone had told her it was new or different.

At my suggestion the Berlin base case officer called on the services of an expert interrogator who arrived from Frankfurt the next day. He brought along his new portable polygraph machine, and Claudia willingly let herself be strapped in and answer questions. The interrogation lasted over an hour and a half, slowed somewhat by the need to have a case officer serve as Polish-English interpreter. At the end, it was clear that she had been issued a new type of document. We later learned from other sources that the Polish government was issuing new documents, but they were appearing slowly, one county at a time, and we would have plenty of time to obtain copies and make our "new originals" as needed.

We congratulated the interrogator, and I commented that he sure could make that polygraph accomplish its purpose.

Oh, he said. "No, not really, I never plugged it in."

For him it was a stage prop.

•••

The technician they called in to join us attached me to the machine with the blood pressure belt on my upper arm, a respiration register around my waist and a little pasty pad to keep in the palm of my hand.

The technician instructed me to listen for the questions, then answer with a yes or no, nothing else. The questions would come at ten or fifteen-second intervals, to give the technician time to view the pen tracks made by the recorder on the continuous-roll reporting tape. We played the usual number recognition game, he asking me to remember a number then asking me with the machine turned on which number it was, and identifying the number. I said to myself that it would be nice if all aspects of intelligence work could be made so simple. After each set of questions, the machine would be turned off and the questions and answers reviewed, before proceeding to the next set. Since the blood pressure cuff became painful to me if left on too long, they agreed on frequent pauses in the questioning, to give my arm a rest.

The course of the questions indicated quite quickly how far from the mark the polygraph would be.

Right off the bat, homosexuality, during that summer in France when I was twelve. The question, seriously asked, was whether there was sodomy involved? I hesitated before my yes/no answer, as I had to think for a moment, what actually was sodomy? I assumed it meant anal intercourse, the old British term "buggery," not an attractive prospect to me under any circumstances. I smiled to myself when I thought I heard the indicator pen scratching away animatedly. The machine may have interpreted my hesitation as reflecting a feeling of guilt, and I noted that the question was repeated once more before the session ended. That is part of the interrogation, to work in a repeat of a questionable answer.

At the break, I reiterated the point I had made to them before, that the record should show that I volunteered the information about Hamilton and my stay with him as a twelve-year old. Regardless, I would later see that the final record would show that the FBI men came upon this as new information, through their efforts alone.

Where was my father born? Germany or Russia? No amount of explanation about life in the musical world in the time of World War I seemed to register. I explained again how the point was reached back then where a German in the U.S. who was not yet a citizen no longer admitted birth in Germany. Particularly after the war began to lap at U.S. shores, as with the *Lusitania* sinking.

What about my father's relatives abroad? I said we were out of touch with all of them, except for my father's brother in France, my Uncle Leon.

So I did have relatives abroad. Why was I hiding information on them? I stated that all my information came from my mother, that they should go interview her.

Next, did I ever knowingly pass information to the Soviet Union? Was there, I asked, any evidence of this that I could comment on specifically? No answer.

Did I ever take classified material home? Yes, sometimes. Did I ever discuss classified matter with my wife or with my mother? Possibly, in that both my wife and my mother had had operational clearances, and my wife's was still valid. Or so I thought.

Did I ever discuss technical equipment matters with my mother? Hardly; she was quite un-mechanical and used to joke about her inability even to change a light bulb.

What was my mother's father's name? Alfried. What was my father's father 's first name? I didn't offhand know, but would be glad to ask my mother, or why don't they ask her directly themselves?

The next round involved photographs, 7x5 enlargements of faces of men all casually dressed, most with bushy hair, some in army fatigue type clothing. The pictures were shown to me one at a time. Did I know this person? No. On the fourth picture, the interrogator noticeably hesitated before showing me the picture, as though giving tacit emphasis to it. Again, I recognized no one.

Afterwards, I could not resist commenting that they apparently wanted me or expected me to react to the fourth picture. I regretted not being able to oblige. They denied that they emphasized any of the pictures when they showed them to me, but did not describe who the subjects were.

They sprang a new name on me. How well did I know SASHA? I said that I knew a Sasha and they all visibly perked up at this, but everybody in the USSR business knew him. I referred to Sasha Sogolow, a highly effective Soviet Russia Division operations man. Finally they asked me if I ever used SASHA as my code name. No, I had not. They obviously assumed I had. What about LYDIA? I drew a blank on that. Did I ever discuss secret writing techniques with someone by that name? No. It seems that LYDIA was a female Russian or East German agent training person who is alleged to have worked with me at some time in East Berlin.

How often did I visit Berlin? I thought every year. Actually, it was only twice in the six years I was in Germany. How often in East Berlin? Only once, in 1951, when I went on a U.S. Army guided tour through East Berlin.

Then came questions about five penetration operations against USSR targets that I must have known about because technical equipment matters were involved. Since all five operations failed, was I the cause of their failure? I recognized only one, an operation of which I had been highly critical when I first heard of it. It involved intercepting five new American cars purchased by the USSR Embassy in Mexico City which were intercepted by the delivery agent. Each car was bugged with the best equipment that the CIA had available, then sent on to Mexico City. Apparently the bugs were detected almost immediately and removed, presumably by their Soviet purchasers. I didn't think the equipment our technical people had available at that time would be good enough to withstand inspection by trained security personnel

Homosexuals came up again, in questions about the number of them serving in Germany in the time I was there, meaning in the early 50s.

"Skip it," I said feeling tired and irritable.

What did I know about the Soviet audio surveillance system used against the American Embassy in Moscow, which the CIA had code-named EASYCHAIR. This was the system where the Russians beamed microwaves through the Embassy building and then planted passive microphones, meaning units that required no power but served to modulate, to affect the microwave screen so that the voices they overheard could be monitored outside the Embassy. I said I was aware of the system and that we apparently had no countermeasures or competitive device as yet.

The session was over. I refused further questions then or tomorrow, saying they were aimless and pointless. My watch said 4:30 and my arm was ready to drop off from the constant exposure to the blood pressure cuff. Applying it as tight as they did, I got a taste of torture. No, I concluded to myself sadly, I'm not the torture-resistant type; tickle my toes and I'll tell you anything if not everything. The relief from tension and the cuff brought tears to my eyes.

We moved to the conference table as the FBI men seriously pondered the scrolls of wiggles recorded by the four sets of pens of the polygraph. There were large purple marks applied by felt tip pens in places on the printout, apparently to call attention to questionable results or items requiring further investigation.

The more they pored over the polygraph sheets and the annotations, the more they expressed concern over serious inconsistencies or actual dissimulation. I suspected this was largely for effect, to make me think that the machine had uncovered some or several lies, despite any efforts by me to dissimulate. Whatever, I was in no mood for further games.

They began a new series of questions. Why did I lie about...and the same series of topics was read out. Again, alleged homosexuality at age 12, my father's birthplace, my relatives abroad, talking to my wife and mother about operational matters, the REDSOX operations that I knew about and that all failed, the EASYCHAIR eavesdropping system. They said solemnly that there were still several areas where I appeared to be withholding information or giving evasive or misleading answers. At this point the situation got the better of me. I recall I had tears in my eyes... tears of futility. I took my identification badge off my neck and tossed it onto the table.

"Well," I said, "that ends my career. What a waste...twenty years down the john." And all this apparently over a series of questions about what has been in the files for all the twenty years I had been in the intelligence business. And no facts, no incidents, no specifics of what I am accused of having done, when, where, how, with whom, involving what. Furthermore, why was no CIA representative here? I got up and asked to be shown the way out.

Neale was almost solicitous, handed me back my badge, saying any action about my status was up to the CIA as they in the FBI were only investigating. When would their report be ready? In the next few weeks. Would I see a copy so that I could comment on it? That's up to the CIA.

Somebody escorted me to the parking lot and I drove home, though I was completely in a daze and remember nothing of the entire trip. Except nosing the Packard into the garage a bit noisier than usual, giving the engine a final loud rev, slamming the car door, uncharacteristically leaving the garage door open, and bursting into the front door where Libby was coming out to meet me, obviously realizing that something was wrong.

CHAPTER 16

STROKE...

After getting over her first shock at seeing me, she told me that she feared I had had a stroke. She wrestled my coat off my shoulders, drew me into the living room and let me sprawl out on the sofa. She disappeared for a moment into the kitchen and came back with a warm cup of coffee. I guess events all caught up with me at once, as I broke down in tears for a moment. It cleared things up for me.

In a voice still husky with emotion, I said what I was thinking: "What a waste! What an unbelievable waste!"

Lib rejoined with an attempt at a light touch.

"You say unbelievable?" she said. "After the past few months, I'll believe anything."

Her reply was predictable.

"Oh come off it...are you serious? Are they serious? Who, the FBI? When? Where? How? Why? You of all people. Why you?"

I remember that I looked down the hall at the Picasso print we had bought on our honeymoon in Paris ten years ago; somehow the distorted red and green eyes of the woman's head, part profile, part front view, seemed to describe my mood.

"Whatever happens," I said, "this means the end of my life with the CIA."

I noticed that I said "CIA" and not "The Agency" or any other affectionate term such as the "Pickle Factory." Was I already beginning to separate myself from what had been my life over the past twenty-plus years? I pulled myself together and reviewed for Lib as composedly as I could the events of the day, the arrival in the polygraph room, the initial conference, Neale's chilling words about my possibly being a Soviet spy. At least, I said with wry gallows humor, if I am to be a suspect, I might as well be the "principal suspect."

Lib was a tower of strength. She asked me if I was too tired to answer some questions about their interrogation techniques. If anything, I'm too keyed up to be tired. She then started systematically: Did they just go down the list of topics they had raised in the four-day preliminary questioning? In other words, did they get beyond the issues of my father's birthplace, the alleged homosexuality, and the operations I might have blown?

For example, in interrogations on which she had helped prepare materials, there always was provision for the sudden injection of surprise topics. Had they used this technique on me? Well, they had, in the sudden introduction of those photos, and how I thought that they expected me to recognize the fourth picture they showed me. Also the name "SASHA" as though this were a code name applied to me. Oh yes, and LYDIA, my alleged female secret writing instructress in East Berlin.

Lib pointed out a glaring gap: At no time did they mention any specific event or date. As close as the questions ever got was about LYDIA; when did I see her? Presumably on one of my trips to Berlin, but no dates mentioned.

Here, then, was the path to take to begin to get a handle on whatever it was we were faced with. Dates. When was what supposed to have happened?

Something else Lib pointed out. If I were to be a real mole, a real spy penetration over the years, I would have kept the data on my personal history forms consistent. In Lib's work with the Agency's SR (Soviet Russia) Division, excess consistency could look as suspicious as some inconsistencies.

Another large question was the absence of interest in Lib herself by the questioners. Yet Lib had been deep in SR Division operations, in fact, in the counterintelligence operations, playing a small but key background role in providing detailed analysis of past statements by suspected agents and drafting questions for the case officers to take up in future interrogations.

So many signs pointed to nothing, to no basis in fact for any of the investigation of me. How could something like this start? Who all knows about it? Obviously the Security Office knew...inevitably also Dick Helms, Tom Karamessines, Liz Dunlevy. What about Larry Houston? None of them gave me a hint of any difficulty. Nor did Dan DeBardeleben, my immediate boss.

Lib suggested I hand in my resignation as noisily as I wished, and leave the business now. She had actually been hinting at this for some time this past year. We talked it over, looking at all alternative courses. I felt strongly that there were no alternatives to staying on and smoking out whatever it was that started this all in the first place. She finally agreed that I could not leave without somehow unraveling this case and clearing my name, whatever this would take.

First thing, it would take a lawyer. Whom? Someone from outside? No, we'd have to start with Houston. It was by then 4:30 in the afternoon. I called Houston at his office, was told he had gone home. I reached him at his home in Georgetown, told him with no preliminaries that I was on my way to see him.

Houston had a roomy, colonial style house in Georgetown not far from P Street and 30th. I was there in less than 25 minutes, said a cursory "hello" to his lovely wife Jeanie, and went to join Larry in his study. I was in no mood for small talk.

"How is it," I asked, "that I am accused...yes, let's use this word...of being a spy? Why this pussyfooting, not alerting me or making the slightest effort to maintain the basic principle of innocent until proven guilty? How did this start and what am I supposed to do about it?"

Houston tried to calm me down, assuring me that this was part of a much larger matter, highly serious in the eyes of top Agency officials. Of course this all may or may not have anything to do with me but the way events developed, it was considered best to take me somewhat by surprise. I snorted at the word "somewhat." Houston asked me to view this calmly and logically, that he was indeed not fully read in on either the operation or its timing. My task now was to write out everything I recall from the interrogation, all the points raised and my responses to them.

I should drop everything, do this report, and come see him as soon as I was done. Meanwhile I should by all means check in with Helms Monday morning to plan strategy, also with the head of the Security Office, Sheffield Edwards, to find out when the FBI report is expected.

Do I need a lawyer? Probably, at some point. I strongly suggested his designating someone from his staff, because if I have to recruit a lawyer from outside I will consider any and all security restrictions on this case or anything about it to be suspended. He would discuss this further with me, and urged me to keep myself under control. I was directly threatened, yet may only be a part of a complex and most serious matter that had arisen and that I would find out about as we go along, and please to be patient.

It was not a satisfying visit. I got to work the same evening pulling my notes together, trying to relax over dinner and wine, then a hot bath and a fitful night of strange disjointed dreams.

●●●

Nine o'clock Monday Morning, February 18, 1963… I was at Dick Helms' office. He would be in a little late this morning. I therefore went over to the Security Office and was shown right in to Edwards' office. He looked terrible. His face was flushed, beet-red and his hands… he had the start of Parkinson's Disease and his hands trembled, particularly when he was excited, as he plainly was.

I asked him what in the world was happening and would he please brief me. Instead, Edwards spat out a litany of vile.

"You are a spy! You are a traitor! It is a matter for the Director to decide if you should be fired or allowed to resign."

It was my turn to blow up. I used such adjectives as sick, super-annuated, and has-been and that I wanted to know what brought this up, what got me involved, and how come am I guilty until proven innocent? What specifically involved me in this mess?

It was a most unsatisfactory meeting and I stomped out of the office outraged. It took a while to pin down a block of uninterrupted time with Helms.

I wanted to see Helms both as a boss and as a colleague and friend of long standing. I told him that, with this kind of vague suspicion circulating around me, it was obvious that my career was over. I had no idea where this started, how it could be stopped, and what I could do about it. He assured me he was not fully brought in on the case. From what he learned of the situation so far, he felt confident I could take care of myself and, of course, he would inform himself and keep his eye on developments. He agreed with Houston's suggestion that I write everything out in detail and hand it in to the FBI, "which had full jurisdiction in this case," he noted as an afterthought.

I told him that Sheff Edwards had literally called me a traitor to my face. What backstopping could I expect from the operating elements of the Agency to counter this? I wanted a hearing or a board of inquiry composed of operations people, not Security people or FBI, so that I could hear the facts in the case and the complaints about me and clear my name. Helms said the next step depended on what the FBI reports conclude.

To say the least, I did not feel encouraged by Helms' response, or rather lack of response. I could not imagine that he lacked the authority to step into my case, either to bring out specific incidents and times, which I could rebut, or to get the case dropped as insubstantial. It was obvious to me that he was not going to take any action on my behalf, regardless of the merits or lack of them of the case.

On my way back to my office I met Barney Bland in the hall. He greeted me warmly and asked me to come with him into his office. He said that he had wanted to talk with me alone and at greater length over the past weeks but wasn't yet sure of his facts. Seeing the anger in my face, he said it was most timely that he give me some background that I badly needed.

Barney was in charge of, as he described it, the care and feeding of Soviet defectors. One such defector, who came out last year over Christmas, identified himself as a KGB Major. The CIA people who handled the defector, his wife and his daughter, described him as "a disagreeable bastard" but he had some hot information on several subjects that might be of major importance to Jim Angleton and the counter-intelligence people.

It seems, Barney explained, that one of the first things he told was that there was a high-level Soviet spy, a mole, that the KGB had planted in the CIA. He described the mole as having a last name beginning with the letter "K" and with a technical equipment background. Also, the suspect had operated in Germany and was of Slavic descent. To Barney's dismay, this was interpreted by Angleton, the vaunted chief of counter-intelligence, and his people as referring to one person and only one... namely Peter Karlow. Just a few years before, several British intelligence officers were arrested for spying on behalf of the Soviet Union and the case was still vividly in mind. Angleton called for urgent, top-level action. National security cases were the mandate of the FBI.

By the time Barney had found out about it, the Security people and their FBI colleagues were well along, swarming all over this one in a sweeping investigation ordered personally by the FBI Director, Mr. J. Edgar Hoover.

"Well," I asked, "who is this defector and wouldn't it be valuable for our people to know that, at least as far as his identification of me is concerned, that he is inaccurate?"

Barney agreed, but it seems that the defector, whose name was Anatoliy Golitsin, had come up with some additional information beyond what he had reported to date, most of it confirmatory rather than new stuff. It was sufficient to convince Angleton that this was the hottest source on USSR matters that had come across since the Penkovski case. Obviously, if the identification of me were not accurate, it would cast doubt on all the rest of Golitsin's reporting.

Barney told me he would continue his snooping around on this case, and also urged me to be discreet but to talk about it to my other close friends in EE and SR Divisions who might shed added light on where the case is going.

My next stop was Jim Angleton's office. He asked me in at once, told me that he was aware of my problem. He begged me to talk to no one about this, and to be patient. I must realize, he explained, that the case in which I had become involved had some highly sensitive angles that he mentioned only in a background sense.

Angleton was well known for his way of explaining a situation so that you felt you were reading a book without text except a series of chapter-by-chapter executive summaries plus infinite detail on otherwise unintroduced names or events. He emphasized that this case was so sensitive that I must be patient until the full FBI transcript can be gone over. He repeated that by all means I should speak to one else about the case.

I assured Angleton that since my life and reputation were at stake, I reserve the right to discuss this as I saw fit, and would keep my own BIGOT list showing the people with whom I have conferred. Angleton barked a final order at me, "Don't talk to anyone," over his shoulder as he abruptly took off through a side door into a back office, and his secretary came in to suggest I make another date to see him.

It took me over a week to prepare a comprehensive memorandum, which I addressed and delivered to Mr. Helms. I started it with a summary of the case as I understood it and ended with a demand for a full hearing in CIA before my peers. My main points were that the so-called discrepancies in the files had been there all of my twenty-plus years of service. I wrote that no specifics were produced, names, places, things to which I could respond, and that I wanted a hearing before CIA officers to go into this whole mess and get my name cleared.

"I realize that, through an incredible error by the FBI, I have come so deeply under suspicion of treason that my career in CIA is ended. I have no intention to end a 21 year intelligence career with any undeserved stigma in leaving CIA or in future job references from CIA or the FBI."

Helms sent the memo on without comment to the Office of Security. I checked there and with General Counsel Larry Houston some days later to see if there had been any report from the FBI. There was. In the summary of my interrogation, one sentence was shown to me:

"Based on the overall interpretation of the [polygraph] charts obtained, it appears that Karlow was under extreme tension and was possibly withholding information on some of the relevant questions which were asked."

The issue was joined. I was facing a determined effort to get me fired with prejudice, at all costs, based only on allegations and irrelevancies. And as for the mole business, I had to disprove something that never existed in the first place!

I demanded a meeting with Houston and the head of Security. Edwards did not come, but sent his deputy, Robert Bannerman, a former State Department security officer who had transferred to the CIA and was openly after Edwards' job. Apparently, because of Edwards' advancing illness, no one wanted to pressure him into retirement.

I demanded specifics: What specifically I was alleged to have done where, and with whom?

Within a few days I was given two dates. Can I prove I was *not* in East Berlin on January 6, 1950, and on August 25, 1951?

Back home, Lib and I labored over calendars and travel receipts. I recall she commented off-handedly that some day I should write a book about this, and should title the book "Don't Keep a Diary," citing a recently issued CIA personnel directive with that title. We found what we needed in a few hours' time:

January 6, 1950 — I was on my way from the U.S. to Germany to start my job of setting up a technical laboratory. I had spent a dull New Years Eve on the French luxury liner *Ile de France* and stopped off in Rheims, between Havre and Paris, to visit Captain Jean l'Herminier and his wife Madeleine. It was a cozy visit, in the course of which l'Herminier gave me an autographed copy of his just-published book, *"Casabianca."* It was the story of his command of the submarine, its 1940 internment at Toulon, his 1943 escape to join the Allies in North Africa, and his missions for the OSS. He presented it to me with a friendly and flowery dedication,

August 25, 1951. This was the date Lib remembered before I did, and I should have reacted faster. It was the day on the weekend when I proposed marriage. We were in Salzburg, Austria for the annual folk festival and stayed at the Army rest center in nearby Berchtesgaden. We sent a telegram to a friend living in Salzburg to do us the favor of going to the rest center, now called the Patton Hotel, to check whether our names were still on the register as proof that we had been there. Apparently they were.

I personally presented a memo on the two dates to Bannerman, with copy to Houston. A few days later Bannerman, Houston and I met again in his office. Bannerman acknowledged having checked both dates. His comment was one I will never forget:

"It shows you must be a high level agent, or you would not be so well documented."

•••

Armed with this insipid comment, I arranged a series of meetings with Houston, with Inspector General Lyman Kirkpatrick, and with Helms respectively. I demanded a letter that would recite my having become drawn into a security case in which I was thoroughly investigated but in which I was not involved. I wanted a further statement that the CIA wishes me well in my future career. Then I could resign.

Every draft that appeared contained an additional clause that I called the "not-not clause." The clause would state that while my involvement was *not* shown, the case was *not* closed by the FBI.

On March 12 I had a note from Helms not responding to questions I had raised, but stating that he thought it "would be preferable if you raised the problems in your note with Larry Houston [and] regard him as your point of contact until matters are resolved."

Bannerman then raised a new question. What about extensive time-off that I was alleged to have taken while chief of TAD, the technical laboratory in Frankfurt, in 1950-51, implying that I had taken the spare time to become a Soviet spy. To rebut this, I presented a copy of a commendation I received from the psychological warfare elements of CIA in October 1950, including wording like this:'

"...Also, at this time, we want to extend our thanks to every one of the personnel...who have been unselfish enough to frequently sacrifice their own time during evenings and weekends in order to produce certain rush orders at our request. In spite of this load of work and lack of sufficient personnel on your staffs, you have produced many different kinds of technical work of high professional caliber. Without such able assistance from the men of [TAD], several operations of value to our program would never have seen satisfactory completion."

I sent a copy of that to Bannerman with a note that "I never, in 21 years of intelligence, drew overtime pay." Another silly question disposed of, I hoped.

By May 9, I had again summarized my position in a memorandum to the Deputy Director, General Marshall Carter. I restated my position, that

"...an exhaustive investigation of me was launched by the Office of Security and the FBI. The investigation produced nothing to show I was in any way involved with the case. Nonetheless, suspicion persists.

"There was nothing I could have done to avoid this suspicion as there was nothing I did to generate it."

Houston summarized his view of the case in a memo to Gen. Carter dated May 13, 1963. He noted my request that my situation "be reviewed in the light of his past performance and his long service...I believe this is a reasonable request, and am informed that [Mr. Helms] is...sympathetic to minimizing the adverse effect this episode would have on Mr. Karlow's future. We are all, I believe, concerned by the fact that if he is completely innocent, as is quite possible, such an adverse impact would be a great injustice."

Nonetheless, pressure continued, as did my refusal to resign under a cloud. On July 3, I received a formal letter, addressed to me at my home, from Kirkpatrick, the Inspector General. The letter expressed impatience over my not yet having resigned. It continued that the acting Director of Central Intelligence (Gen. Carter) would decide–

> *"as to your termination under his statutory authority in section 102(c) of the National Security Act of 1947, as amended. As all aspects of your case have been discussed with you in great detail over the past four months, no further proceedings are contemplated except to notify you officially of the final decision."*

> *"Sincerely,*
> *Lyman B. Kirkpatrick*
> *Executive Director"*

–but with source initials "LRH" showing as author, meaning Houston.

CHAPTER 17

CHECKING OUT...

On July 5 I was called into Houston's office. Bannerman was there and officiously demanded I surrender my plastic building pass, then escorted me out of the building with a large plastic "Forgotten Badge" around my neck. More psychological pressure.

Houston called me into his office three days later, on July 8. I got as far as the main lobby at the Langley headquarters, but I could not, of course, get into the building without my building pass. I refused to come in on a visitor's badge. Houston's secretary came down to the lobby to beg me not to be stubborn on this. I said I would wait until someone brought me my badge, which was presumably in Bannerman's office. An impasse of one and a half-hours resulted while I waited patiently in the lobby. I sat on the bench staring at the gold lettering on the opposite wall, the quote from the Bible, "You shall know the truth and the truth shall set you free."

We finally compromised. I would come upstairs on a visitor's pass, but my building pass would be returned to me upstairs. The badge was duly found and returned to me.

At the meeting, I handed in text for a resignation that I would find satisfactory, including sentences like "The investigation did not show he was involved in the case in any way" and "the case has left no stigma on his CIA record." Trouble was that some people, who were doing some alternate drafting, still wanted to include a second sentence, that the investigation "did *not* show he was *not* involved."

The final letter was completed by Houston and shown me on July 18. It included a sentence about my "long and valuable service to intelligence." I was to take three months leave without pay to see if this case would blow over by then, also to give time for CIA early-retirement legislation finally to pass Congress. With 20 years of service, six overseas, I would qualify for the operations officer's pension at age 50.

I approved this letter; it became Executive Registry document number ER 63-5743, and it was agreed, as I requested, that a copy would be stored in safe hands *outside* CIA. The safe hands were agreed to be those of former deputy director Frank Wisner, now retired. Wisner was a leader in building CIA's psychological action structure.

•••

As part of my round of farewell calls in the Agency, I stopped to see Dick Helms in his office. He greeted me warmly. It was a brief meeting. He said, in parting, that I would never know how valuable my work has been to him and to the Agency. I agreed; I tartly said that I would probably never know.

•••

On September 24, 1963, I drafted a letter of resignation to General Carter, noting that this was the 22nd anniversary of the day "when, in 1941, I began my 22 years of continuous service in intelligence." I added a paragraph:

"I would also like to express to you my appreciation for the long discussion we had on the subject of the memorandum of 18 July 1963 (ER-63-5743). I should have insisted on seeing you much sooner about this matter, and regret that my only direct contact with you concerned my decision to resign from the Agency."

This letter was sent by registered mail, return receipt requested, to assure its delivery.

•••

The transition from working for government to working for business was more difficult than I had expected. First of all, there were ingrained security habits for me to overcome. It took me a while to get used to talking in practical terms about what I had been doing professionally. Secondly, business attitudes towards intelligence are very different from those in government.

My first challenge came when I was officially "processed out" of the CIA in the last week of September 1963. The Security Office and the Personnel people had developed a standard checkout procedure and, apparently, every employee who left the CIA for whatever reason had to go through it. The whole operation could take up nearly two full exasperating days to live through.

The idea was to protect CIA's security by impressing upon the resignee that security constraints on such things as writing or talking about CIA activity continued in effect even after separation. In addition, it was part of the personnel "debriefing" or relocation procedure that the Agency conducted, to help a person like me who was leaving the Agency to prepare a resumé and to describe my various jobs in a way that protected CIA but also helped the individual. Well meant, but the end-product "resumé" was blissfully vapid and all in gritty government-ese. It never mentioned "CIA" but referred to obscure offices in the "Department of Defense," giving actual room numbers in the Pentagon and working phone numbers that would when called look up your name and take a message for someone to call back. I tried it out, reached a pleasant female voice that took only about fifteen seconds to find that I was not at my office and could she take a message?

The resumé itself was replete with terms like "implementing the coordination," or "comparative analyses of priorities" or "developing interrelationships between staff and line elements." It was a transparent attempt to hide rather than to inform, done by people who had no apparent experience of hiring in the private sector.

The checkout procedure had its sad but comic overtones. For example, for my checkout I was turned over to a junior clerk from the CIA personnel office. She tried to be helpful but it was hopeless. I finally asked her to go back to basics: How could anyone judge my qualifications for a job if I could not describe what I had been doing? Anyhow, even if I told with some degree of accuracy what I had been involved with, it didn't offhand mean much to people with whom I interviewed while I was looking for a job. The Hungarian revolt? Special weapons? The Berlin Wall? The State Department Operations Center? The OSS War Report?

Then came a questionnaire on my feelings about leaving the CIA. What were my positive memories? What did I think could be done to overcome shortcomings? I said I had no comments.

The final item on her checklist was to brief me on how to apply for public unemployment compensation. At this I cut our conversation short.

The next and greatest challenge was that I literally had to learn how to talk to "outsiders" about CIA work. It took some time to work out for myself ways to describe my past activities in generic terms. I engaged the help of a professional counseling firm. I learned a great deal from people like a former Navy submarine captain who had just retired from the Navy. He used a description of how the responsibilities of a submarine commander were entirely comparable to those of a plant manager. This gave me some good ideas. My function could safely and informatively be described as obtaining basic operating information on foreign countries, mostly for free, from government resources. Much of this was a matter of knowing where to get it, and then organizing it together with other information so that the results will be useful to the company's executives in their market planning and international operating responsibilities. Then I added some wrinkles about international government relations, and the identification and measurement of risks to investments in countries abroad.

I found a temporary job with Worldwide Information Services, a New York based business news network relying on newspaper "stringers", correspondents working for the existing news services who in addition contributed articles on demand. My main use to WWIS was in Washington to take clients to meet congressional staffers and committees. It took some eight long months of feeling around, networking, travelling and interviewing. I finally received two job offers in the same week, one from Xerox in Rochester, and the other from Monsanto in St. Louis. I picked Monsanto.

The introduction to Monsanto developed through my friend and colleague from OSS days, Edwin J. Putzell. Ned was General Counsel to Gen. Donovan at the end of World War II, and was currently general counsel at the St. Louis based company. He wanted some more executives in Monsanto with formal intelligence awareness. He felt strongly that an intelligence background gave good training in decision making for key people in all parts of the company.

We got together in Washington to discuss my joining Monsanto and developed an immediate rapport. I made it a point to brief Putzell on the circumstances of my leaving CIA, which he appreciated. Actually, he had heard generally about it, but he promptly checked on my situation and me with people who had close CIA contacts. I was somewhat apprehensive about how CIA would vouch for me, and was pleased to have him say that he found nothing that would stand in the way of my having a successful career in Monsanto.

We moved to St. Louis in August 1964. It was for us a new place with new people and new challenges, out of the morass and unhappy memories of the last days of our Washington lives. I was with Monsanto for better than thirteen years, thirteen very interesting and exciting years for me. I was able to go deeply into the similarities and contrasts in intelligence requirements between business and government, where the two were at irreconcilable odds and where each was indispensable to the other, like it or not.

Business views of an intelligence function were much more immediate and tactical than those in government. The basic ground rules were so different. In government you developed a function or a process that was designed to augment an existing overall program. The key measure was in the number of people involved. In business the pressure was on you to earn your keep, and the key measure was in the net financial results of your efforts, and would they cover expenses and more, if not in this quarter then in a projected but not too remote future quarter. In government the idea was to provide a service. In business the name of the game was growth.

I was fortunate that for my early days at Monsanto my immediate superior, Shea Smith III, became an invaluable mentor for me. A long-time executive with the company, he had served in various plants and division headquarters and as Corporate Secretary. Smith, a stocky redhead, was an unusual combination of chemical engineer and global political scientist. He was an energetic sportsman what with yachting, fishing, hunting, and travel. Smith started me off with a three months familiarization program, going down the corporate organization chart and marking key people in each division for me to meet. He wanted to let me brief people in person on what I could do to help them, and on what type of information they needed.

There were some surprising results. For example, the Inorganic Chemicals division wanted to update its market survey for toothpaste use in Venezuela. One product sold worldwide by the division was a phosphate base for toothpaste. How could we better estimate the consumers' habits and needs for toothpaste all over the country and not just in Caracas? I had no idea how to get this type of detailed information, and set off to Washington to make calls.

If U.S. business needs this type of information, should not our Government have it somewhere and make it available? I wasn't sure, but began to look around. I contacted the Venezuelan desks of Commerce and State departments. Commerce had some nine-year old information on consumer use of soaps and toiletries. Since no one had shown any interest in this reporting, it was not renewed. If I would send in some specific items to investigate, they would be glad to oblige.

State Department did even better. There I was introduced to a veteran U.S. Public Health doctor who had just returned from three years in Venezuela, and had traveled around that country extensively. I pricked up my ears when he mentioned his views that poor local dental hygiene habits were a good reflection of local economic development. He cited his informal surveys of how people brushed their teeth (using tooth brush, fingers, sand, soap, leaves, cloth) and I immediately was on the phone to the Inorganic people suggesting they invite the doctor to St. Louis for consultation. They did, and later commended me for coming up with such a good information source on such short notice. With this, my reputation began to spread, as someone who could walk on water when it comes to finding answers to obscure questions.

Actually, it was a mutual learning process. I had to learn that the product directors were top dogs in the corporate pecking order, particularly in a multi-product-diversified company. Each product or product group had its own fiefdom with a broad degree of autonomy and distinct ground rules. For example, the Agricultural Chemicals Division knew in great detail the main areas where wheat, corn, and rice grew, as basis for selling herbicides specifically designed to increase yields in these crops.

The problems the divisions faced lay in such external factors as revolutions, political boycotts, and controls over trade through tariffs or artificial product standards. Every division had regular judgment days in the form of the profit/loss statements that inexorably came out every quarter. After all, the company's performance as a whole was largely the sum of its product parts. I found many of the product executives really broad-gauge in their view of the world but, in their drive to maximize short-term and long-term results, they had to concentrate on the larger, richer, more developed markets of the world and, politically, favor continuation of the familiar *status quo*.

Here was a key factor: the operating and planning people in the business world placed deep importance in factors of stability, continuity, and predictability. A business could be run under all but the most dogmatic political systems, provided there be continuity, some assurance that the rules for business would not change frequently or without warning overnight.

The concept of market share was also new to me and not a factor taken into account in government planning. For a good-sized company like Monsanto, at least a 25% market share would prevent other suppliers from setting prices or from destructive competition or dumping on the market. This introduced the whole area of competitor information... who else could or possibly intend to develop the same market? Instead of national intentions, what were the intentions of your key competitors? In business, this needed a dual approach, by specialists in the product and by area or market study. The latter aspect was what International Division was expected to produce. The specialists after all attended professional meetings, exchanged papers, and generally knew what their colleagues were about. In contrast, governments were notoriously changeable.

The whole subject of business-government relations in the area of intelligence covers the whole scene from obtaining information to outright lobbying. This all has received increasing attention over the past decades, and changes somewhat with changes in national administrations in Washington and the growing political sophistication in major and middle-sized companies. It deserves detailed and continuous study.

And what about the position of an International Division within a company? Should it be a corporate staff function emphasizing strategic planning considerations? Should it be a profit center, actually selling corporate products or would this compete rather than complement the role of the product divisions? How to develop a balanced staff/line relationship with the operating divisions?

I traveled widely for Monsanto, to Europe, to India and Pakistan, to South Africa, and to the Philippines and Hong Kong. By 1970 the information collection program was well under way, with growing awareness in the major corporate divisions and staff elements. The emphasis of my work changed to international government relations, and in 1970 I was relocated to Washington. I was 49 years old. The next year, 1971, I would be 50 years old, and eligible to start receiving my early retirement pension from CIA. I had a strange foreboding that this would not be easy. I was sure, however, that my being in Washington rather than St. Louis would inevitably be an advantage.

• • •

In early 1971, we had comfortably settled in a handsome home northwest of Washington in the near suburb of Bethesda, out River Road just inside the newly built Beltway. Lib was engrossed with work in the national headquarters of the League of Women Voters and was elected to membership on its National Board. She was also active with, and ultimately elected president of, an offshoot of the League, the Overseas Education Fund. The Fund supported programs of self-help for women in certain developing countries in Central America and Africa. Jim and Alex were both thriving in Montgomery County's excellent high school system.

My job had been for the past year in Monsanto's Washington Office as International Affairs Director. Sam Pickard, the able head of the Washington Office, was a great help to me in learning the ways of the city from the business standpoint. When I outlined my program to him, he asked how many other companies had people in Washington with functions like mine. I knew of about a dozen, including Mobil, Dow, General Motors, 3M, John Deere, Caterpillar Tractor, Ralston Purina, TRW, Eastman Kodak, Union Oil, Bechtel and IBM. I felt the numbers were growing as more "Washington reps" were being given increasingly near full-time assignments on international business problems. Pickard mentioned the importance of working jointly with others and not working alone. Government officials concerned hesitate to assist an individual company but welcome joint or industry-wide approaches. It was an excellent suggestion.

I began by setting up monthly luncheons with individual government officials as guest speakers, people involved in some way in matters that affected international finance or trade. In short order the group developed into an interesting and lively informal international business/government meeting place, with regularly scheduled luncheons either at the International Club at 18th and K Streets or in the offices of one of the attending companies. As the group grew to a membership of over twenty, all of them international representatives of Fortune 500 companies, it began to require a growing share of my time.

I welcomed an offer from Bill Barton of Business International to take over management of the group. Barton had been the senior Midwest representative for BI, a highly useful source of international business data for over three hundred company clients. He used to call on me frequently while I was in St. Louis and provide useful information on developments in the international investment field. He had just been appointed BI's head-man in Washington, and proposed to make the group an industry-wide service complete with scheduled events, newsletter, and consulting services. Out of this grew International Business/Government Counselors, emphasizing multi-company activities. Another group, International Business Affairs Council, broke away when Dick Barovick, the editor of Barton's publications and an outstandingly well-informed reporter of the Washington business scene, concentrated on an *International Trade and Investment Letter,* which attained a circulation of over 500 major companies, including US, German, British, and Japanese firms. I subsequently joined Barovick as IBAC's director of consulting services.

CHAPTER 18

BREAK-OUT...

March 1971. My fiftieth birthday came and went with no word from CIA as to starting to send me my retirement pay. I learned from CIA people that the chief of personnel was now Harry Little, an able former colleague from Europe Division days. He told me that approval of my request was discretionary with the Director of Central Intelligence. Richard Helms was then the Director of Central Intelligence, and would certainly be the most logical and receptive point of contact. I wrote him a personal letter:

August 30, 1971
Mr. Richard Helms
Director of Central Intelligence
Washington, D. C.

Dear Dick,
There is an administrative matter concerning my status under the CIA Re-
tirement Act of 1964 that, as I understand it, must come to your attention.
The Act is applied at the discretion of your office to employees who reach
age 50 and have over 20 years' service of which 6 were overseas. My tenure
with CIA and predecessor agencies covers over 21 years service with over
7 years overseas. My 50th birthday was in March. Request your favorable
action for my inclusion under provisions of the Act.

With all good wishes,
Sincerely,

I never got a reply from Helms, but did receive a letter from a deputy director of the Personnel Office, Mrs. de Felice, a lady who had been a junior but well-informed Personnel employee eight years ago when I left the Agency. Her letter, dated September 13, 1971, stated flatly that:

"It is with regret that I must inform you that you are ineligible to be included
under the provisions of the Central Intelligence Agency Retirement Act of
1964 for Certain Employees. In order to be eligible...you must be on duty

*in an employee relationship with the Agency. Not only are you currently
ineligible, but with a separation date of 27 September 1963, your employment status terminated...prior to the passage of the Act on 13 October 1964.
There are no provisions in the Act to designate former employees as participants in the System."*

So, there it was. No automatic inclusion in the early retirement act, in fact, no
inclusion at all. I rechecked all my notes on the negotiations for my resignation, and
realized that there was nothing explicitly in writing about my inclusion in the Act. And,
simple eligibility in terms of twenty years service, six of them abroad, was not enough.

I felt this was arguable in any case, but my time was absorbed elsewhere.
There ensued a very busy period of my activity for Monsanto, including my being
chair of a business committee arranging for reception of the first trade mission from the
Peoples Republic of China. Then there was monitoring the developing difficulties for
business in South Africa, watching for international currency adjustments, checking
the possible adverse implications for business with Cuba from Monsanto Chemicals
Ltd. in the U.K., coping with the Arab Boycott of Israel, and other such subjects.

By 1975 I had taken the time to consult lawyers and specialists on security
matters, on Civil Service procedures, on personal damages, to collect recommendations on courses of action open to me to be covered by the Early Retirement Act.
One proposal stood out...to get a private bill through Congress. This assumed a
fully cooperative response by the CIA and the FBI.

This increased my concern that it was an indicator of something else. Were
other factors involved in my retirement, not just the security case? But why should
other factors affect my receiving retired pay? I had been kept on the CIA books for
three added months without pay in the expectation specifically so that the Early
Retirement legislation would be through Congress and would apply to me by the
time of my retirement. The bill had been working its way through Congress for
nearly a year. While reference to the three months leave without pay idea was mentioned in several letters and memos, the fact that this was to give me a chance to get
in under the provisions of the bill was apparently never specified in writing. I only
had two references in memos for my files that I jotted down after two meetings with
Larry Houston during the negotiations. But notes in my files by me would hardly
carry the day in a legal contest.

I tried another approach: Monsanto had a policy of annual physical exams. The
doctors in St. Louis were shocked not to see any report in my medical records of a
strong heart murmur, from an enlarged wall in my heart. Left unreported and untreated,
it could lead to sudden complications, and the doctors in St. Louis regarded it as badly
unprofessional, to the point of possibly being legally actionable for the CIA not to have
paid direct attention to it. I wrote the medical department at CIA to ask for copies of any
EKG or other medical records; I knew an EKG had been taken in 1961 when I reached
the age of forty. The reply I received was prompt and bland:

*"Your request for information about your last physical examination was re-
ferred to the Medical Office. They stated that your records are not available
at this time since all their old records have been sent to the Records Center.
As soon as the Medical Office obtains the information, it will be sent to you."*

Despite several follow-ups by me, nothing was ever made available to me. So
much for making this the basis for a claim by me for medical-based retirement, an idea

that frankly had crossed my mind as a way to attract renewed attention to my case.

By 1973, I had my confirmation from several sources, colleagues who took the time and effort to find out that my case had long ago been closed in the FBI. I was never notified of this officially, nor in the inquiries I made at various times with CIA people. In fact, I was told that the FBI had "cleared" me even before that mid-July date in 1963 on which my resignation document, ER63-5743, had been signed. I was never officially notified of this. Was this news deliberately buried and not passed on to senior CIA officials at the time?

I applied for documents under the Freedom of Information Act, following the necessary procedures to describe what I was looking for. This led to a series of letters for over six years from Freedom of Information officers regretting the delay in meeting my request, citing overwork and the complexity of obtaining multi-agency clearances for some of the material I requested, and was I still interested despite the delay? Each time I replied that yes, I was still interested. I wondered if I was being deliberately stonewalled. Was it legal to do this? I saw no way to challenge it except to keep asking and renewing requests.

By 1975, I had several proposals from lawyers that I had consulted for drafting and submitting a private bill to go through Congress. I had little stomach for this, or at least for doing it alone. I felt that the CIA was still sufficiently immune from a congressional attack to offer any expectation of success in this endeavor. And up to this point, I had had no way to find out who, if anyone had been adversely affected by whatever evil had affected my status and forced my retirement.

Then came a period of major changes in my life. My bosses at Monsanto called me back to St. Louis, as I had been in the Washington job over six years. A new vice president for corporate affairs had been designated, but his priorities were US corporate matters such as the environment, equal rights, toxic substances and job discrimination. International topics such as relations with governments or government sponsored unions, policy towards South African *Apartheid,* the Arab Boycott of Israel, and growing anti-multinational corporate moves in the United Nations and the developing country world were still secondary. At the same time, with the establishment of the central corporate function, International Division lost interest in my public affairs work. After several talks, the consensus was that I take a line job in St. Louis for three years as valuable experience, then join the vice president for public affairs as his international man. Lib and I decided we would prefer to remain in Washington, and that my international affairs function would work better based in Washington with another company or as a consultant on my own.

I accepted a generous early retirement package and resigned from Monsanto in late summer, 1976. I landed several consulting jobs and joined what became International Business Affairs Corporation with my friend Richard L. Barovick to produce a newsletter on international-business related developments in Washington. Barovick was one of the best-informed reporters in Washington specializing in this field.

In October 1976 Lib had an attack of strange muscular pains. Still a championship equestrienne, fox-hunter and horse show competitor, she thought it had to do with physical strains. Prior to leaving for our annual Caribbean holiday in January, Lib had a complete physical at Bethesda Naval Hospital with a double check at the National Institutes of Health. The diagnosis was cancer in the spine and breast, probably still metastasizing. We decided that a week in the Cayman Islands could only do us good. On our return Lib started radiation and then chemotherapy. It was badly debilitating but the spinal cancer was stopped and biopsy of the breast was no longer positive. However, a spot was detected on the liver.

She had taken a final spree in a horse competition in April. She and Alexandra came back rain-soaked to the skin, flushed and happy. Between them they had won all the silver cups for which they were eligible as females. It was Lib's last ride on horseback.

We spent two weeks in Maine at Tall Timbers in August but by Labor Day Lib's strength left her. She became progressively bed-ridden, but still the manager forever keeping lists and schedules, she wanted to plan for the future. Would I go back to work for a company? What financial matters were unfinished? One of our cars was in her name and I should trade it in or re-register it in my name. After her death, she said; I should remarry and she listed several candidates. At this, I prepared a counter-list of more controversial and far less acceptable candidates, and we laughed over it and agreed the humor held off the end by days if not weeks.

I was in a daze of total denial. I could not believe she would die. One day before I left for work, she pulled me to her, put her arms around me and said, "Peter, you've been terrific." I was crying so uncontrollably that I ran out of the house to the doctor's office, also called on a college classmate who had become a leading hematologist on the National Science Foundation. Both told me soberly that we were off the bottom of the drawing board of our knowledge of controlling cancer, and that the end was near. Alexandra came down from college to be with us. Lib died quietly in her sleep Sunday, October 31 at age 51.

My son Jim came in from his new job in Memphis, and my sister Sonja and Lib's sisters Barbara, Nancy, and Ginny took turns staying with me for a few days at a time until I could pull myself together. We had a memorial funeral service at the Navy Chapel on Massachusetts Avenue with nearly one hundred attending - people representing the League of Women Voters, Overseas Education Fund, Potomac Hunt, the Naval Historian, friends from Swarthmore and Smith colleges and Monsanto and other company colleagues. It was a basic Navy service, as she would have wished, complete with the Navy hymn and, at my request, a piano solo of "Willow Weep for Me," played as a mournful song but one we had always felt was "ours."

Alex went back to Smith College and wrote me from there that she had left so quickly to come to Washington that her clock radio was still on. As she returned to her room, it was playing "Willow Weep for Me." "It was," she wrote, "as if for a moment Mother was there in the room with me, saying that everything will be all right."

Despite the loving support of family and friends, things seemed to hit bottom all at once.

CHAPTER 19

TURN OF THE TIDE...

Things began to loosen up by 1979. There were an increasing number of references in the media to alleged improper action by CIA operations officers. Since the flamboyant and critical hearings in the Senate about CIA in 1976, the sanctity of CIA and its activities had begun to wear thin.

The first break came in the late summer of 1980. Talk was widespread in the media of the excesses committed by counter-intelligence chief James Jesus Angleton, and his exploitation of a Soviet defector named Anatoliy Golitsin. The wave of protests against Angleton in and out of the CIA had risen to a crescendo by 1978. Word got out that Angleton had traveled to Paris that year, called on the head of the French intelligence, the corresponding agency to the CIA, and told him that the senior CIA officer then stationed at the U.S. Embassy in Paris was a Soviet double-agent. When the Director of Central Intelligence, Bill Colby, heard of Angleton's accusation, it was the last straw. Angleton was summarily fired.

Only then did the damage inflicted from Angleton's paranoia become evident. False accusations against a dozen or more CIA officials, unsubstantial intelligence blown up into sinister plots involving a number of Allied country national intelligence services—British, Canadian, French, West German and Australian. File documents taken out of the CIA building to the house where Golitsin was held, so that he could "review" them.

The first comprehensive public revelation of the situation appeared early in 1980 in "Wilderness of Mirrors," a book by *Newsweek* correspondent David C. Martin. Here was a broad recounting of CIA activity in anti-Soviet counter-intelligence work culminating in the defection of Soviet KGB officer Anatoli Golitsin late in 1961.

"The CIA appeared to have been handed a major triumph," Martin wrote. "The amount of information we got from Golitsin in the first forty-eight hours of his interrogation established in most people's minds that he was 'for real,' a CIA officer said. The biggest problem with Golitsin was not his bona fides but his behavior.'...'He just refused to cooperate with a whole series of case officers who he insisted were idiots. He demanded access to the highest levels of the US Government.' He 'basically insisted that he wanted to deal only with the President of the United States.'"

"Finally," Martin continued, "Golitsin was handed over to Angleton, commencing one of the most extraordinary relationships in the history of the secret war between the CIA and the KGB."

Martin's was the first reporting I had seen about the second defector situation. "Golitsin warned Angleton that the Soviets would attempt" to discredit him and "would send false defectors" to undermine him. Indeed, "in June of 1962...Yuri Nosenko, a KGB officer with the Soviet delegation to disarmament talks in Geneva, contacted the CIA" and subsequently defected. In the extensive interrogation that ensued, "Nosenko's information tended to negate or deflect leads by [Golitsin]." Was Golitsin the real and informed defector he claimed to be? Was Nosenko a "provocation, part of a desperate Soviet effort to sidetrack the hunt for the mole?"

This was all a revelation to me. While I had heard some of this from my friends still in the CIA, I had not paid too much attention as it was hard to equate how all this related to me. Martin's book seemed to spell this out: Golitsin had told Angleton of how the KGB had "penetration at high levels" in Western countries including the U.S. But "Angleton's search for Soviet spies in the CIA's ranks was not meeting with spectacular results. According to Golitsin, the KGB had a source named SASHA who had penetrated the Agency's German operations. 'At first, everyone became frantic,' [a CIA officer] said...'No one's going to name an agent by his true name."

Then came a key paragraph for me:

"Besides, Golitsin had a better lead to source SASHA's true identity. He could not recall his name precisely, but he was certain that it began with the letter "K." An investigation of CIA officers whose names began with "K" and who had served in Germany failed to uncover any Soviet agents, although it did result in the resignation of one officer *for mishandling of Agency funds.*

Was that what the record shows on me? I wondered, Had I been described as mishandling agency funds? Was that the adverse report that the Inspector General made on the Technical Aids Detachment in 1953, where my supply officer and his German assistant were making expense money from the deep discounts they received from German suppliers?

In early summer of 1979, I had a phone call from a lawyer representing two other CIA employees who had been adversely affected in the mole case. They were Paul Garbler and Richard Kovich, both Soviet Russia Division operations officers. I did not know either one personally, but was interested that there were others openly identified with the case and that they were contemplating action. Would I join in with their effort to draft legislation to be presented in Congress to authorize the CIA to make amends to employees whose careers had been harmed or worse by the mole scare?

While I was glad to hear that the effort was being made, I drew back from getting involved in a legal suit against the Government or the CIA. Garbler and Kovich were both in SR Division and so more logical possible targets. I was now more convinced than ever that my being dragged into this was entirely random and that my having negotiated my resignation letter, the ER 63-5743 document, put me into a different category. If I could get that document recognized as the only thing that applied to my case, I would not need any lawsuit or legislation.

Upon his inauguration in 1980 President Carter appointed Admiral Stansfield Turner to be Director of Central Intelligence. Turner worked a provision into the annual CIA Appropriations Bill. This was the famous section 405(a), the so-called "Mole Relief Act." It contained a provision authorizing the Director of Central Intelligence to grant monetary or other relief to employees or former employees wherever the Director determined that an employee's, or former employee's, career had suffered due to unjustified personnel or administrative action...only during fiscal 1981 and limited to "those cases resulting from allegations concerning the employee's, or former employee', loyalty to the United States."

The Act entered into effect on October 1, 1980, the start of the Government's fiscal year. On September 30, 1980, I sent in a formal request by registered mail. The documents were prepared by Ned Putzell, the former General Counsel at Monsanto who had by this time retired to private practice in St. Louis and Naples, Florida. Citing my request, he wrote *"pursuant to the Privacy Act for access to his entire personnel file and to the Agency's files relating to [his] termination of employment in or before September [1963]."* Putzell followed this with a second certified letter on December 18, 1980 which pointed out that a parallel request for information under the Freedom of Information Act had been filed but that neither formal request had elicited any response to date, except to advise of the substantial delay to be experienced in responding to such types of request due to the large number awaiting by personnel of the Agency.

Putzell's letter continued:

"Findings by the Director of Central Intelligence...must be made during the current fiscal year. We will be unable to file such a claim on behalf of Mr. Karlow until we have access to the files and documents referred to in our letter of September 30, 1980. Therefore, we respectfully request that the two above mentioned applications for files and documents be taken out of their present position in the long queue of such requests and be given priority handling. Otherwise, our ability to present our claim fully and in detail and in timely fashion for a finding by you in this fiscal year will be severely hampered, if not entirely frustrated."

The bland stonewalling by the FOIA people continued. Every six months, I would receive a letter thanking me for my patience as things were still in the process of being cleared. I never received a single document through the Freedom of Information protocol.

I sat helplessly, in utter frustration, as the days ticked by and the deadline for the expiration of the authority in Section 405(a) came ever nearer. I prepared a final and near-desperate appeal directly to Director Casey...urging him to please review the facts of my case. *"After 21 years of continuous and repeatedly commended service in COI, OSS and CIA, my career was abruptly ended. My name was brought into a security case unbeknownst to me. It hit me like a loose brick falling from a rooftop. Nothing I did caused this, nor could I do anything to defend myself...or is there something else? If so, in all fairness, give me the chance to set this to rest, whatever it may be."* I went on to refer to a *Newsweek* article whose author had called me *"one of the most prominent victims"* of the mole hunt.

The first of October came and went.

Casey's reply was dated October 7, 1981 and read as follows:

Dear Pete,

I am aware of your case and of the relief which you have sought. Let me assure you that your claim received very careful study after a thorough examination of the underlying facts. Members of my legal staff, moreover, were in contact with your attorney, Ned Putzell. As you know the law under which your claim was brought is quite specific and relief can only be granted when an individual's career has been damaged as a result of a particular type of circumstance. The facts and circumstances under which you left the Agency were not such as to allow me to provide you with relief under this law.

Sincerely,

Bill Casey

I was quietly furious. I felt completely stymied and frustrated, but knew I had to keep my cool as best I could. General de Gaulle's war cry came to mind: "We have lost a battle, but we will win the war." As for how...it seemed like I was in a three-cornered firefight. On one hand there was indisputable language in legislation that had passed Congress. There was also the *Newsweek* article that described my situation as a person whose career had been adversely affected by unjustified allegations against my loyalty.

In the other hand I held a numbered and signed CIA registered document (ER 63-5743) which stated that my career was compromised since I had been drawn so deeply into a security situation that did not involve me. And now, Casey's letter falls into my lap and informs me that *"after careful study"* I am not included in the terms of the legislation.

I could only conclude that the basic Executive Registry document (63-5743) had never made it into my file, despite my frequent references to it. Or could it have been removed from my files? I had frankly begun to wonder about this possibility, but anyone must know that a numbered Registry document has a master copy in the Central Registry files. Of course, I had a copy...the copy specified in the agreement with me that would be kept in safe hands outside the physical confines of the CIA. Now I wondered how I could succeed in getting the document directly and unmistakably to Mr. Casey's attention. If I sent him a copy through the mail, would this backfire in a charge against me for misusing classified documents? By this time, I was ready to believe anything.

Years would pass and the struggle continued. One evening, in 1983, I was invited to New York to attend a formal dinner given by Veterans of the OSS. I managed to get in a brief word with Casey and tried to bring up my problem. He just snapped at me and said that the matter was settled and he couldn't reopen it.

Late in the winter of that same year, Ned Putzell made a date to visit Casey when both vacationed not far apart in Florida. They were personal friends from OSS days. In one conversation, Putzell would later inform me that Casey referred to inconsistencies in the files as a partial reason for my problems. Putzell told me that it sounded like there were other issues that had come up and Casey alluded that these would be hard to get at.

I felt all along that the other questions about me had been settled before I resigned, as I had been turned down in my formal request for a hearing on any other security-related points that might still be "open" in my case. I recalled to Putzell that both Larry Houston (former General Counsel) and Mr. Bannerman (former Deputy Director Office of Security) had informed me that no further hearings "were necessary". But in view of Casey's attitude, Putzell was pessimistic that there was any way open to me from here on.

I turned back to my contacts with outside lawyers to see what suggestions they would now have for courses of action. Again, what about a private bill? I saw little chance for this paying off without a long spell of litigation and publicity, and I was a bit diffident to the approach. A member of the CIA General Counsel's staff made it clear to me that the CIA would back me in working towards such a bill only to the extent of vouching for my having rendered "satisfactory" service over the period of my employment...nothing further.

I tried another approach to the General Counsel's office. Since I had been cleared of any association with the mole case, would not this remove any reluctance by CIA to re-hire me? What about having an arrangement whereby I would be re-hired for a day, and then be allowed to resign and meet eligibility for retirement?

My point was that I was fully eligible for the early retirement in terms of length of service...which included a minimum of six years service overseas. The question was how to start it for me. This was duly considered by the General Counsel's office, but an action to hire someone just to let him resign did not appear appropriate for a government agency, particularly one in a period of transition to a new director. During the discussion, I listened for any reference to "inconsistencies" or other unfinished residuals in my record. Nothing was ever mentioned.

•••

Meanwhile, there were other major developments in my life. Shortly after leaving Monsanto I had some consulting work for Business International regarding international terrorism and the responsibilities placed on U.S. executives in coping with and protecting employees abroad. My part centered on Europe and the Middle East while others took Latin America and the Far East. I traveled to England, concerned with the IRA crisis; France, with its "open door" policy towards terrorists; Germany, which had its "Red" faction; Italy, with its "Red" Army; then Lebanon, Iran and Israel, with their growing threats of Muslim insurgency.

Iran was different; I did not realize it at first, never having lived through a genuine revolution. I still thought that if the seeming well-equipped and loyal army held together, the Shah's regime could survive. I stayed with my friend, Dorothy Robbins Mowry, who was a senior Public Affairs officer at the US Embassy and an inveterate "yenta" who wanted me to meet a lady who might interest me. She had in mind the lady President of American-backed Damavand College for Women which was located on the outskirts of Tehran. The President was facing growing problems as Muslim fundamentalism increased in strength and hardly approved of Americans to educate their Iranian women.

We were unable to meet in Tehran, but did get acquainted in Washington after both Embassy and College were closed as U.S. personnel were ordered out of the country. It took a while, but Carolyn Davis Spatta and I eventually got our schedules together. I had warned her with some gallows humor that she might be dealing with a Soviet spy and mole. It didn't faze her; after her stint during the early phases of the Iranian revolution in Tehran, she was inured to crisis. She gave me her full support in pursuing what she viewed as a deliberate effort to undermine my CIA retirement entitlements. Carolyn and I ultimately had a July wedding in Arlington, Virginia.

My next move was to attempt another approach to Congress. What about the Congressional Intelligence committees and their newly developing oversight functions? I engaged the services of a former CIA lawyer and operations officer, Stan Gaines, who had been involved in drafting the 405(a) legislation. Gaines contacted the executive director of the Senate Oversight Committee, Mrs. Virginia Toensing, and interested her in going to Langley and reviewing my case. I prepared a briefing paper that Gaines would direct to Mrs. Toensing.

"I still cannot believe," I wrote, "that somehow, some distorted information, its nature unknown to me, may have entered my files somewhere. As I told you, I never had a hearing despite my requests over the years..."

A reply came via a letter to Gaines from Toensing- September 14, 1982

> United States Senate
> Select Committee on Intelligence
> 82-2061
> Dear Mr. Gaines,
>
> *This letter is to formalize in writing when I informed you that, in this Committee's oversight capability, a review was conducted of the Central Intelligence Agency's administration of your client, Mr. Peter Karlow's claim under {405}, Intelligence Authorization Act FY1982 (sic). We found no basis to disagree with the Agency's denial of that claim. We reviewed both the procedures used by the Agency to carry out the Act and the substantive reasons for the Agency's request in 1963 for Mr. Karlow's resignation and, this, the basis for the decision that he had not been treated "unfairly." You are an excellent advocate for your client and I know you have pursued this matter vigorously. However, we have found the facts in this case do not support a decision in Mr. Karlow's favor.*
>
> Sincerely,
> /s/Victoria Toensing
> Chief Counsel

Gaines and I did a post-mortem. It was now obvious that there was something in CIA's files that I did not know about...something which completely undercut my case. It also seemed to have replaced ER 63-5743 as the basic document in my files. Could I possibly get to Stanley Sporkin, the General Counsel, whom Director Casey brought on from the Security and Exchange Commission? Could I get to Ernie Meyerfeld, the Deputy General Counsel? Gaines called on Meyerfeld and was predictably stonewalled.

What about Freedom of Information? I had received nothing except some more apologetic letters that requested my continued patience. On this facet, I directed Gaines to call Ms. Toensing. His response: "I raised the question of two years elapsing since you asked for Privacy Information and your not having received anything, despite the Director's having stated [in his letter] that your case had been very carefully studied. Her reply was simply that the information in the reply was made up by administrators not well acquainted with you[r] case, not by the lawyers who reviewed your case."

We could only conclude that Ms. Toensing's replies were incredibly naive, particularly for someone in her Congressional Oversight position. Either this, or she had simply been blown away by the snow job hurled by the CIA.

There must be a deliberate concealment or frame-up here, I pondered, for what are they making me a scapegoat or is this a deliberate misleading of the Congressional Oversight process?

I had to get at Bill Casey directly. Nothing else would do.

I started off the year of 1986 full with determination to get something from the Freedom of Information procedure. I felt this would be vulnerable to legal action. I reviewed the five years of evasion and outright stalling and proceeded to write a sharp letter to the "Information and Privacy Coordinator" of the CIA:

January 6, 1986

Mr. John Wright
Information and Privacy Coordinator
Central Intelligence Agency
Washington D.C. 20505
Dear Mr. Wright,

This letter confirms my continuing interest in obtaining access to the information that I formally requested five (5) years ago. At the time of my original request, I was under a one-year deadline of September 30, 1981 to file a request under Section 405(a) of The Authority to Remedy Unjust Personnel Actions. I did not receive any materials even though the material was all together and the Director, Mr. Casey, wrote me personally on October 8, 1981, to say that my file had been reviewed by him at that time. Since this request has now been in your hands and those of your predecessors and colleagues for all these five years...I request this initial requested data be made available to me by or before February 1, 1986, or an explanation given as to why the Freedom of Information Act does not seem to apply in this case, or to the CIA as a whole.

I followed this with a second registered letter and a Western Union telegram that stated I would be in Washington on Monday, February 24th, and would like to meet with him that day at 10:00 in the morning, at the CIA Building in Langley. I received the following via special delivery:

...processing of your request was continuing and, thus, we were not yet able to accommodate your request...since, as we mentioned, other information was forwarded to other government agencies for review and coordination and since this will involve considerable time...we must decline your invitation to a meeting on 24 February. When all the processing has been completed, we will prepare and forward our final response to you.

Thank you for your continued interest.

(signed) Lee S. Strickland

A friend at CIA agreed to pass word back to the General Counsel office reporting that I was reopening my case and had engaged new and expensive legal counsel for my effort. Whether that had any effect, I could never tell for sure. I put out other "feelers" through intermediaries, people such as former OSS veterans who knew both Casey and me, but this also failed to elicit a response.

In September of 1986, a conference was held at the Mayflower Hotel in Washington. The theme was The Role of General William Donovan in Shaping the National Intelligence Structure. Various agencies sponsored the event, including the National Archives, but the spark plug for the entire affair was Maximillion Corvo, the brilliant and controversial head of the OSS Italian SI section and its widespread operations on the Italian mainland in World War II. Corvo invited me to speak on Donovan and the History of OSS. I noted that Director Casey was also on the program, as the keynote speaker on Donovan's legacy.

I worked hard on my speech, and indeed it was well received by the audience of nearly 200 people. I aimed much of my speech directly at Casey, knowing how he regarded Donovan as his mentor and ideal. I recounted how Donovan had greeted me when I returned to Washington. I told of French Navy Captain l'Herminier and how Donovan arranged for his medical rehabilitation. I told other stories that were circulating about Donovan's special virtues as a people person, and his insistence on fairness.

After the program, Casey came over to me to compliment me on my talk. He finally said, "OK Pete, what is this about your case?"

I gave him the reference number ER 63-5743, as the critical document in my case, and since he had obviously not seen it, would he please look it up? Three weeks later, early October of 1986, the phone rang on my desk in San Francisco. It was Bill Casey and he wanted to know when I was coming to Washington. He said that he had looked over my case and there are two things.

There's the security thing, and that's all right and settled, he said, But there are other things that you may not even know about.

He went on to say that he had instructed his general counsel, David Dougherty, to see to it that I was shown everything about the case, and to prepare a report on the basis of which he could impose his authority.

The door had opened.

I went to Washington a few days later, and met with what turned out to be a roomful of somber-faced people. They were the ad hoc committee on my case, and included one or two representatives each from the Operations Directorate, counter-intelligence, Freedom of Information office, Security Office, and public relations.

Dave Dougherty, the General Counsel, chaired the meeting. Steve Hermes of the General Counsel staff accompanied him. A tall, slender, serious younger man in his late thirties, Hermes had read deeply into my case and played a key role in its resolution.

Dougherty opened the meeting with a starchy statement of objectives that he proposed for this ad hoc committee. He wanted to review points brought up about me in the investigation conducted back in 1962-63 and respond to any discrepancies and inconsistencies that had appeared in the investigation.

My objection was quiet, but immediate, and firm. Holding up my copy of ER 63-5743, I stated that this was the governing document in my case. After all, it bore the signatures of then Deputy Director Gen. Marshall Carter, of the then Inspector General Lyman Kirkpatrick, and then General Counsel Lawrence R. Houston; no other document or consideration had any room in this discussion.

In the sharp argument that ensued, the committee acknowledged that ER 63-5743 was the overarching guide today, but I was prevailed on to go over the charges and put them to rest, realizing that these factors had played a part in past decisions on my case.

And here they came, the same allegations that I thought had been rebutted back in 1963. My father's birth place: Why did he equivocate about this? I pointed out that a team had found his actual birth certificate in civic records in Germany, which should put the matter to rest, once and for all. Five or six failed REDSOX operations, and was I the common cause for their failure? What was my "homosexual experience" at age twelve and how did it affect me? Did I discuss operational matters with my wife or my mother?

I took the occasion to ask about the two specific dates that had been given to me to prove that my whereabouts on those days were not in East Berlin being taught secret writing by case officer "LYDIA." I hammered home that this was the only specific data that had come up in the entire case, and that I had had no difficulty in establishing where I was on those two dates. Why was there no reference to these dates in my files? These were, after all the only hard facts in the case against me, and I demanded they be made part of the active record.

Then I turned the conversation to ER 63-5743, and why was it missing from my files? Isn't tampering with files a Federal misdemeanor of some sort? There was some shaking of heads at this, as if reality were beginning to dawn.

It may have been.

I continued: Why was no one, as far as I could tell, informed in a timely manner of the FBI giving me clearance after my interrogation in 1963? No response on this.

Why had I not received a single document from the Freedom of Information (FOI) procedures? The committee was ready for this, and happily handed me a thick batch of over 150 pages of photostats, FOI documents "sanitized" for release to me. That meant, possibly still sensitive sections blacked out, even if this meant blacking out all but the "To" and "From" in some memoranda. The group sat and watched me as I went through the documents page by page. This was not easy, as I noted that the documents were as though they had been shuffled; they were numbered but in no order, almost deliberately so, even though related documents like travel orders were included with operational memos. I proposed that I study the documents at home and return as soon as possible with my analysis. I took them back to California and sorted them out with the aid of my computer. I listed the ones that pertained to the case, some seventy-five documents; the others were all administrative, meaning moving orders, promotions, matters concerning office allocation, efficiency ratings, and even security violations such as leaving safes unlocked or documents exposed, a chronic hazard of everyday life in CIA.

I engaged the services of a seasoned and senior Washington lawyer, Arnold Levy, whom I met through a friend and with whom I established immediate rapport. Levy's specialty was in labor relations and as head of his own firm, he had long experience in dealing with governmental bureaucracies. His contribution to my life was enormous. Just as I was nearing total frustration, Levy provided me the sage wisdom of a skilled negotiator and the reassurance of his confident support. In very little time, he was outlining my case to me lucidly. I had sent him some material, the Executive Registry document, the *Newsweek* clipping, etc. He had done some phoning on his own (to whom, I wondered?) and had been able in short order to corroborate some of the things I had said. Levy sensed that I was not up against bureaucratic bungling but a deliberate series of moves over the years to blackball me, for whatever reason was not yet clear. He modestly described his position in the Yiddish term *Suppenloeffle*, meaning the large ladle used to stir the soup, the ladle that added nothing except a new motion, a new mixing of the ingredients which would improve the taste.

I reviewed the analysis I had made of the FOI documents with Levy and Simonds, and they appreciably sharpened up my presentation. Sidelining all irrelevant documents, we had now a body of some thirty documents from back in 1963 that actually summarized my case and the word-for-word build-up in preparing what became Executive Registry Document 63-5743.

Chapter 20

Smoking Gun...

Missing from the collection of documents was the specific recommendation made to Director Casey not to include me under the original §405(a). Levy urged me to demand a copy of whatever document or action accomplished this. I placed my demand before the committee the next meeting that I had with the members. There was obvious reluctance to meet my demand, but equally obvious realization that it was a perfectly proper demand by me.

It took nearly two months to "find" the document. When I received it, I immediately notified Simonds:

"We have the smoking gun," I wrote.

And, indeed, it was just that.

It was an outrageous memo from General Counsel Stanley Sporkin to Director Casey that noted my claim for inclusion under §405(a). He wrote that I had been duplicitously encouraged in that belief but that actually, I did not come under §405(a) as review of my files shows me ineligible for employment in CIA. I noted that the memo, addressed to Director Casey, was marked "From Stanley Sporkin," but bore the signature of Fred Duesenberry, the deputy General Counsel. It had not actually been signed by Duesenberry, but only by his name marked by initials, as though someone else had entered his name in his absence. The initials were not clear enough on the photocopy to be legible or identifiable. To all intents and purposes, this document was a forgery, or at least contrived, very possibly, without knowledge of either Sporkin or Duesenberry.

I also met with Larry Houston in Levy's office. Houston stated flatly that he was the person in charge of handling the legal aspects of my case back in 1963 and, while the Office of Security at the time insisted that my dismissal was imperative, this was not the reason for my being asked to resign. It was purely and simply the fact that my name had been drawn into the security case. Houston volunteered to prepare a statement to this effect, and duly gave us a four-page paper. Presented to the committee, this paper, together with the questionably signed Sporkin/Duesenberry paper, cinched the case for me.

It was over.

I met again with the committee. The committee agreed I came under the original authority in §405(a) of the 1981 Act, and would recommend accordingly. I was asked to submit a summarizing paper documenting my case, and promptly submitted the paper Levy and Simonds had helped me prepare.

As the meeting broke up, Ray Reardon of the Office of Security made a final comment to me about the case. He expressed his congratulations that the case was now resolved, but he still had a question about my Father's birthplace, that he still did not understand my Father's inconsistency about "this Russia-German business." I was about to snap at Reardon to tell him that, judging from the question, it was obvious that he and his colleagues had learned nothing about how my case was mishandled. But I didn't; I wanted a complete settlement first before I rocked the boat any further.

Then came Bill Casey's collapse as the brain tumor finally took its toll.

The question became how to handle this case in view of Mr. Casey's death. Mr. Gates, the interim DCI, was not about to handle hot leftover cases, if any of them were indeed ever presented to him. Therefore, Steve Hermes, a deputy general counsel, was assigned to my case.

Everything was on hold until finally Judge William Webster was installed as DCI. Webster brought with him a team of FBI administrative officers to attack the backlog of unfinished business including my case. Authority had to be obtained first from Congress to release funds for me, that is, to reopen the authority in the 1981 Act. Finally, a formula was worked out. The next CIA enabling act contained a sentence that read:

"The authority for the Director in Section 405(a) of the Act of 1981 is hereby reopened for one individual for one year."

When this legislation passed the Congress, Hermes and I sat down to negotiate the settlement. I had felt that the need to go back to Congress for authorization for the funds was a stalling tactic. Hermes assured me it was not; that the authority in the 1981 Act meant that the Act, in effect Congress, had to be the source of the funds, that settlement could not come from within current Agency funds or elsewhere.

How do you measure the damage in dollars and cents terms? Suffice it to say that Hermes obtained agreement on a sum that I would accept as reasonable.

One thing was still missing, I pointed out. I need an open, public sign of recognition that this case was over. We agreed that a CIA decoration would be appropriate, at a date to be set. I suggested to Hermes some activities in which I had been involved that might have merited this kind of recognition, had my career not been interrupted.

By this time, it was late on a Friday afternoon. I took off from the Langley building for Washington by Metro subway. Suddenly I saw the time and, in checking my wallet, found that I didn't have Metro rush hour carfare to get to the bank before closing time. Here I was with a six-figure government check hot in my hand but not even money for the Metro or for cab fare or, for that matter, for dinner. I located a taxi and asked driver to stop and let me call the bank from a roadside pay phone. I asked them to have someone please meet me at the bank's front door not just to help me open an account but to bring change to pay the cab fare and the bank obliged.

•••

The CIA protocol office called me to set a date for the decoration ceremony to be to be held at the Langley building. Some fifty people, family, friends, former colleagues, were invited and a simple ceremony was held. I wanted to treat it like a retirement party, commenting in a deliberate low key on how gratifying it was for my generation to see the Agency continue and in younger hands. It was perhaps a little saccharine but as far as I was concerned the Mole matter was closed and I was prepared to leave it that way.

Prior to the ceremony, Carolyn and I were invited to meet with Judge Webster, the Director of Central Intelligence. He commented to me on how effectively he felt Hermes had followed through on resolving my case. Another person who was briefly there for a handshake was Gus Hathaway, the Chief of Counter Intelligence, meaning the person whom now occupied Angleton's former job. I believe he came just to see what I looked like, I being the only survivor of the Mole frenzy to emerge with a decoration, I thought wryly.

The ceremony opened with the presentation of the decoration.

I was surprised at the commendation, the wording of which was so vapid, especially for the circumstances. I did a double take when I heard, and read, its terms:

> *"Mr. Karlow demonstrated inspired leadership, operational wisdom, and good judgment throughout his career, reflecting credit upon himself, the Central Intelligence Agency, and the Federal service."*

Dick Stoltz, Deputy Director for Operations awarded the medal to me. He had been a junior officer, and a very effective one, whom I first met in the 1950s in Germany. I was told he went out of his way to be designated as the officer who should award me the medal. I was glad he had.

Then my group of invitees joined by other friends migrated to the International Club's main reception room for a buffet and get together. I was pleased that Dick Helms joined the party. I talked to him briefly only about generalities, what he was doing professionally and what my plans were. We did not mention my case. He left early.

As with the decoration ceremony, at least until the citation for the decoration was read, I looked on the occasion like a retirement and reasonably sedate party. This was not to be. My good friend Harry Rosiztke was toastmaster and started right off to make this party a roasting.

"Peter," he began. "The name comes from *Petrus* meaning the rock. Regardless of what flowed over him, he remained solid and anything that hit him just foundered."

Then came banter about past events in Germany or here, names of former colleagues, references to past activities and to the numerous humorous situations we had all faced. He called on perhaps a dozen in the group who came up with breezy stories.

...Of the operations officer in Karlsruhe in the early 1950s trying to phone Munich and in his frustration sprawled across the top of his desk. He was screaming into the German telephone, and the German phone system was still pretty shell-shocked then, the immortal German-English word mixture: "Operator, *bitte* (please), *bitte*, God damn it, *bitte!*"

...Of the Munich operations officer whom for weeks was openly savoring his scheduled weekend trip to Paris where he intended to propose to a girl with whom he was in love. He returned after the weekend. No, he didn't propose to her, he reported. He didn't need to.

...Of the young GI truck driver who, on his first trip to Munich, ended at the Austrian border. The only road signs he had seen pointed to "MUENCHEN" and why were so many towns called "AUSFAHRT" (exit)?

To climax the festivities, Rositzke regained the floor. Then he looked around at me and, as though making a toast, he said, "Look. You licked them. You beat them. This is more than just a ceremony. It's a celebration, for all of us."

A victory celebration! It became just that, as stories of past activities and encounters flowed. Like old times. I had rejoined the group. Or what was left of it. The twenty-six year nightmare was over.

Where is the wisdom we have lost in knowledge? Where is the knowledge we have lost in information?
-*T.S. Eliot*

EPILOGUE...

What went wrong? Once it was shown that I was not involved in any way, why was such an effort made to get me out of the Agency as quickly as possible, and at all costs? How could something like this get so badly out of hand? Larry King asked me these very questions in a television interview. "Was this the result of stupidity?" he asked. I recalled for him a reason for the paranoia: the infamous British spies, Burgess, McLean and Kim Philby who had been uncovered only a few years before. The effects of their penetrations were still being investigated.

Looking back as dispassionately as I can, three particular facets of this fiasco have yet to be explained.

First, little or nothing should be of higher priority to the CIA (at any time) than looking for a high-placed penetration agent in the Agency. What became known widely as the "Mole Hunt" should have been a most carefully controlled security case, managed by a special, top level, across-the-board task force that reported directly to the Director of Central Intelligence. Instead, action was left to the controversial Counter-Intelligence staff.

Secondly, the case became a political issue between hard-liners who feared a build up by Russia (or Russia and China) would lead to a World War Three. In contrast, the main body of the Agency regarded it possible (if not probable) that Russia might well join the family of nations as a competitor, but not necessarily as a potential military adversary. The point is that intelligence must be as neutral as possible and not exert influence *a priori* in the collection process. When Angleton's activities virtually destroyed the CIA's Russian operations, he was essentially influencing U.S. policy in the direction that he personally considered as correct. He had simply been granted too much autonomy. It was hard to counter his high-pressure briefings, his blinding knowledge of minutiae, or his arguments about disinformation. Under Angleton, the CI staff became nothing less than a rogue element, making its own rules. No senior CIA official cared to tackle the problem it presented because of the powerful momentum and mystique built up by Angleton. He nurtured the conviction that anything done to restrict CI's mandate might weaken the security of overall clandestine operations and it worked as senior CIA officials were loath to exercise supervision over his staff.

Third, has an adequate evaluation been made of Soviet defector Anatoly Golitsin? Does his outright subversion of Jim Angleton make his the most successful and hostile penetration of the CIA on record? When Golitsin arrived, Angleton was delighted to find a new and potent ally because he supported Angleton's hard-line views. Angleton worked to have Golitsin's *bona fides* accepted as quickly as possible. When Golitsin produced vague allegations about a mole whose name began with the letter "K," my name was picked and Angleton called for top-priority action and the personal attention of J. Edgar Hoover. Angleton ultimately came to rely on Golitsin as an advisor. Golitsin could not have asked for a better reception.

The reality of Golitsin begs for clarification. It is possible that he was specially picked and trained for the job of crossing the lines, getting to Angleton, and exerting influence over him? That would indeed be a coup. After all, Kim Philby was available in Moscow and knew Angleton sufficiently well to coach someone (like Golitsin) on how to exploit his weaknesses. Golitsin would have been privvy to all sorts of details on Angleton... from his political positions to his drinking habits.

Numerous classified studies have been made of Golitsin in CIA and elsewhere; I have not seen them. All I know is that Golitsin defected in Helsinki with his wife and daughter, something that is unusual since families were not usually allowed the chance to accompany their KGB husbands near borders (lest they abet a defection). Upon arriving in Washington, Golitsin gave out some operational information that was accurate and of value, but much of it was confirmatory; all might have been build-up material, information the KGB would have been glad to give away to help establish Golitsin. I understand one nugget was that Golda Meir was a KGB agent, but this was not taken seriously.

As my case was an internal U.S. matter, it was necessary to refer it to the FBI, but the speed in which they dealt with it was extraordinary. Golitsin came out about December 15th and within three weeks, was delivered to the United States, interrogated, and already able to implicate a "principal suspect" in a case that was turned over to the FBI as quickly as January 8th. Anyone who knows the workings of the government would appreciate the near panic that Angleton aroused in this situation. Nothing much traditionally happens in the U.S. government over the Christmas holidays.

Once in FBI hands, my case was presumably assigned to the best personnel the Bureau had available. It is hard to judge how good these people were from their approach. Given the absence of any evidence, all they could do was mount a fishing expedition, to conjecture and watch, hoping that I would reveal my hand or try to make contact with my supposed Soviet spymasters.

Looking back, I can never forget how I was told that I was the principal suspect. I immediately looked for a logical explanation of how I became involved. To my horror, I quickly came to realize that there were neither facts nor logic in this, that it was a rogue activity that could not be stopped or diverted. Even though it did not involve me, once it headed towards me... it swept me along like a tree in the path of a hurricane. I have, however, been able to construct or reconstruct much of what happened through information from former colleagues and from informed outside sources such as David Wise, the author of *Molehunt,* Tom Mangold (*Cold Warrior*) and David Martin (*Wilderness of Mirrors*), all authors of detailed analyses of the period.

After a full year's investigation in 1962 and the detailed interrogation in February 1963, all the FBI could produce were indications of possible "discrepancies or inconsistencies" in my life, or in data concerning me. The case on me was reportedly closed by summer. Did the CIA Security Office prevent this news from reaching top CIA levels? It seems so. Failing to find a security-based reason for removing me, Angleton's efforts concentrated on isolation...getting me out of the way, immediately. One approach was to show me to have been ineligible for recruitment by

CIA in the first place. This is where items came up... like my father's apparent confusion as to his birthplace, my being loose-mouthed with information, my alleged homosexuality at age 12, etc.

Here is where tradecraft should have entered the scene. Tradecraft is an intelligence term for doing things right, professionally. If indeed my leaving the scene in 1963 was considered esssential, how much easier it would have been to call me in and offer something like three years' pay or a leave-with-pay situation, with my pension intact when I reach the proper age. I would have gone off to business school and started my second career with no hard feelings or need for further attention by the Agency. It was within the power of the senior echelons of the Agency to work out such a formula with me as a man well known to them after 22 years service. It certainly would have saved on time and hurt feelings while preserving security... much better than leaving me to fend for myself and take legal action against the Agency.

Angleton's motives became obvious... the identification of me by Golitsin was one of the first pieces of information provided. Had this been shown as false, it might have discredited Golitsin thereby discrediting Angleton. Awaiting confirmation of the verbal evidence collected. Angleton was loath to admit that his principal new source of information was giving inaccurate information.

In the end, Angleton's suspicions led him increasingly to question most of CIA's active penetrations of the Russian Government... penetrations that were considered among the most valuable of our operations. He eventually deluded himself in the notion that these operations only produced disinformation at best and viewed everyone who surrounded him as some sort of double agent. His breakdown is wonderfully described by Bill Buckley in *Spytime: The Decline and Fall of James Jesus Angleton,* a scathing appraisal of Angleton whom he knew from Yale days.

As it worked out, Angleton and Golitsin formed a strange team that decimated the work of the SR (Soviet Russia) Division, and reduced the defenses of all concerned with Soviet operations. They opened the way for real penetrations of CIA Russian operations. One was uncovered in 1994. This was the Aldrich Ames case. More recently, an FBI man was fingered for having been a Russian agent for many of his 15 years of service. The full details of the Robert Hansen case have yet to be revealed, but I cannot help wonder if both Ames and Hansen are minor when compared to Golitsin. The very idea of a defected KGB Major having access to our nation's most coveted intelligence...that he could so easily pull the strings and make Angleton an unwitting puppet...it makes for a spy penetration that is surely second to none.

If this was his goal...he certainly made his mark.

As long as human intelligence activities, meaning agent operations, are the vital ultimate resource for secret intelligence work, there must be a highly responsive human resources program. The intelligence professional must, to a large degree, be his brother's keeper. I would rather see the CIA's operating element accused of paternalism or of being a "good ol' boy" network, than to again see the day when a dedicated veteran of the agency feels he could fall under a cloud of suspicion...merely on the smoke of false innuendo and unfounded accusations.

I hold no malice toward the CIA or any of the persons involved in my case– only sorrow and regret that this breakdown in management was allowed to go on as long as it did. The CIA is too important to national security to let an operational lapse like this go unchecked.

THE PLAYERS...

Anatoly Mikhailovich Golitsin, the KGB officer who defected in Helsinki in 1961, touching off the hunt for Soviet moles inside the CIA that lasted for almost two decades.

James J. Angleton, the reclusive chief of the CIA's Counterintelligence Staff, became obsessed with finding the Soviet mole who he was convinced had burrowed deep inside the CIA.

THE SUSPECT...

S. Peter Karlow (today), former officer targeted by the CIA as a Mole in the early 1960s.

A DISTINGUISHED CAREER...

Karlow was comissioned as Naval officer, Washington, 1943.

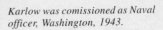

The United States of America

Central Intelligence Agency

Citation

SERGE PETER KARLOW

is hereby awarded the

INTELLIGENCE COMMENDATION MEDAL

In recognition of his more than twenty-two years of devoted service to the Central Intelligence Agency. He distinguished himself in a series of increasingly responsible assignments both at Headquarters and overseas. Mr. Karlow demonstrated inspired leadership, operational wisdom, and good judgment throughout his career, reflecting credit upon himself, the Central Intelligence Agency, and the Federal service.

CIA Medal Citation awarded Karlow, 1989.

General Donovan awards Bronze Star Medal for Valor to Lieutenant Peter Karlow, Washington, May 1945.

"For Peter Karlow, in small recognition for an outstanding professional career of a great gentleman." Dick Stolz, May 26, 1989.

Former CIA director Bill Colby and Peter Karlow meet with President George Bush at dinner of Veterans of OSS, Washington.

THE OSS...

Italian Navy PT boat used by Karlow on the fateful re-supply mission to OSS outpost on the island of Capraia off the Italian coast, February 1944.

Map of Corsica with Capraia Island to the northeast.

General William J. Donovan

OFFICE OF STRATEGIC SERVICES
WASHINGTON, D. C.

5 October 1944

Lt. S. P. Karlow
U. S. Naval Hospital
Philadelphia, Pennsylvania

My dear Peter:

        Thank you for your letter of 2 October.
I am more than pleased that you are getting on so
well, and I look forward to seeing you here.

        I talked to Bill Langer the other night
about you. I told him that we were anxious to have
you here, whether you were in Naval or civilian
status.

        I don't need to tell you in what respect
and affection you are held here, or how glad we'll be
to have you back with us. There is still a big job
to do.

                            Sincerely,

                            William J. Donovan
                                Director

Letter from OSS Director Bill Donovan

THE CIA...
A WEDDING IN PARIS...

French Navy hero Captain Jean l'Herminier attending Peter and Libby Karlow's wedding in Paris, May 1952. Front row from left: Roswell and Louise Rausch, Libby, Ferida Karlow, Fred Flott (Embassy), Capt. and Madeleine l'Herminier.

Peter and Libby with Captain l'Herminier

ON THE LIGHTER SIDE...

State Department cartoon impression of Operations Center. Center face is that of Ambassador Theodore Achilles, director of the Center, Washington, 1961. Karlow was CIA officer there 1961-62.

OSS training sketch, circa 1943, to show difference between "open" propaganda (that may turn the listener off), and "black propaganda" (psychological warfare).

Book reveals mistreatment of falsely accused CIA moles

HUNT FOR SPIES: An upcoming book reveals that some CIA employees became victims of the agency's hunts for moles in the 1960s and early 1970s.

By DAVID JOHNSTON
N.Y. Times News Service

WASHINGTON — Three years ago the CIA gave S. Peter Karlow a small bronze medal, a citation in a blue leatherette binder and a check for close to $500,000. It was the agency's way of saying there had been a terrible mistake.

More than two decades earlier, the CIA had falsely branded Karlow as a suspected mole — a spy, within the agency's ranks.

"I walked down the street and a flower pot fell off the roof and landed on me," Karlow, who is now 71 years old and lives in northern California, said in an interview.

His case, and those of other CIA employees who became victims of the agency's hunts for moles in the 1960s and early 1970s, are detailed in a book by David Wise, "Molehunt: The Secret Search For Traitors That Shattered the CIA." The book will be published by Random House on March 16.

After 10 years of research and more than 650 interviews, Wise writes that the agency paid Karlow and two other former employees a total of more than $700,000 to com-

Paul Garbler, the CIA's first station chief in Moscow who also received a payment from the agency, spent years in professional exile after he was suspected of being a mole.

Richard Kovich, who recruited Soviet spies for the CIA until his career slid into limbo, also received compensation. Three other unidentified CIA employees sought payments, but the agency rejected their claims.

Mark Mansfield, a CIA spokesman, said agency officials declined to coment on Wise's book because they not yet seen it. But he added, "Several agency employees did receive compensation under what has often been referred to as the Mole Relief Act."

The cases of the three former officials were known from news reports and previous books about period. But Wise, a longtime ington reporter who has written eral books on espionage, intelligence, documents vestigations and their employees involved reporting that pai paralyzing distri Soviet Division ble for spying st

were actually investigated and a least 16 were treated as serious suspects, although former directors of central intelligence, like William F. Colby, say that not a single Soviet penetration was ever uncovered

The mole hunt had cost K Garbler and Kovich their tions, betrayed their loy damaged their careers. Garbler hired lawyers Congress for a com which was signed i ber 1980 by P Carter.

Garbler an received con Karlow, w at Monsa agency agency cision lia 1970's

More the C.I.A. Karlow as a within the er pot fell off the me," Mr. Karlow, years old and lives California, said in an i His case, and those agency employees who victims of the agency's hun 1970's, are detailed in a book David Wise, "Molehunt: the Secret Search For Traitors That Shat tered the C.I.A." The book will be published by Random House on March 16.

Into Professional Exile
After 10 years of research and more than 650 interviews, Mr. Wise writes that the agency paid Mr. Karlow and two other former em ployees a total of more than $700,000 to compensate th having wrongly accuse disloyalty. The pa made under an became know as the "M Pa

---

Espionage

Victims of CIA's hunt for moles win vindication

© 1992, New York Times service

Washington, D.C. — Three years ago the CIA gave S. Peter Karlow a small bronze medal, a citation in a blue Leatherette binder and a check for close to

landed on me," Karlow said in an interview. He is now 71 and lives in northern California.

His case, and those of other CIA employees who became victims of the agency's hunts for moles in the 1960s and early 1970s, are detailed

total of mor compensate wrongly accus The payment obscure law within the CI Act."